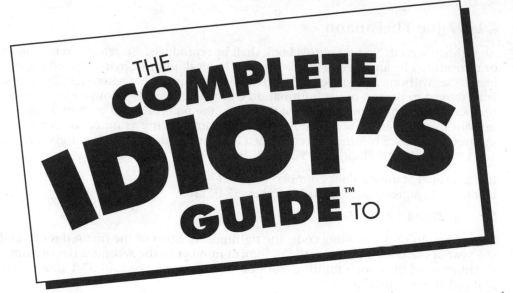

THE COMPLETE **IDIOT'S** GUIDE™ TO

Understanding Football Like a Pro

by Joe Theismann
with Brian Tarcy

alpha books

A Division of Macmillan General Reference
A Simon & Schuster Macmillan Company
1633 Broadway, New York, NY 10019

International Standard Book Number: 0-02-861743-6
Library of Congress Catalog Card Number: 97-071183

99 98 97 8 7 6 5 4 3 2

Interpretation of the printing code: the rightmost number of the first series of numbers is the year of the book's printing; the rightmost number of the second series of numbers is the number of the book's printing. For example, a printing code of 97-1 shows that the first printing occurred in 1997.

Printed in the United States of America

Editor-in-Chief
Richard J. Starn

Editorial Manager
Gretchen Henderson

Director of Editorial Services
Brian Phair

Editor
Lisa A. Bucki

Production Editor
Brian Robinson

Cover Designer
Michael Freeland

Cartoonist
Judd Winick

Illustrators
Bryan Towse
Marvin Van Tiem III

Designer
Glenn Larsen

Indexer
Chris Wilcox

Production Team
Angela Calvert
Linda Knose
Daniela Raderstorf
Megan Wade
Pamela Woolf

Contents at a Glance

Contents

4 Every Player Has a Different Job 39

5 Coaching: Win or Get Fired 51

6 Understanding the Lore 61

10 The Running Backs: Great Ones Control Games   107

11 Strategies: A Lot of Ways to Go 80 Yards or One   119

Foreword

The athletes who play pro football are among the best in the world, and certainly among the bravest and toughest. The thrills they provide on a weekly basis are unparalleled, and the twists and turns of plot in almost every game is a script that Hollywood wouldn't, or couldn't, write.

Pro football is unique in that fans can rehash Sunday's game until Wednesday, then start to get revved up for the following Sunday's game. Anticipation plays a big part, and with each team playing only 16 regular season games, every one of them is crucial—and special.

It's fun for us at ESPN to get inside the game, to talk with players and coaches and really understand what's going on. It's also fun for us to relay the information to our viewers. But the best part of Sunday is the six hours we spend watching all the NFL games— sometimes eight or nine at once. In that way, we're no different than anyone else.

Watching football on Sundays has become almost a religious experience in the U.S., and understanding it just a little bit better makes it more fun to cheer, debate, exhilarate, and suffer with your favorite teams. That's where Joe Theismann comes in.

Joe had the good fortune and great talent to engineer one of the best offenses in football, the Washington Redskins of the early and mid-1980s. He won a Super Bowl and helped the Skins set records. He lost a Super Bowl and had his career end on the most graphic injury anyone can recall—a broken leg. He certainly knows the ups and downs, and as a broadcaster, he knows how to communicate them to fans eager to digest information.

You don't need to know every play call, every defensive alignment, or every player's stats to understand and enjoy pro football. You just need a couple of tips, basic facts, or a brief refresher course in the game and you're ready for action. Joe has provided that refresher course in the pages that follow.

Enjoy the book, and I can't wait to see you next Sunday.

Chris Berman, ESPN's Mr. Everything

Introduction

Take your wildest dream, the thing you want to happen more than anything else, the thing that you absolutely can't live without, and then make it come true.

Stand at its doorstep. That's what it feels like to be standing in the stadium tunnel waiting to play for the NFL Championship in the Super Bowl. It's like a first kiss.

The game is bigger than life.

My first Super Bowl was in Pasadena, California before more than 100,000 people. It was surreal, like going on that first date, waiting for that first kiss. I was so excited. It is the greatest thing to ever happen to a player, and yet, I don't remember the first three or four minutes of the game. It was almost paranormal—I went into a zone, an absolute zone.

That's football. Three or four days later I watched film of the first few minutes of the game and I didn't remember any of it. Yet I functioned. I called plays, threw passes, and gave hand-offs. I completed passes. But I don't remember any of it. After getting kicked in the head, though, I remember it all. Yes, I remember it all.

This book is about what I remember of NFL football. It includes everything but the first three minutes of that Super Bowl. I know and love the game and I want to share that knowledge and love with you.

How to Use This Book

This book is divided into five parts, just like a class on football. But don't worry, no boring lectures. This is a book about football. It doesn't get any better than this.

Part 1: "Learning the Rules and the Lore" deals with the foundation of football—the rules. In this part, I will discuss the field, the ball, the players' jobs (in general), and the role of coaches in this most emotional of games. I will also give you a quick primer on the lore of the NFL. The lore doesn't end. Watch the games. You are bound to see something amazing happen.

Part 2: "Learning the Offense and the Penalties" deals with the offensive side of the ball—what teams try to do to score. This part will go through the roles and duties of each offensive player, position by position. It will also cover strategies. By time you finish, you will have an advanced degree in offense and be ready to complain about the play calling by the third quarter.

Part 3: "Learning the Defense and Special Teams" deals with the defensive side of the ball, where a group of guys is trying to stop the other team from scoring. It covers the role and duties of all the players on defense, and it will tell you of basic and advanced defensive strategies so you can second-guess your defensive coordinator if he blitzes on first down.

Part 4: "College and Pro" deals with the structure of the game. The college game is, in many ways, like a minor league for the pros, and that relationship will be examined here. In addition, the NFL will be considered. This part will deal with why the NFL is the pinnacle of the game, how teams advance to the Super Bowl, as well as the business of the game—which no fan can ignore. It will also discuss the relationship of the media and the game.

Part 5: "The Essentials of Fandom" deals with your life as a fan. I will discuss clothing, joy, and rivalries here. You want to cheer? Hey, this part tells how. As a fan, you do make a difference.

Some Play Calls to Help You Understand

This book provides a few gems of wisdom and lore that will help you understand the game even more. These boxes give you extra information:

Joe's Rules

This kind of box will detail the rules of the game, on and off the field.

Joe's Tips

The information included in this type of box will help fans enjoy the experience of being a fan.

Joe's Record Book

These boxes include interesting facts from the game, so you can stump your friends.

Joe's Gridiron Talk

These boxes define common and uncommon football terms.

Acknowledgments

I would like first thank all of my former coaches and teammates for giving me an opportunity to make a dream come true.

I also want to thank my wife, Robin, for her patience as I relived my years on the gridiron.

And in particular, I would like to thank three gentlemen who made me the football player that I was. I want to thank Joe Walton for his guidance and driving discipline, Jack Pardee for believing in me and giving me a chance to compete, and Joe Gibbs for putting me in a system that allowed me the opportunity to achieve the ultimate dream.

This book could not have been completed without the expertise of Russell Baxter, ESPN Research, who helped us get the facts straight, and Vince Casey, who helped us understand the Collective Bargaining Agreement. We also thank Tricia Trilli of the Professional Football Hall of Fame in Canton, Ohio for her help with our research.

Finally, I would like to thank my collaborator, Brian Tarcy, who did an excellent job turning thoughts into words. I hope he gets his Cleveland Browns back soon.

Trademarks

All terms mentioned in this book that are known to be or are suspected of being trademarks or service marks have been appropriately capitalized. Alpha Books and Macmillan General Reference cannot attest to the accuracy of this information. Use of a term in this book should not be regarded as affecting the validity of any trademark or service mark. The following trademarks and service marks have been mentioned in this book:

Wilson

NFL and all NFL teams are trademarked.

All broadcast networks are trademarked.

Part 1
Learning the Rules and the Lore

On Sundays in the fall, you cannot avoid professional football. Who would want to? The game has everything—gladiators, bright colors, physical confrontations, and a vivid joy that is nothing short of pure exuberance. It has excitement and drama and it is played by the biggest and most spectacular athletes in the world. It is pure competition. Football is about winning.

This opening part of the book will explain why so many folks love the game. And then it will detail how it works—from where it is played, to the ball it is played with, to how teams actually get to win. This part will also talk about the folks who run the games—these great generals called coaches. And finally, this part will give you a sense of the history of football. When something wonderful happens on the football field— and something always does—it reminds fans of something else. Football is rich. Check it out.

Chapter 1

So You Want to Be a Monday Morning Quarterback

In This Chapter

➤ Why the game is so loved by so many

➤ How emotion plays into the game

➤ The connection between football and community

The best part of the National Football League (NFL)—if you don't get to play—is acting like you know something about it. Football is all about opinions. *My team is better than your team.* It's true. Professional football is a *topic.* It is love and hate, power and pride, all the *stuff*—the competitive *stuff.* And professional football is *professional*, so it also deals with money, which is a fun ingredient to throw into any mix if you are looking for drama. Yes, there is plenty of drama in the NFL.

This is a step-by-step book about the drama of professional football. You see, football is a step-by-step drama—how good is this? It's great. If you can understand the game, you can argue more effectively; and if you can do that, just think of the friends you can make. Well, think of the arguments you can win. Think about how smart you will look to all those so-called football geniuses at the office. Truthfully, one of the true joys of football is standing around the drinking fountain, discussing the play calling in the third quarter of yesterday's game. But, if you don't know what a third quarter or a play call is, you could have some trouble participating in the conversation.

This football stuff really isn't hard to learn. Football is actually a fairly simple game with a complex language and a violent temperament. But don't worry, I am going to teach it to you, one step at a time.

Think of the first step this way: There are two teams. Each wears different colors and each is trying to get the football into opposite ends of the field.

Okay, that's enough for now. Go get a drink of water and impress someone with your new knowledge. When you get back, in this chapter, I'm going to tell you about the lure of the game, the passion of football, and why violence is such an integral part of it. Finally, I will talk about the connection between community and team because that is really the most special part of the attraction.

The Lure of the Game

So much of what is loved about this game has to do with our childhood fantasies. Heck, it's a kids' game. Many of us remember throwing, running, and playing on the sidestreets, backlawns, and open playgrounds of America. From New Jersey to Ohio to California, kids play football because football is a game of *heroes*.

Joe's Record Book
William (Pudge) Heffelinger, a former Yale All-American guard, became the first professional football player when he was paid $500 in 1892 to play a game for the Allegheny Athletic Association against the Pittsburgh Athletic Association. He was worth the money. The AAA won the game after Heffelinger returned a fumble 25 yards for a touchdown.

Think about it: You wear the jersey of your favorite player and, for a brief while, you are that player. It's true. If you want to know what football is to so many, it is the opportunity to experience the emotional extremes in this most emotional of games. Football is full of special moments.

Some of us are lucky enough to live those fantasies out. Others live those fantasies vicariously. Regardless, we all enjoy the game for what it is—a chance to go to your emotional well, chance to vent, and chance to celebrate. For the fans and the players, game time is a chance to act like you would never dream of acting in the real world.

As you start to follow the game, you will soon learn that the sport has a rich history laced with gigantic names that have taken on legendary stature. Nevertheless, football is a game of NOW.

Each fan in a 60,000-seat stadium brings his or her own set of memories, but when the quarterback slings the ball downfield you can hear a pin drop until it is either caught or dropped. When the ball goes in the air, possibilities and opportunities are up there with it. When it comes down you hear either "Awwwwwwwwwww," or a loud roar. Something happened and everybody knows what. In a situation in a stadium, there is no hiding. Everybody reacts.

The lure of football is deep and multi-faceted, but a lot of it is tied up simply in what happens when the ball flies in the air. Don't breathe, just watch.

But the allure of the game is also about those gigantic names: Jim Thorpe and Jim Brown, Bart Star and Joe Namath, Joe Montana and Brett Favre. There was once a kid growing up in New Jersey who was convinced that Joe Namath was the coolest person ever to walk the planet. That kid was me, and I grew up to play against Joe Namath. That's just one example of how football can make kids' dreams come true.

Football is about dreams that come true. It is about the pursuit of dreams. It is, in fact, a celebration—a very violent celebration—of the pursuit of dreams.

The lure of the game is the opportunity it offers to be a part of history—to say, "I was there." You were there? Wow, that must have been something.

I can remember being in the stands in Giants Stadium in 1962 when everybody took their hankies out and sang "Good-bye Allie" to Y.A. Tittle as he limped, bloody, off the field. I'm very proud of that. It is something that will be with me forever.

You have to understand—football players are gladiators. You have two titans, representing a city, a culture, and a segment of the country, and they are going at it 'til the end.

Joe's Tip

If you don't know who to root for, consider that there are 30 professional teams in the National Football League. Also, consider that I played for the Washington Redskins, so that team would be a good choice. And then ask yourself:

➤ Do you like the name, colors, or city of any particular team?

➤ Do you live near a team?

➤ Do you like the current players? (This is not as important because the players will change.)

➤ Do all your friends cheer for one team?

➤ Where did you grow up?

There is something primal about the look of football. The colors. The huge men. The ferocious meetings. This whole football thing really is simple. It's each guy saying, "Look, I'm better than you. I want to prove that I am better than you are."

Joe's Rules

In 1880, a Yale rugby player named Walter Camp invented modern football by suggesting the rugby scrummage be changed to a scrimmage. This had one effect. It let a team take possession of the ball before play began. Rugby was a spontaneous game. Football, as Camp envisioned it, would be more orderly. The scrimmage meant that teams could plan what they wanted to do and then do it. The *line of scrimmage* is the imaginary line across the field that is the location of where the ball is placed at the beginning of the play.

The Passion

Football is 15 percent physical and 85 percent mental. The mental is not merely intellectual. In fact, the mental part of the game that is most important has less to do with intellect and more to do with force of will. Football is a game about engine power, so rev it up.

If you are going to understand the game of football, you have to understand the emotional energy that it takes to play the game. When you see someone cheering for a football team, that person is living their life vicariously through a player or the players on the field. And the players on the field are playing on overdrive.

Joe's Record Book
The NFL is very popular. In 1996, 14,497,014 people attended NFL games, for an average attendance of 60,404 per game. Also, about 80 million Americans watch NFL football on television every Sunday. A whopping 128.9 million Americans watched Super Bowl XXXI on television, while more than 800 million people worldwide watched the game.

Joe's Tip
If you are going to try for the full emotional experience of being a fan, be careful of the effects of alcohol. It can cloud your judgment and you may end up doing something in the heat of the moment that you could later regret. Always be a smart fan.

The human heart is endowed with the capacity to push the body to incredible limits. Football is a game that epitomizes the power of the will. There is only one way to play the game: all out. There is no speed but full speed. When football players talk about giving 110 percent, they really mean it.

You see, football is a game that requires its participants to ride the wire of emotion. Why is the game so emotional? There are a million reasons. The biggest reason is that there is a great fear factor in football. It is a macho game. It's each player saying, "I don't want to let you show me up."

Each player is trying to overcome his own limitations (playing past the point of exhaustion or doing something that's a personal best, for example) and that each team is overcoming the emotional challenges in playing as a unit. Noble reasons—men striving to be better individually and as a team—are what push these titans.

The game appeals to the most base emotions of the human psyche and it allows for a healthy release of those emotions—for both players and fans.

Players lay it all out on the field—right in front of an average of 60,404 fans. The players put it all on the line. And for fans, Sunday afternoon is a chance to do the same thing: Take your emotions out of hiding and let them go for a three-hour ride. When you tie your heart to a team and then watch a game, that's what happens. You go on a three-hour ride that ends in either pure ecstasy or pure agony.

Fans understand. Just take a look at any stadium. You are not seeing insanity in action. Nope. Just think of it as some folks who want to share in the passion of the moment. If you are a football fan, I have one thing to say: You people are nuts. I mean that in the nicest way.

I remember instances during my career where I was coming out of the locker room thinking I was pretty excited—until I looked at the fans. All I could think was, "Thank God they're on my side." When it was the other team's fans, I tried not to pay attention. The truth is, football is a very interactive game. Both fans and players feel the power of the passion. It is a game that boils the blood and makes the heart do jumping jacks inside your body. Fans feel the power coming from the players, but players also feel it coming from the fans. Actually, I think players feel it more. It is like a plug full of energy—pure power.

> **Joe's Record Book**
> In the 1880s, linemen (the big guys who initiate contact on each play) could do anything to each other. "It was the heyday for the good boxer and the slugger type of player, for there was no penalty for rough work," said Amos Alonzo Stagg, who coached the University of Chicago football team for 41 years.

Fans are definitely part of it. In fact, they are a huge part. The fans are a part of your family, and you are a part of theirs. If you hurt, they hurt. Fans all know the players on a first-name basis.

There are 30 franchises in the NFL. Therefore, there are 30 hero-making machines (teams) across the country. I get 15-year-old kids coming up and saying, "Joe. Hi Joe." They know me by first name. Those of us who have played pro football are more than entertainers. We represent our fans' city, their culture. Their enthusiasm and passion are tied to the team and its accomplishments. Thus, there is a bottom line to that passion. The bottom line is winning.

Why Is It So Violent?

Somebody wants to go someplace where somebody else doesn't want them to go. That's football. It's as simple as a bully saying, "I don't want you to go across the street."

Oh yeah?

Yeah.

The question of violence in the game is not a question at all. Football, in fact, is violent. It is physical. It is a culture, a world, a society of its own. There are rules in that society, and you must understand them before you enter because the rules allow some form of violence.

Of course, that is part of the appeal of football. Who can deny the traffic accident effect that occurs on highways all across the country, when you can't resist slowing down and looking. There is even a term for it—rubbernecking. Well, the NFL is designed for all the rubberneckers in America. The picture only becomes clear when you see the colorfully clad gladiators lined up face to face. There's a traffic accident in Washington, and look, it's scheduled for one o'clock on Sunday afternoon.

The thing about football violence is that it is extreme and continuous. It is two men repeatedly running at approximately 30 miles an hour and crashing right into each other. Imagine the sound, then watch a game. It can rock your bones. Trust me, I know.

Joe's Rules

There are a number or penalties (rules violations) that pertain to the illegal use of violence. Although the game is physical, players cannot try to intentionally hurt other players.

Football, you see, is not really part of the real world. It's more like the surreal world, but it is all happening in real time. In the game, the violence is not evil or malicious violence. It is competitive violence.

But that violence can sometimes come across as evil violence if you compare it to the rules of society. In fact, if you did the things that we did on the football field on the street, such as hitting another play so hard he blows *snot bubbles*, you'd be in jail today. That is not a brag or a macho statement or anything of the sort. It's just the truth.

The game is not promoted as a violent game, but that's what it is and every player and every fan recognizes this. Violence is part of the appeal. There is no way to down-play the fact that you have large, fast, agile men running into each other at what they hope are precise angles.

Joe's Gridiron Talk

Snot bubbles are a sensation that is created by a big hit. When you actually have bubbles coming out of your nose after you have been hit, you know you have been hit good. And, thus, it is a good thing to give another player a case of snot bubbles.

Sometimes the hits cause injuries, and the truth is even those are part of the appeal. I know. I suffered a broken leg in a Monday Night game against the New York Giants in 1985. It was a fairly gruesome affair. And it taught me a bit about the appeal of the game.

Now, on the night when my leg was broken, many people saw it live. But later, it was played over and over on every sportscast in the country. Inevitably, the announcer said something like, "You might not want to see this, but look…" And a lot of people did.

The Connection Between Football and Community

When a football team goes into formation, from the stands, it can look like a flag. The set formation has colors and patterns all its own. It almost makes you want to stand and salute (at least in the cities that have winning teams).

There is no doubt that a football team belongs to a specific city or region. It's our team, our colors, and our tradition. It belongs to us. (Of course, it doesn't, it belongs to somebody with a bunch of money who is called an owner, but that's another story.)

Football, because of the pure man-on-man nature of the event, is the sport that best exemplifies the civic nature of modern athletics—our guys versus your guys. That's football, and many people take it very seriously.

It is a game and it is a business. But football is more. Mostly, I think, football is about the relationship of the team to the community. Football is a great game because a team can represent what the cavalry represented in an earlier era—a chance for individuals to move on in the world, and a chance to defend the honor of a home city. A football team can exist somewhere in the pulse that runs through a community, and when it does, there is no sporting relationship quite like it. It is not an understatement to call it a love affair.

> **Joe's Record Book**
> The NFL supports local communities in many ways besides simply giving folks a team to root for on Sundays. In fact, in 1996, NFL Charities donated $5 million to local charities in each city.
>
> In addition, more than 50 players have their own charities in their local communities.

It's not hard to figure out. Just watch a game. The connection is total and it is not faked. The emotions spent by the fans and players are real for both sides. Fans may be surprised to know (but they shouldn't be) that players get a tremendous amount of energy from fan support. That's not a line. That's the truth.

Fans offer the players a chance to be part of their family. We feel that we really are welcomed into fans' families. We feel the energy from the roar of the crowd, and it effects us. It really does.

The impact of fan support is especially magnified in football—more so than in other sports. First of all, there are only eight regular season home games a year. If a player is playing well at home, all is right with the world. If that player can have eight good games a year in front of the hometown fans, that player can do nothing wrong. The limited opportunity to play in front of the fans amplifies the devotion for a couple of reasons. First, there are fewer home games each season than in other sports, and thus more pressure not to mess up; fans don't want to spend that rare chance watching their team lose. Additionally, there is more of an opportunity between games to build into a frenzy. When there are only eight home games each regular season, a game is an event.

Joe's Record Book
As a player, I knew my performance had a lot to do with the mental attitude of my fans for a week. When I played for the Washington Redskins, if we had a bad game on Sunday, Congress inevitably had a bad day on Monday. I couldn't make this stuff up if I wanted to. It's true.

But a home game is even more than a sporting event. It is a civic event. When your team trots out on the field wearing your colors, the players are not just out there to entertain. Sure, football is entertainment, but it is much more. When that team goes on the field, the players are going to war and the fight they are fighting is for your honor. The honor of your city. The honor of your place.

Players really do get it. We understand.

Football is more than a mere spectator sport. It is a national passion that is part of 30 different civic cultures across the land. Football teams are really like armies sent out to defend a city. There are rules to the battle, but it is nevertheless a battle.

Fans also are quick to recognize what football players actually do for a living. Are football players overpaid? Sure they are. But then again, they are paid exactly what they are worth. Go figure.

The truth is that fans don't much care about the money part of it and are more intrigued by the gladiator aspect. There is a connection there that I have felt as a player and that I have felt as a fan. I know both sides, and I know for a fact that the connection exists.

Joe's Record Book
In the early days of professional football, teams were congregated in a few places in the East and Midwest. In 1904, the state of Ohio had seven professional teams. Talk even surfaced about forming a statewide league, but nothing ever came of it.

It really is tangible.

I have had people come up to me and show me autographs that I signed 20 years ago. I had no idea these people kept the autograph in their wallet all these years. But they pulled it out, and when something like that happens, you can't help but feel a sense of obligation to the fans and community.

That is why so many players volunteer to do things such as appear at a children's hospital. We know it means something. The player is the person that the child saw on television. On television, that person is bigger than life. When the player shows up, it is life (the players usually seem bigger than life in person too), and that has an effect.

Football is a game of confidence and raw emotion. We players understand what our presence can mean to someone fighting an illness because we know what the presence of cheering fans does when we are fighting out on the field. Vocal support means a lot. So yell, and yell loud. We like it.

In the 1996 playoffs, the Carolina Panthers came back out of the locker room and did a lap around the field, that was not a curtain call asking for more cheers. That was not the Carolina Panthers looking for adulation. It was, instead, the players wanting to show their gratitude to the fans. And when the Jacksonville Jaguars returned from beating Denver in the playoffs, they were not taken from the airport directly to their cars. No, instead, they were brought to the stadium at 1:30 in the morning so they could be welcomed home by 40,000 fans. This is at 1:30 a.m. Communities and football teams are involved in nothing short of a love fest. Believe me, players understand. They get it.

The thing to understand about the connection between the players and the community is that before we played in the NFL, every one of us watched the game on television. We all had heroes.

In my first year in the league, I was the third-string quarterback for the Washington Redskins. That year, we played the New York Jets and Joe Namath was the quarterback. After the game, I went up to him and said, "Mr. Namath, my name is Joe Theismann and when I was growing up in New Jersey, you were my hero."

"Nice to meet you," he said, and he shook my hand.

"I would be honored if I could carry your helmet to your locker room," I babbled.

"That's all right, kid," said Namath. "I can carry it myself."

The Least You Need to Know

➤ When you learn about football, you will be capable of engaging in scintillating Monday-morning conversation.

➤ Football is played on overdrive and cheered at the same speed.

➤ Football is a violent game, and that is part of the attraction.

➤ Football teams are like gladiators representing a city. The connection between a team and the home fans is a remarkable bond.

➤ Players and the NFL show appreciation for fan support by trying to win, and by supporting local charities.

Chapter 2

Looking at the Field and the Ball

In This Chapter

➤ Sizing up the field and the ball

➤ The pros and cons of artificial turf

➤ Why the final 20 yards before the end zone are special

This is a weird game. On one hand, you have a rectangular field with specific dimensions, and you have precise, measured rules. On the other hand, you've got this odd-shaped ball. When you put the two together, you get organized chaos. It's perfect.

Both teams in a football game make attempts at precision in the midst of chaos. If you watch, you will see that football is in some ways a finite art. The lines are always in the same place.

But inside those lines is another world. The game is designed to create excitement. That's why the field is big. Think about it. What is the absolute perfect measurement of big? Ever heard something like, "That aircraft carrier must have been about three football fields long." That says it all. The football field is a measurement of big.

This is a chapter about where the game is played and about the ball it is played with. Okay, I admit it, these are not the most exciting parts of football. But they are key basics, and as your coach, I think it is important that you at least glance at this stuff.

Why Is the Ball Shaped Like That?

The football evolved from the rugby ball, which evolved from the soccer ball. And in other countries, folks refer to soccer as football. So, you see, there is a connection between the two games. One game just stopped evolving.

In 1875, an egg-shaped ball was used instead of a soccer ball in rugby. The new rugby ball became the official ball of football until 1896, when the term *prolate spheroid* came to define the shape of a football.

The average early football looked like an elongated pumpkin. At first, there were no official dimensions. Just an official description of the shape—a prolate spheroid. Pat O'Dea of Wisconsin kicked many of his collegiate records at the turn of the century with the original prolate spheroid ball.

Today's more elongated football is shaped to be easy to throw. I can wrap my hand around the ball with some of my fingers on the laces and my thumb on the back side of the ball, and I feel in control. The ball is designed to inspire confidence. It always works for good players.

With its tapered ends, a football is aerodynamically designed to spin after it is thrown. Although it is quirky in the way it bounces, it is quite true in the way it flies. A football is perfectly engineered to be a football. There are no design flaws, although there were days when I'm sure I could have found plenty, but more on that later.

The ball itself is also easy to grasp if I want to run with it. I can put my hand around one end of it and tuck the other into the inside of my elbow and I am able to maintain a running rhythm. The folks who designed this thing were geniuses. You can even kick it.

Today's ball looks like the following picture.

Today's regulation NFL football is designed for straight flight.

The ball is made of pebble-grained leather, which makes it easy to grab and, at least in dry conditions, easy to catch.

The home club supplies the balls for each game, and must have 36 balls available in open-air stadiums, while 24 must be available in dome stadiums. The referee is the sole judge of whether a ball meets the requirements. Unfortunately, quarterbacks are given no say in the matter. Go figure.

Joe's Rules

The official NFL game ball is:

➤ Called a "pigskin" but made of leather.

➤ A "Wilson" bearing the signature of NFL Commissioner Paul Tagliabue.

➤ Inflated to between 12 $\frac{1}{2}$ and 13 $\frac{1}{2}$ pounds.

➤ Between 11 and 11 $\frac{1}{4}$ inches long.

➤ 28 to 28 $\frac{1}{2}$ inches in circumference around its long dimension.

➤ 21 to 21 $\frac{1}{4}$ inches in circumference around its shorter middle dimension.

➤ Shaped like a prolate spheroid, tapering at each end.

The Object of The Game

You want to win, of course. But in order to win you have to score more points than the other team. You score by controlling the ball and moving it all the way down the field into a designated *end zone*. The ball must stay on the playing field. The game involves a series of *plays*, in which live action begins when one player *snaps* the ball to another. The play usually ends when a person carrying the ball, a *ball carrier*, is tackled. A ball carrier is *tackled* when he is brought to the ground while he is being touched by an opponent or he runs outside the boundaries of the playing field. A play also ends if the ball is thrown forward and is not caught. A play can also end when the ball lands after it is kicked toward the goal posts in an attempt to get points. See Chapter 3 for more details on how the game proceeds on the field.

The Dimensions and How They Figure into the Game

The playing field is a rectangle—360 feet in length and 160 feet in width—a big rectangle. At each end of the length of the rectangle, there is a 10-yard long box. This box is called the *end zone*. Look again at the illustration of a football field.

The dimensions of a football field are awesome.

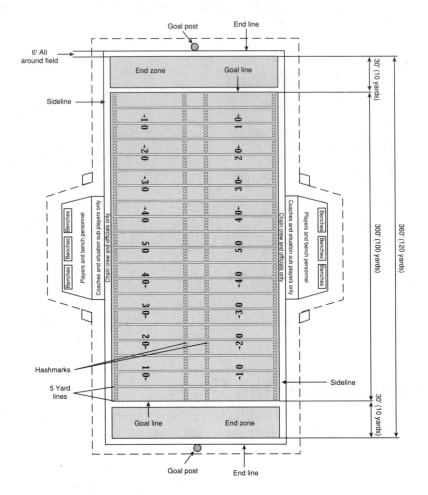

There are two end zones, one, as I said, at each end of the field. End zones are very important in the game of football. There is an eight-inch line that separates the playing field from the end zone. This line is called the *goal line*.

An end zone is not just a box on a field. It is more like a candy store. The end zone is a special place for many reasons, not the least of which is that you can only score touchdowns in the end zone.

Touchdowns are good. They are worth more points (6) than any other type of score. Therefore, the end zone is the promised land, because that is the only place a touchdown can happen.

The rest of the field, that part between the end zones, is where the battle is fought.

The field between the end zones is 100 yards long. If you look down the field, you will see a series of lines running all the way across the field. Those lines, parallel to the goal line, are *five-yard markers*. Every other one has a number by it—a multiple of 10.

The middle of the field is the 50-yard line. The highest number on the field is 50. So, how come the biggest number is 50 but the field is 100 yards long?

Simple. It is a distance of 50 yards from each end zone to the middle of the field. So, when you are 40 yards from one end zone, you are on that 40-yard line going towards the 30, 20, and 10 yard lines, each of which you will reach before the end zone. But if you are 60 yards from one end zone, you are on the other team's 40-yard line, and you must cross the 50 first when heading toward the end zone before you come to the other 40, 30, and so on.

> **Joe's Record Book**
> In order to re-sod Green Bay's Lambeau Field for a 1997 playoff game, sod was shipped from Maryland to Green Bay in 28 heated tractor trailers. The new field cost the NFL about $150,000.

> **Joe's Gridiron Talk**
> Unless you are on the 50-yard line, the yard line belongs to either yourself (your team) or your opponent. The yard lines between your *defensive end zone* (the end zone you want to keep your opponent out of) and the 50-yard line are *your yard lines*. If the other team has the ball 30 yards from your end zone, they are on your 30-yard line. If they are 70 yards away, they are on their own 30-yard line.

There is one other marking on the field. Two yards before each goal line (on the playing field, not in the end zone) and in the middle of it, there is a one-yard-long line that is parallel to the goal line. This is the line on which the ball is placed for an extra point or a two-point conversion after a touchdown. (I'll explain what extra points and two-point conversions are in Chapter 3.)

Joe's Rules

Here are a few more facts to know about the football field:

➤ The line around the field is a six-foot solid white border.

➤ Players and coaches on the sidelines are only allowed to stand between the 32-yard lines.

➤ The goal line is eight inches wide.

What Is a Crossbar?

At the back of the end zone, there is something called a *goal post*. It is a pole-like structure. There is a bottom or base pole that rises straight up from the ground. At the top of the base pole, there is another pole that is attached, parallel to the ground. The second pole is called a *crossbar*. Your team has to kick the ball over the crossbar to get points (3 for a field goal, 1 for an extra point—see Chapter 3 for more about how to score by kicking).

Joe's Gridiron Talk

A ball kicked *over the crossbar and between the uprights*, is worth points (the number depends on the situation—see Chapter 3). If a kick is *wide left*, the ball flew to the left of the left upright. *Wide right* means the kicked ball went to the right of the right upright. If the kick is short, the ball didn't make it over the crossbar.

At each end of the of the crossbar are two more poles that rise perpendicular to the ground. Kicks must go over the cross bar and between these two poles. These poles are called *the uprights*.

The crossbar is:

➤ 18 feet, six inches in length (so it spaces the uprights to that distance apart).

➤ 10 feet off the ground.

When teams win big games, rowdy fans sometimes try to tear these the goal posts out of the ground and carry them around. This is not really a good idea.

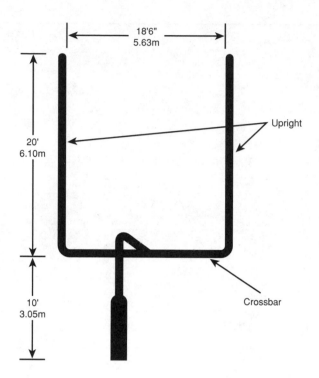

18'6"
5.63m

20'
6.10m

10'
3.05m

Upright

Crossbar

To score points, the kicker must kick the ball over the cross-bar and between the uprights of the goal post.

Hashmarks

In between each of the five-yard markers, there are two sets of four short lines, with each pair designating a one-yard increment on the field. All plays begin in between the two *hashmarks*, toward the center of the field.

Hashmarks were added to football fields in 1933 as a way to bring the start of the play away from the edge of the field. If a ball carrier is tackled between the hashmarks, the ball is placed where the ball landed when the player was tackled. In other words, it stays between the hashmarks.

But, if a ball carrier is tackled outside of the hashmarks, or if the ball goes out of bounds, it is brought to the same yard line, at the hashmark nearest the side of the field or side-line where the ball ended up.

*Hashmarks be-
tween each five-
yard line indicate
one-yard incre-
ments. Each play
must begin in the
center area between
the hash marks.*

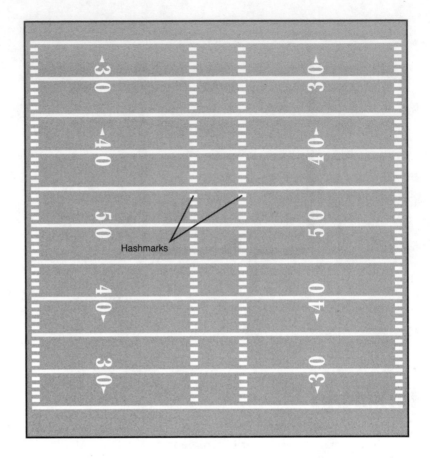

Hashmarks

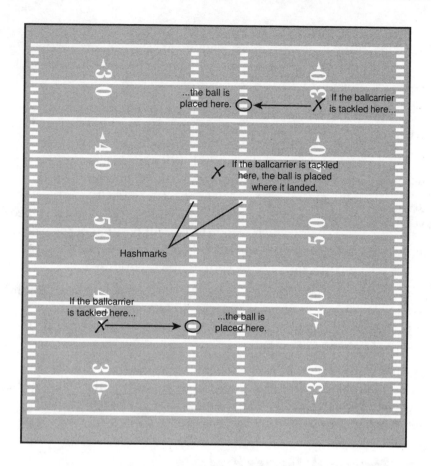

The purpose is to bring the ball closer to the middle of the field. This gives a team a better chance to direct the play in either direction. In 1972, the hashmarks were moved even closer the middle of the field to create more opportunity for excitement.

The Chains, the Sticks

If you are on the chain gang in the NFL, you've got a great view of the game.

You see, a football game is designed to essentially take place in 10-yard increments. If your team can move the ball forward 10 yards within four plays, the team is allowed to keep it again. And so, 10 yards is a very important measurement to know.

The 10-yard measurement is so important, in fact, that there are people in charge of keeping it marked. They keep it marked with special equipment called chains or "the sticks." Each person has a stick. The two end sticks are held together by a 10-yard chain.

These chains (really only one chain, but never mind) mark where a series of downs begins. A series of downs is the four plays you have to move 10 yards; we use the term *down* because each play ends when the ball or the player is knocked to the ground. One chain end marks the beginning of the series of downs and one marks 10 yards past the beginning. There is a third stick, which is not attached to a chain, which marks the current position of the ball at the beginning of a play. This is stick has a number at the top that displays the current down—from 1–4.

Joe's Gridiron Talk
First down occurs with change of possession of the ball, or when a team moves forward 10 yards toward its scoring end zone from where it began. A team is then given four more plays to move forward another 10 yards. If it does not do so (each play is numbered consecutively) in four downs, the other team is given the ball (given possession) and it is first down for them.

If the team that possesses the ball moves it 10 yards toward the team's scoring end zone in four plays, the team is rewarded with a new set of four downs. It becomes first down.

If there is a question whether the ball moved far enough, the two people with the chains that measure for first down run onto the field and measure right next to the ball. This can be exciting and nerve-wracking because sometimes only an inch or two makes the difference in whether a team gets to keep the ball.

Artificial Turf or Natural Grass?

Football is played on two basic types of surfaces: artificial turf and natural grass. Both are green, although not the same shade. Artificial turf can be darker or lighter than real grass, depending on the kind of turf—but it always seems to be brighter.

Natural grass is exactly that. It is grass. Just like on the lawn or at the playground or in the outfield—natural, only better because it is cared for by the NFL.

Joe's Record Book
In the National Football League, 15 stadiums have grass and 15 have artificial turf. Parity lives.

Artificial turf is more like a carpet. It is what the name suggests—it is not real. It does not grow. There are not artificial turf farms across Kentucky. Artificial turf is synthetic material placed on a pad that is set upon asphalt. It is like a carpet, and when playing on it you can even get carpet burns. When I was a kid, we played ball on driveways or in the street and sometimes you took a spill on the ground. You would end up with a long, deep, red scrape that we called a "raspberry." Well, you get a lot of raspberries playing on artificial turf, especially on your elbows.

The original intent of artificial turf was to allow a game to be played indoors at the Houston Astrodome—the first domed stadium. Once it was shown that Astroturf (artifical turf) could be used indoors, it was then considered for use outdoors for one simple reason—it kept the uniforms clean.

In games on grass, players sometimes became so dirty and muddy that the fans could not read the uniform numbers. Owners wanted the fans to know who was out there, so for a while teams switched to artificial turf.

Another reason for artificial turf is that it is a relatively low-maintenence surface compared to grass, which must be cared for, fertilized, and mowed. In addition, there are many cities that have multi-use stadiums with artificial turf for both baseball and football. In these cases, artificial turf has extra economic value.

But recently, there has been a trend in the other direction. Some outdoor stadiums have gone back to natural grass.

The game is different on the two types of fields. The game is so different that teams actually pick their players based upon what kind of surface the team plays on for home games.

On artificial turf, the game is faster. Thus, teams that have artificial turf on their home fields want faster players. The footing on artificial turf is so sure that it is sometimes tough to believe what you have seen from the players. It causes the players to have a little different running style. On artificial turf, you have to pick your feet up when you run. You can make cuts (sharp turns and sidesteps) on artificial turf that would almost seem humanly impossible on grass.

On artificial turf, you are sticking every single step. I've never run with suction cups on the bottom of my shoes, but to me, that's the feeling of running on artificial turf. The footing is unbelievable. Think of the phrase, "turn on a dime." The cuts really are unbelievable. The footing is precise.

> **Joe's Gridiron Talk**
> The footing on artificial turf is so sure that there is actually an injury called *turf toe*, in which the big toe is jammed into the ground because you have stopped too abruptly. It is like a stubbed toe, except you are wearing a shoe.

> **Joe's Record Book**
> Teams will do anything they can to win. This includes the grounds crew. For instance, if a fast team is visiting a field with natural turf, the grass will be grown a little longer so the guys move a little slower. You know, "Maybe I didn't cut it on Sunday. Maybe I didn't cut it since Friday. Well, oops, I forgot." That's just another part of the strategy of winning.

Sometimes, I think it is too precise. Artificial turf is a tough point with some players, and I believe there is some merit to the argument that it shortens careers.

Football is a tough job. All players recognize the risks. Injuries happen on both kinds of turf. But still, the game's field and equipment should all contribute to minimizing injuries where possible. Artificial turf, I believe, shortens careers because it produces a wear and tear on the joints—especially the knees.

Standing on artificial turf for a few hours gives me a backache. When you move on it repeatedly over an extended period of time, your knees and ankles will begin to feel the wear.

I like football on grass. To me, it is just like the schoolyard stuff we used to play on years ago when mud or snow just made the game better. Sure, on grass you may be a bit slower, but there's just something about playing football and getting a little mud on your jersey. It makes you remember the look on Mom's face when she saw you return from a day of playing. Yes, Mom's famous football-laundry face. This indeed is a game of childhood fantasies and memories.

Indoors or Outdoors

Football was originally designed to be played outdoors in the fall. But, a number of stadiums are now designed to keep the temperature at a cozy 72 degrees for the entire game. A lot of stadiums are now enclosed—what is called a *dome*.

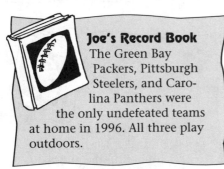

Joe's Record Book
The Green Bay Packers, Pittsburgh Steelers, and Carolina Panthers were the only undefeated teams at home in 1996. All three play outdoors.

Domes are big stadium buildings with a roof on top. Indoor football is always played on artificial turf. Artificial turf, as you may remember from the last section, is like a carpet. So, here's what you do. Clear out your living room of furniture, invite 22 of your biggest friends, give them a football, and, voilà, you have your own domed stadium.

Well, okay, it's a few hundred-million dollars more complicated than that, but you get the idea. Dome football isn't quite the same as football outdoors.

Indoors, you don't have to deal with the elements—wind, rain, snow, cold, or heat. I personally think it makes you soft, so when you do have to face the elements, you're not prepared.

Football is a very mental game, and the way you build mental toughness for the elements of nature is to be out in the elements. Look, if I'm a mountain man and I've lived in the elements and I want to play a football game in the mountains against you, and you've lived in a house all your life, your reaction to the weather is going to be different than mine.

I don't believe the weather gives you a home field advantage on game day. The advantage weather gives is in the preparation. Look, it is as cold outside for a quarterback from Green Bay as it is for a quarterback from Tampa. But if the quarterback from Green Bay is used to cold weather (and he cannot help but be used to it), then it is less of a negative or distraction for him. Mentally, he is prepared for it.

Joe's Record Book
No team that plays its home games in a dome has ever won the Super Bowl.

But fans, especially fans in cold weather cities, seem to revel in bad weather. They believe it gives their team an adavantage and they love to be part of the experience of surviving the wrath of Mother Nature.

The Red Zone

The red zone is the area between the 20-yard line and the end zone. You are only considered to be in the red zone if you are within 20 yards of scoring a touchdown. There is NOT a red zone within 20 yards of your defensive end zone. *The red zone is not marked on the field, other than by the 20-yard line. It is simply a figurative area that coaches and players refer to as critical.*

So why is the final 20 yards so important? Why give it a special name and color?

Well, the thinking is that if you can bring the ball all the way down the field to get in this zone, you'd better take advantage of the opportunity and score a touchdown. If you get into the red zone and only score a field goal, you have given your opponent—who was trying to stop you—a psychological edge, and you never want to give those.

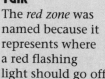
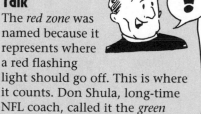

Joe's Gridiron Talk
The *red zone* was named because it represents where a red flashing light should go off. This is where it counts. Don Shula, long-time NFL coach, called it the *green zone* because that was where the money was made.

Think about the importance of that area this way: If you score a touchdown and convert the extra point, the other team can drive down the field twice, kick field goals both times, and you are still up by one point.

One reason why the red zone is different than the rest of the field is that it is actually a smaller field, therefore cramping both the offense and defense in closer quarters. With the smaller field, the defense has less to cover, making it more formidable. But still, when you are in the red zone, you need to score a touchdown for it to be a successful visit.

The Least You Need to Know

➤ The ball is designed to fly true when thrown, plus it fits neatly into the crook of your arm, between your hand and inside of your elbow, when running.

➤ The field is big to create excitement.

➤ There is an end zone at each end of the field. That is where touchdowns are scored.

➤ The lines on the field help you figure out how far to go to reach the end zone.

➤ The game is faster on artificial turf because it offers better traction.

➤ The weather is always perfect inside of domes. Yet, teams that have outdoor home fields are more accustomed to varying weather conditions.

➤ The red zone is the final 20 yards of the playing field before the end zone. It is considered a critical area of the field, although it is not marked on the field.

Chapter 3

OOHM...

You Get Six Points To Do What?

In This Chapter

➤ How do you get points?

➤ How do you keep time?

➤ Why you need a coin

In football, you want to win.

No kidding.

So how do you win?

You win by finishing with more points than the other team.

So how do you get points?

Ah, good question.

That's what this chapter is about—how to score points and keep track of time. By the time you are done reading this chapter, you will be able to keep score of a football game all by yourself. Is this a great book, or what?

Touchdowns

6 points.

Touchdowns are the best thing that can happen to you and your team in a football game.

Your team scores a *touchdown* by having possession of the ball in the other team's end zone.

If you don't know anything about football (or, for that matter, baseball) let me put it this way: Touchdowns are like home runs in baseball, only better. Touchdowns are a really big deal. This must be clear if you want to understand football. Touchdowns are the best.

So say this, "*I love it when my team scores a touchdown.*"

There you go. You are now talking the talk.

Joe's Rules

A touchdown was originally worth only 4 points. In 1898, a touchdown was changed from 4 points to 5, and in 1912, it was changed again to 6 points.

Joe's Record Book

Three players have scored six touchdowns in an NFL game. And all three games involved the Chicago Bears:

➤ Ernie Nevers of the Chicago Cardinals versus the Chicago Bears, November 28, 1929.

➤ Dub Jones of the Cleveland Browns versus the Chicago Bears, November 25, 1951.

➤ Gale Sayers of the Chicago Bears versus the San Francisco 49ers, December 12, 1965.

Touchdowns are worth 6 points, and there are a few different ways to score one: you can carry the ball into the end zone running, you can catch it in the end zone, or you can fall on a live ball. If you have possession of a ball and both of your feet are in the end zone, or if the ball is in your possession and it crosses into the air above the end zone, you have scored a touchdown. In fact, the ball does not even have to be in bounds. If your feet are in bounds before the goal line and the ball crosses plane of the goal line, even if the ball is out of bounds, it is a touchdown. Also, if you're carrying the ball and the ball itself breaks the plane of the goal line with your upper body, but a defender pushes you back before your feet cross, you still score.

Let's review:

Touchdown = hold the ball in the other team's end zone (the end zone the other team is defending).

Touchdown = 6 points.

The great thing about a touchdown is what it represents. It is more than just 6 points. It says to the other team, "We have gotten the highest score possible this time down the field." It is a statement.

There have been people or groups who have made a celebration in the end zone quite entertaining. Ickey Woods, who played for the Cincinnati Bengals, had one called the Ickey Shuffle. For a group celebration, the Washington Redskins had seven guys who used to get in a circle and on a count of three, jump up and touch hands after anybody scored a touchdown. They were called the "Fun Bunch."

If you think about it, the originators of football were really smart when they designed its scoring system. Giving more than one point for a touchdown makes the game seem even more exciting. For instance, consider a game that ends 21-7. If you counted touchdowns by 1 (and for the moment disregarded extra points), the score would be 3-1. Now, what would you rather watch? A 21-7 game, or a 3-1 game?

Joe's Gridiron Talk
The *touchdown dance* is a celebration players do in the end zone after scoring a touchdown. There is a fine line between spontaneous joy and arrogant showmanship. A little of both makes for a heck of a dance.

Joe's Tips
When your team scores a touchdown, that's when you are supposed to scream, yell, give high fives, and hug all your friends and neighbors. If the other team scores a touchdown, pull out your four-letter word dictionary and yell a few choice phrases at the opposing quarterback—you will feel much better.

Extra Points

1 point.

An extra point has the perfect name: extra point. That's what it is—extra, and worth 1 point.

An *extra point* is one of two ways to score after a touchdown. You have to score a touchdown first, or you cannot get an extra point opportunity. If you score 6, you can then try to go for 1.

See, the more you learn about this game, the better it gets. It just makes perfect sense all the way around. It works like this: When a team scores a touchdown, the ball is placed on the other team's 2-yard line (the 2-yard line right in front of the end zone where the touchdown occurred). The kicker for the team that scored the touchdown then must kick the ball off the ground through the uprights of the goal post, over the crossbar.

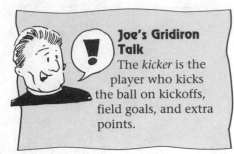

Joe's Gridiron Talk
The *kicker* is the player who kicks the ball on kickoffs, field goals, and extra points.

Joe's Record Book
Here are a few extra point experts:

➤ George Blanda, who played professional football for 26 years, holds the record for the most kicking extra points—943.

➤ Tommy Davis, who played for the San Francisco 49ers, kicked the most consecutive extra points without a miss—234.

➤ Pat Harder, of the Chicago Cardinals, kicked the most extra points in one game—9.

To complete the extra point kick, the ball is snapped from the 2-yard line by a player, called the center, to a kneeling player. That player, called the holder, is seven yards behind the line of scrimmage. The line of scrimmage (LOS) is the starting line for each play.

The holder, when he receives the snap, places the ball, one pointy end down and the other up, on the ground. The holder holds the pointy end that is up with one finger.

The kicker then kicks the ball.

If it goes through the uprights on the goal post, it is worth 1 point. You can only get this 1 point if you first scored a touchdown. Remember, it is called an extra point. For this reason, it is sometimes called a *point after*.

The extra point is that little way of punctuating the big event, which is the touchdown. It says, "You could come back and score a touchdown and match my big event, but if you miss the extra point, I still have you." The extra point is indeed extra, but it is not really a bonus. It is more of a must. If you don't make it, you lose some of the psychological advantage of the touchdown.

The extra point is so much of a given, that sometimes you will hear announcers refer to a touchdown as 7 points. A touchdown is worth 6. The extra point is 1.

Two-Point Conversions

2 points.

After you score a touchdown, you have a choice. You can kick the safe extra point, or you can live dangerously and try for not just 1 extra point, but 2.

After a touchdown is scored, the ball is always placed at the other team's 2-yard line. The team that scored the touchdown can kick an extra point for 1 (see the preceding section), or they can go for a *two-point conversion*. Got it?

If you want to score 2 points after scoring a touchdown, your team must move the ball forward two yards into the end zone by having a player carry the ball over or having the quarterback throw the ball to a player in the end zone—and you only have one play to do it.

One play. Two yards for 2 points: the two-Point conversion.

The two-point conversion is also called "going for 2." Say, *"I think we should go for 2."* Be careful when you say it, though. Most times it is not smart to go for 2. It is usually safer to say, *"I don't think we should go for 2."*

Even coaches need a little help deciding when to go for 2 and when to go for the much-safer 1. They usually use the chart in Table 3.1 for reference.

Table 3.1 Chart for Deciding When To Go for 2 Points After a Touchdown, Based on the Current Score

If your team's ahead by:	You should:	If your team's behind by:	You should:
Even	Kick	Even	Kick
1	Go for 2	1	Kick (depends on time, consider going for 2 to win)
2	Kick	2	Go for 2
3	Kick	3	Kick
4	Go for 2	4	Kick (but consider going for 2 to win with field goal)
5	Go for 2	5	Go for 2
6-10	Kick	6-8	Kick
11	Go for 2	9	Kick (but consider going for 2 because you'd only need a touchdown to tie)
12	Go for 2	10	Go for 2
13-18	Kick	11	Kick
19	Go for 2	12	Kick (but consider going for 2 because then a touchdown and field goal could tie)
20	Kick	13-15	Kick
21	Kick	16-18	Go for 2
22	Go for 2	19-20	Kick
23-24	Kick	21	Go for 2
25	Go for 2	22-24	Kick
26-28	Kick	25-26	Go for 2
		27	Kick
		28	Go for 2

Table 3.1 is only a guideline. Coaches use their own judgement in deciding what to do, but this chart gives them a basis to start thinking from so they don't have to mathematically evaluate every possible scoring outcome while the game is being played.

Teams don't usually go for 2 because they want to, but rather because they must in order to tie or win.

Let's say your team is behind, but you just scored a touchdown with three minutes to go in the game. You know you are probably only going to get the ball back one more time to try for another touchdown. The touchdown you just scored makes the score 24-14. If you get 2, it is 24-16. If you can then score another touchdown and two point conversion, you can tie the game. If you had kicked the extra point earlier, you would need 9 to tie the game. And you can't get 9 at once. By going for two, you have given yourself a chance to tie the game with another touchdown and 2-point conversion.

You probably didn't think football was that complicated, did you? Now you can appreciate how tough it is for coaches to make decisions. That's why coaches use the above strategic chart.

Field Goals

3 points.

This is the exact same action as an extra point—a kicker kicking the ball through the uprights off of the ground—only it occurs in different circumstances and is worth more points.

Joe's Record Book
The longest field goal in the history of the NFL was kicked by Tom Dempsey of the New Orleans Saints against the Detroit Lions on November 8, 1970. Dempsey, who was born with half a right foot and wore a special shoe, kicked the ball 63 yards. Alex Karras of Detroit didn't even rush to try and block the kick. He just laughed.

A *field goal* is easier to get than a touchdown, but it is worth half as much. A field goal is scored when a team kicks the ball through the goal post uprights from the field of play. On any down in an area close enough to the goal post, the offensive team can elect to kick the ball through the goal post uprights. This usually occurs on fourth down, but not always.

There are a couple things to keep in mind about field goals. First, the goal post is at the back of the end zone, which is 10 yards farther than the front of the end zone. And secondly, the ball is placed about seven yards behind the line of scrimmage when it is kicked. Therefore, a kick is always 17 yards farther than the yard line where the line of scrimmage lies.

So, if the line of scrimmage is the 20-yard line, the kicker will try a 37-yard field goal.

Because most kickers' range ends between 40 and 45 yards, it is safe to say that the 30-yard line is the most distant spot of a kicker's field goal range.

See Table 3.2 to see how often NFL kickers make field goals in various yard ranges.

Table 3.2   1995 Field Goal Kicking Peformance by NFL Kickers

Field Goal Length (in Yards)	Kicks Attempted	Kicks Made	Percentage Made
1-19	19	18	.947 (94.7%)
20-29	265	243	.917 (91.7%)
30-39	318	262	.824 (82.4%)
40-49	261	189	.648 (64.8%)
Over 50	91	46	.505 (50.5%)

The other thing to realize about kicking a field goal is that it requires tremendous coordination between the snapper (a.k.a. the center), the holder, and the kicker. The entire process takes approximately 1.4 seconds.

Snap, hold, kick.

That quick.

Safeties

2 points.

A safety is a *gotcha!*

A *safety* is scored by the defense, the team that doesn't currently have possession of the ball. Quite simply, if the defense tackles the offense in its own end zone or gets the offense to commit a penalty in its own end zone, the defense scores 2 points. Another way to get a safety is for the offense or a team receiving a kick to run out of the back of its own end zone with the ball—if a team crosses behind the back line of the end zone (behind the end line), it's an automatic safety. The defense can also score a safety if it blocks a punt out of the end zone, if the offense fumbles the ball out of the end zone, or if an offensive player runs out of bounds in the end zone.

But it gets better. The offense then must go to its own 20-yard line and kick the ball away. This kick is called a *free kick*, in which the kicking team can either punt it or kick the ball off the ground.

The bottom line to a safety is the defense gets 2 points and then gets the ball—not a bad deal.

There is also a tremendous momentum swing that occurs with a safety. To either be sacked in the end zone or lose yardage, resulting in a safety, also says that the offense can't handle the defensive pressure. It can be morally taxing.

Quarters and Halves

Keeping time in a football game is an easy concept to grasp. The game is broken into sections, which are then broken down a little more. It's like this:

1 game = 60 minutes

1 game = 2 halves

1 half = 30 minutes

1 half = 2 quarters

1 quarter = 15 minutes

A quarter is also called a period. Okay, just like there are four quarters in a dollar, there are four quarters in a game. The first two quarters, together, are called the first half. The last two quarters, together, are called the second half.

There is a two-minute intermission between quarters in each half. There is a 12-minute intermission between halves, unless otherwise specified. Half-time is longer for playoff games and the Super Bowl so the television networks can run more commercials and make more money.

Now check out how easy it is to keep track of the current quarter. The first quarter is called *the first quarter*. The second quarter is called *the second quarter*. It continues like that all the way to the fourth quarter.

Game Time Doesn't Include Commercials

There are aspects of a football game that are a bit more complex than counting to four: for instance, the way time is kept. Time in a football game is not real time. No. It is *game time*. Real time includes commercials.

Instead, an official carries an official game clock, which stops and starts at different times. A stop of the clock means that the countdown of time left in a quarter stops, and doesn't resume until the start of the next play. Here are the instances when the game clock stops:

➤ Change of ball possession

➤ Incomplete pass, when the quarterback throws the ball to another player but that player doesn't catch it (more on what each player does in the next chapter)

➤ Penalty

➤ Ballcarrier goes out of bounds

➤ A team calls a time-out (more on these shortly)

➤ Injury

➤ An official calls a time out to measure for a first down or to spot the ball

➤ A team scores a touchdown, field goal, or safety

The Two-Minute Warning

The final two minutes of each half are considered special. Thus, when there are two minutes left in the game, there is an official time-out. Both teams can confer with their coaching staff.

And then, in those final two minutes, there are some special rules.

➤ On a kickoff, the game clock (also called *the clock*) does not start until the ball is touched by a player in the field of play. In all other cases, it starts with the kick.

➤ If a ball is fumbled in the last two minutes, it may only be advanced by the offensive player who fumbled the ball, or by any defensive player. No other offensive player may advance the ball.

➤ If a player is injured in the final two minutes, his team is charged a time out. At any other time in the game, his team is not charged a time out.

Overtime

If a professional football game is tied at the end of four quarters, it doesn't end. Instead, teams play to *sudden death*, in which the team that scores first wins. They play for 15 minutes, called an *overtime period*. If no one wins by the end of an overtime period, the game ends as a tie.

Got it? Good, because it doesn't always end as a tie.

In playoff games and the Super Bowl, teams keep playing overtime periods until one team scores and wins.

The Play Clock

The NFL wants there to be lots of plays (you'll learn more about plays soon). Thus, teams are given 40 seconds from the end of one play to start another.

If, however, the officials become involved for any number of reasons, teams are given 25 seconds from the time the officials finish their business (and blow their whistle) until the team must start a play.

Time-outs

Teams are given three *time-outs* per half. A time-out is exactly that. Just like you give to your three-year-old.

It means we on the team want to stop and think about it. No need to act hasty. Actually, it could mean we panicked, we don't have the right guys on the field, or any of a million other things too.

Time-outs serve two purposes: They let the coaches and the team think about the upcoming play—usually an important one—and, they stop the clock.

Teams are only given three time-outs each half. You cannot save the ones from the first half for the second. If the game goes to overtime, each team is given two time-outs per overtime. If there are any timeouts left from the second half, they do not carry over.

Play the Game

So, you've got points, you've got quarters, and you've even got time-outs. But how the heck do you start?

Well, you start with a coin.

That's right, you flip a coin to see who gets the ball first. The visiting team gets to choose heads or tails. Whichever team wins the coin flip can choose whether they want the ball or whether they want to defend a certain end zone. They can't do both. Sometimes, because of wind or weather conditions, teams may choose the end zone. Every quarter, teams switch end zones and go the other way.

But usually, the team that wins the toss elects to get the ball. But if they don't want to decide they can *defer* to make the choice until the beginning of the second half. Usually, the team that kicks off in the first half receives the ball to start the second.

When it is decided which team gets the ball, the other team lines up on its 30-yard line (the 30-yard line it's defending) where the ball is placed on a *kicking tee*.

To start each game, one team places the ball in a kicking tee like this, then its kicker kicks the ball.

The other team receives the kick and runs it back until it is tackled or forced out of bounds. That team then starts with *first down and 10 yards to go.* This is common lingo for the current situation in any game. When a team has the ball, it wants to get a first down. It has a certain number of yards it needs in order to get a first down, and, in fact, the current situation carries with it a down. It is either first down, second down, third down, or fourth down. So, if it is *second and seven,* that means it is second down with seven yards to go until a first down.

If a team does not get a first down in three plays, it will usually elect to *punt,* which means that it will kick the ball to the other team. A punt is a different kind of kick than field goals, extra points, or kickoffs. A punt is a kick in which the punter (the player who punts) receives a 15-yard snap and then drops the ball while, in a coordinated manner, he kicks it from the air. When a player on the punt receiving team receives the punt, he can run it back until he is tackled. It then becomes first and 10 for the team that just received the punt.

Joe's Record Book

In Super Bowl XX, Walter Payton was the captain of the Chicago Bears. He was told by the official tossing the coin to "call it in the air." He didn't. The official tossed the coin. It landed. It stopped. Payton then said, "Heads." The Bears got the ball and went on to win 46-10. Despite that, I don't think the coin flip affected the outcome.

The Anatomy of a Play

A *play* is the offense's attempt to move the ball, and for each play there is a "plan" dictating what each player should do.

Each play starts with a huddle in which the *offensive* team (the team that has possession of the ball) gathers around the quarterback a few yards behind the line of scrimmage, where the ball came to rest at the end of the previous play. The quarterback gives the team the strategy for the play (the plan the team will follow to make the best progress during the play). The offensive team then comes to the line of scrimmage and lines up, and the defensive team lines up across from them. Offensive players must get into a *set position* meaning they must set their bodies steady until the play begins. The quarterback then calls signals. At a certain sound uttered by the quarterback (usually the words "Hut two!"), the play begins. The offensive players follow the plan for the play, trying to advance the ball as far as possible. The defensive players try to stop the offensive players from advancing at all. The defensive players have a plan of their own. They also try to stop the offense from making a first down or scoring a touchdown.

The Least You Need to Know

➤ Touchdown = 6 points

➤ Field Goal = 3 points

➤ Safety = 2 points

➤ Two-Point Conversion = 2 points

➤ Extra Point = 1 point

➤ Time is kept on a game clock. Each game is 60 minutes long; those 60 minutes are divided into four quarters. Halftime occurs after the first two quarters (called the first half).

➤ The winner of the coin toss usually gets the ball first.

Every Player Has a Different Job

Football players are not just a bunch of big guys. Well, they are a bunch of big guys, but there is much more to the story.

In fact, football is a game with diverse skill and size requirements. There are 11 players on offense. There are 11 players on defense. There are teams for punts, kickoffs, and returns of both. There are short-yardage units on both offense and defense. There are other specialized groups, each of which has 11 players and each player has a different job.

This chapter is an introduction to the different types of players that make up each team, what they wear, and what they do. It will outline some very different jobs. The truth is, this chapter will not cover every detail of every job. In fact, entire books could be (and, in some cases, have been) written about just one position. This is one chapter about all of the positions.

But first, start with the uniform. After all, everybody's gotta wear a uniform.

The Uniform

The psychological effect of the uniform is immense. When you're wearing your football uniform, you look large to the other team. You feel large to yourself. The colors are vivid, and are either urban and hip, or historic and legendary.

The colors alone make the game seem like a clash of titans. I'm not exaggerating. Watch a game. The players look like knights in armor attacking each other. The padding amplifies this perspective.

Although all players must wear helmets and padding, different players holding different *positions* (jobs on the field) wear different types of helmets and padding.

The basic uniform looks like this.

Professional football players wear this uniform, which offers a substantial amount of protective padding.

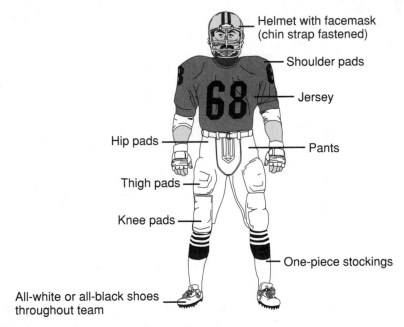

Helmet with facemask
(chin strap fastened)

Shoulder pads

Jersey

Hip pads

Pants

Thigh pads

Knee pads

One-piece stockings

All-white or all-black shoes
throughout team

Helmet and Facemask

The helmet and facemask of the uniform are designed to protect the head and face.

Helmets come in many different sizes for different sized heads. Thus, some helmets (big ones) weigh more than small ones. In fact, one player, Steve Wallace, offensive lineman of the San Francisco 49ers, wears a *cap* on top of his helmet. The cap is essentially a second helmet fitted on top of the regular helmet. It softens blows for Wallace, who has had a concussion.

All helmets come with a facemask, which is a bar or a series of solid plastic bars that act like a rollbar for the face. They protect the face from pokes and hits and damage that comes from falling on your face.

As for facemasks, I wore a single bar. I wore it specifically because it helped me to see better. No quarterbacks wear them anymore. I was probably the last one to be stupid enough to wear one. If I were playing now, I'd still wear a single bar, but most players now wear much more protection for the face.

Shoulder Pads, Hip Pads, Knee Pads, and More

This is basic science. The shoulder pad is worn to protect the shoulder. The hip pad is worn to protect the hip. The knee pad is worn to protect the knee. Guess what the elbow pad protects? The elbow…very good. See, you're no idiot.

All the pads simply protect the various body parts from the ferocious blows that are delivered in football. The idea is to make it a game about the power of muscle, not the ability of the body to absorb *everything*.

Flak Jacket for the Ribs

A few types of players that you'll learn more about later in this chapter—quarterbacks, running backs, and wide recievers—can wear flak jackets. These items look like a vest and they protect the ribs. They don't hurt mobility, but some guys don't like them. Sometimes running backs don't like to wear them because they cannot feel the football next to their body as they run.

It's Gotta Be the Shoes

Players wear different types of shoes for different types of playing surfaces, which makes sense.

On a grass field that is wet, you need to dig in more, so you wear a longer cleat. (The term *cleats* refers both to the blunted spikes added to the bottoms of shoes for traction, and to shoes that have cleats.) On a dry grass field, you still want some dig so you still wear a cleat but just not as long.

On artificial turf, though, you wear something akin to a basketball shoe; you don't need cleats for extra traction, because the surface is already "sticky," as I explained earlier. Or maybe, on outdoor artificial turf, you could wear a shoe that has rubber nub cleats on the bottom, for a little bit more traction.

And, depending on the condition of the grass field, you could change the length of the cleat as the game progresses. Normally, you go out during warmups and try out different shoes. In cold weather games, if the field has just been uncovered, you are able to dig your spikes in, but then, as the game goes on and the field starts to freeze, you may want to consider changing spikes to give you better traction.

The following illustration shows some typical cleat sizes NFL players may choose for playing on grass fields in different conditions.

Cleats give NFL players better traction in varying conditions.

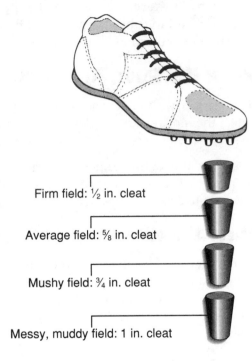

Firm field: ½ in. cleat

Average field: ⅝ in. cleat

Mushy field: ¾ in. cleat

Messy, muddy field: 1 in. cleat

Jersey, Pants, and Socks

These are the clothes players wear when they play. There is great uniformity to what they wear. That's probably why it is called a uniform.

There are several specific rules that pertain to the uniform. Here are a few:

➤ The jersey must be tucked in at the waist.

➤ Towels can only be eight inches long and six inches wide and must be tucked into the front waist of the pants.

➤ The exterior sock must be one piece, solid white from the top of the shoe to no higher than midpoint of the lower leg.

➤ Sleeves cannot be torn or cut.

➤ The uniform pants must meet the socks below the knee.

➤ Tape used on shoes or socks must be either transparent or of a matching color to the team uniform.

The clothes that players wear are governed very closely by the NFL. The jersey must be tucked in to the pants. If it is not, the NFL will fine a player. In fact, the NFL is such a stickler for style that it even governs the color of tape you can use on your socks. That tape must match the color of the uniform. If it doesn't, the NFL will fine the player.

Offensive and defensive lineman (the guys you'll learn about shortly who line up opposite each other at the beginning of a play) will often wear jerseys that are skin tight, and the players need help getting them on and off. Because lineman are allowed to grab a jersey in certain instances, the players want to give as little to grab as possible. Some guys have even been known to use a silicon spray on their jerseys to make them harder to grab. It is like putting Pam on a skillet before you cook—no stick, just slick.

Always 11 on a Side

Okay, they wear uniforms and protective equipment. But what do they all do?

Well, to start with, there are always exactly 11 players on the field for each team: 22 in all. If your team has more than 11, your team gets a *penalty*, which is the formal name for a violation of the rules. You are charged five yards for having too many men on the field. That means that if your team has possession of the ball, you're pushed back five yards, and have to travel that extra five yards to make a first down. If your team doesn't have the ball, it means that the opposing team will have five fewer yards to travel to make the first down.

If your team has less than 11 players on the field, it is not a penalty. It can be merely a competitive disadvantage. And it is a big competitive disadvantage. While it is a big disadvantage to have only 10 on the field, ironically enough, Tony Dorsett set the longest run from scrimmage—99 yards—against Minnesota when Dallas had only 10 men on the field.

Joe's Record Book

Players cannot wear any piece of clothing with a logo or personal message on it. Jim McMahon, the irreverent quarterback of the Chicago Bears during that team's 1985 Super Bowl run, didn't like the rule. So to protest commissioner Pete Rozelle's enforcement of the rule, McMahon wore a headband with the word "Rozelle" written on it during the Super Bowl. Rozelle thought it was funny.

Joe's Tips

Who is where, and when? Through the course of a game, there is a lot of substitution. It takes great coordination to get every player to know where he is supposed to be on every play. Some guys play on some plays, some guys play on others, some guys play on all in the same position, and some guys play on all in different positions. As simple as it sounds, there is great choreography in that 11-man show.

The Offense

The 11 guys that have possession of the ball are called the offense.

The offense's job is to try to score points. On the way to scoring points, the offense tries to move the ball at least 10 yards every four plays to make first downs and keep possession of the ball. See, this is easy to understand.

Generally, the offense consists of:

➤ 5 offensive linemen

➤ 1 quarterback

➤ 2 running backs

➤ 1 tight end

➤ 2 wide receivers

Other than the quarterback and offensive linemen, there is a great deal of flexibility in how the offense lines up. For instance, instead of the above configuration, the offense could have no tight end, only one running back, and four wide receivers. A team would employ this alignment if it faced a play where it most likely needs to throw a pass. Regardless of who is lined up where, the offense must always have only 11 players on each and every play.

One rule that you should be aware of is that the offense must have at least seven players lined up on the line of scrimmage (LOS). In other words, no more than four players can line up behind it.

Here's a quick review of how the offensive players line up, and what each type of player's job is:

➤ *Offensive linemen* line up in front of the quarterback. There is a *center*, who snaps the ball from between his legs to the quarterback. Two *guards* line up next to the center. There are also two *tackles*, who line up on the outside of the guards. All five linemen are responsible for blocking defenders from getting to the man with the ball, making running lanes for the man carrying the ball, or creating throwing lanes for the man throwing the ball.

➤ *Quarterbacks* call the signals and take the snap from the center. Their primary job is to throw the ball, hand off, and provide leadership.

➤ *Running backs* usually line up behind the quarterback. Their primary job is to take the ball from the quarterback and run with it as far toward the goal as possible.

➤ *Tight ends* line up next to the offensive tackle. Their job is two-fold—to block like a lineman and to catch passes like a receiver.

➤ *Wide receivers* line up on the line of scrimmage, to the right or left, away from the offensive line. Their job is primarily to catch passes thrown by the quarterback. But they also block on running plays.

The chapters in Part 2 of this book provide a more detailed look at the various players on the offense.

Joe's Rules

Players cannot just pick their favorite number. As with the rest of football, there are rules governing what number they can wear:

Positions	Numbers
Quarterbacks, punters, and placekickers	1-19
Wide Receivers (if 80-89 are taken)	10-19
Running backs and defensive backs	20-49
Centers	50-59
Centers (if 50-59 are taken)	60-69
Offensive guards and tackles	60-79
Wide Receivers and Tight Ends	80-89
Defensive lineman	60-79
Defensive lineman (if 60-79 are taken)	90-99
Linebackers	50-59
Linebackers (if 50-59 are taken)	90-99

The Defense

The 11 guys who try to stop the offense from scoring points are called the defense. On every play, the defense lines up across from the offense, on the opposite side of the line of scrimmage and tries to stop the ballcarrier by tackling him.

Generally speaking, the defense consists of:

➤ 4 linemen

➤ 3 linebackers

➤ 4 secondary players (also called defensive backs)

Of course, just like the offense, the defensive configuration can vary quite a bit. In fact, it is almost as common to see 3 linemen and 4 linebackers as the other way around. It all depends on how a team wants to play. And on passing plays, teams may take out a linebacker or defensive lineman and replace him with an extra player in the secondary.

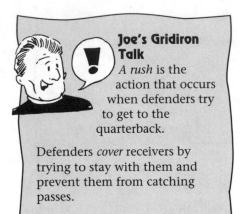

Joe's Gridiron Talk
A *rush* is the action that occurs when defenders try to get to the quarterback.

Defenders *cover* receivers by trying to stay with them and prevent them from catching passes.

Take a look at how the defensive players line up, and what each player does:

➤ The *defensive linemen* line up directly across from the offensive line. There are usually four defensive linemen—two *tackles* in the middle, and two *ends* on the outside of the tackles. The linemen are responsible for stopping the run and getting to the quarterback.

➤ *Linebackers* are the most athletic players on the field. They line up a few yards behind the line. Their job is to sometimes stop runs, sometimes rush the quarterback, and sometimes defend against passes.

➤ The *secondary* consists of two *cornerbacks*, who cover wide receivers, and two *safeties*, who help out on coverage where needed.

If you're curious to learn more about the players on the defense, consult Part 3.

Skill Players

As you can probably tell by now, there are many different names and labels in the game of football. One of the more misleading may be the term *skill player*, which simply refers to players who handle the football.

The truth is every player in the game of football is a skill player. In fact, the position of offensive line, which is naively thought by some to be a position of mere brute force and no skill, is in fact one of the most difficult positions in all of football to learn.

Skill players are, as I said, those who handle the football. On offense, that includes running backs, quarterbacks, and receivers.

On defense, the skill players are the players in the secondary because they are the ones who are in a position to intercept passes and generally get their hands on the ball.

The Trenches

Think of the term *trench warfare* and you will get a sense of what the announcer means when he talks of the trenches in football. The trenches are where the big guys do battle.

The trenches are the area where the offensive line battles the defensive line. Say this: *"If we win the battle in the trenches, we will be in good shape."* There is much truth to that statement, so say it often.

A big part of the offensive line's job is to create holes for ballcarriers to travel through and passing lanes for the quarterback to throw through. The line must also protect the quarterback so he can safely deliver the ball. Conversely, the defensive line wants to get to the quarterback, or free up holes for the linebackers to blast through. Put simply, if your big guys are able to push their big guys around, your skill guys have a chance to show off their skills. If not, forget it.

Special Teams

Special teams handle any play that does not involve your offense or defense. But many of the players on the various special teams also play offense or defense as well. Chapter 19 will discuss special teams in more detail.

Simply, special teams play during:

➤ Kickoffs

➤ Punts

➤ Field goals

➤ Extra points

Joe's Record Book

Who makes the most money? Quarterbacks, of course. In 1996, seven of the top ten paid players were quarterbacks. Troy Aikman, quarterback of the Dallas Cowboys, was the top 1996 money man, earning $5.371 million.

Joe's Record Book
In the 1997 Super Bowl, Desmond Howard of the Green Bay Packers won the Most Valuable Player Award as a special teams player. Howard finished with 244 return yards, including returning four kickoffs for 154 yards and six punts for another 90. The big one, though, was a 99-yard kickoff return that came on the heels of a New England Patriots touchdown.

➤ Two-point conversions (offense may also be involved in these). In these plays, both sides put out a group of 11 players. No matter what side of the play they are on, each group of players is called a special team. The truth is, about one-third of the game involves special teams. These plays are just as important as those involving offense and defense. Good teams realize this, and work hard to have competitive special teams.

There are two positions on special teams, besides the kicker, that are extra special. Those positions are the kick returner, and the punt returner. These two positions, specialists on punts and kickoffs, receive kicks and run them back. These players must be quick and elusive.

Joe's Rules

Special teams have the potential for some of the most exciting plays in football. However, in recent years, as kickers have gotten stronger, kickoffs were often going into the end zone and not being returned. The NFL remedied that in 1994 by moving the kickoff back five yards, from the 35-yard-line to the 30.

The importance of special teams, besides being involved in one-third of all plays, is that the outcome often dictates *field position*. This means, where you start when you get the ball. If your special teams are good, you will end up with better field position on offense, and you will give the other team bad field position when you go on defense. There is a lot of truth in the simple idea that the farther a team is away from scoring, the harder it is to score.

Kickers Are Different

There are two types of kickers. There are punters, and there are place kickers. They both are part of special teams, and they both kick the ball, although they do it in different ways.

Place kickers are responsible for kickoffs, extra points, and field goals. They kick kickoffs off of a tee (see Chapter 3). They kick field goals and extra points from the ground in a situation in which the ball is held by another player. Kickers are not allowed to use a tee when kicking field goals or extra points.

Punters kick punts. When they kick a punt, it is called *punting the ball*. See, once again, a lot of this is simple. In a punt, the ball is snapped back to the punter, who, while dropping the ball from his hands, kicks the ball in a continuous motion from the air.

Kickers and punters are different than other football players. It is weird. Football is probably the ultimate team game, yet kickers and punters are off in their own little world. In many ways, kickers are like athletes who compete in individual sports. They are like tennis players, golfers, and bowlers. In this emotional game, their job is non-emotional. They must stay steady. Not get frazzled. Although they rely on coordination from others, their job is very individualistic. They rely on themselves.

Rookies and Veterans

A first-year player is called a *rookie*.

Everyone who has played a year or more is a *veteran*.

There is more of a difference between rookies and veterans than you may first imagine.

Rookies come into the league having been a superstar at the previous level, college, and suddenly find that everyone they play against has out-of-this-world skills. (Plus they learn that the rules in pro football differ a bit from college football.) I look at it this way: The jump from Pop Warner (or Pee Wee, or any of a few other names for little league football) to high school is a big jump. The jump from high school to college is a bigger jump. But the jump in talent level from college to the pros is the biggest by far. The talent level in the pros is so high that it takes even the best rookies a little while to get acclimated.

Now, of course, there are exceptions to every rule. Dan Marino, the great quarterback of the Miami Dolphins, had great success in his first year. On the other side of the coin, many players take years to become successful. Still, the NFL is paying young players so much money now that they often feel pressure to leave college and start playing earlier than perhaps they should. Often, these young players do find success.

But there is one position that just takes longer than the others to learn—quarterback. Generally, there is a four-year rule when it comes to quarterbacks. The first year, he learns his team's offense. The second year, he learns the opposing defenses. The third year, he learns how to use his offense against opposing defenses. By the fourth year, he should be ready to perform at the most competitive levels. For example, Troy Aikman of the Dallas Cowboys won the Super Bowl in his fourth year. And Drew Bledsoe of the New England Patriots took his team to the Super Bowl in his fourth year.

The Least You Need to Know

➤ Uniforms must be worn exactly as described by the NFL or else the league will fine players.

➤ The offense is the team that has posssession of the ball.

➤ The defense does not have the ball, and tries to keep the offense from scoring.

➤ Special teams handle about a third of the plays, including kickoffs and extra points, and usually involve kickers.

➤ Skill players refers to those who handle the football.

➤ During a player's first year, he's called a rookie, and has a lot to learn to play successfully with the best players in the world.

AND WHEN YOU GOT THEM ON THE RUN YOU GOTTA KEEP 'EM ON THE RUN! WIN! WIN! WIN!

Coaching: Win or Get Fired

Coaching is one of the most brutal professions in the world. There are a lot of ways to do it, but it almost always requires an ulcer. You see, football is a bottom-line business. All businesses are, but this one is exaggerated because of the public nature of the job. There are only two choices: win or go away.

The bottom line, of course, is winning, and to win in this game of strategy, motivation, and, yes, deception, coaches have to dedicate their entire lives to the profession. What does this mean? It means what it says. Coaches don't have a life. Well, not a life outside of football anyway.

There are coaches who literally live at the football facility. From July to January, they see much more of their wide receivers than they do their wives. They breathe game film, dream of offensive and defensive schemes, and recite speeches in the shower. Coaches in the NFL, despite the glamour, lead quite unglamorous lives.

This chapter is about this most brutal of professions. It is about how coaches design game plans, and how they motivate players. Coaching is not a one-man show, and this chapter will examine how coaches rely on assistant coaches for help. It will also look at the different philosophies that work, and how a team takes on the personality of its coach. And if you knew some of the NFL's coaches, that's a scary thought.

Xs (or Vs) and Os

Part of the job of a coach is to design a strategy for running a football game. This is called dealing with the *Xs and Os* because when coaches draw up plays on a chalkboard, they usually use an O to designate offensive players and an X or a V to designate defensive players. Some coaches get creative and use the O to designate defense and the X or V to designate offense. But you get the idea. They draw up plays.

The standard offensive/defensive set serves as the basis for plays created by coaches.

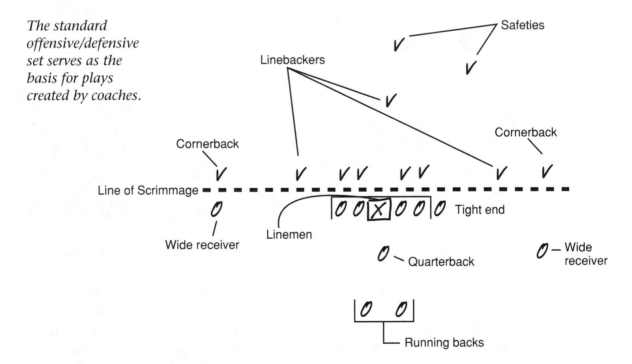

From this standard setup, coaches then can dream up any number of plays by drawing arrows showing where the players should go. If the standard setup looks like a sort of chess match, that's because that's exactly what it is—a matchup of wits between two generals who command comparably equipped armies.

But drawing up plays is not by any means the primary job of the coach. In fact, coaches are responsible for a much more complex process that is known as a *game plan*. The game plan is the approach that a team will take to an entire game. The coach may also want to develop a detailed list of the first several plays for the game. This is called *scripting the plays*.

Coaches try to cover every possible scenario and situation that will occur in games. It is not just a matter of figuring out which plays to run. It is a psychological war with the other coach.

Coaches are always thinking about different situations. Which plays should they run on first down and 10 yards to go? Which plays to run on second down and seven yards to go, second down and 10, second and more than 10? For every situation, there is a standard strategy and a lot of options. The options are almost unlimited. Plays on third down and short will be different than plays on third down and 12 yards to go.

It gets trickier. You see, all coaches know the standard type of plays that teams will run in various situations. So, they try to outthink the other team.

Follow this example line of thinking, and you will get an idea of how a coach's thought process goes: *He thinks that I'm going to do ABC. But I know that he thinks that I'm going to do ABC, so I'm going to do XYZ instead. But wait, he probably also knows that I know that he thinks that I'm going to ABC, so he is probably expecting XYZ. So, maybe, I really will do 123. Or, maybe, I'll do* **something else** *entirely.*

Got it? See, it's a head game, a battle of wits, and a chess game all in one. And the good coaches are always a few steps ahead of the others in thinking what the other guy is thinking.

Joe's Record Book

How much does a coach mean to a team's success? In 1997, the New York Jets, in a complicated negotiation, hired Bill Parcells who had been coach of the New England Patriots. To get him, the Jets gave the Patriots the rights to pick four college players in the future. Was he worth it? The Jets think so: Parcells has won two championships.

Joe's Gridiron Talk

The San Francisco 49ers under former Coach Bill Walsh began every game by knowing which 15 plays the team would run first. This was known as *scripting the plays*. The idea was to have a good idea how they would begin and then make changes as the game warranted. It was quite successful. Walsh won three Super Bowls, and now many teams script their opening plays.

Film Study

If you watch a movie more than once, you are going to see things you didn't see the first time. You will see nuances, things placed in the background for subtle effects. You have the same experience when you repeatedly watch film of a football team.

Joe's Tips

Some offenses are much more complex than others. Some teams run more than 500 different plays in their offense. Other teams only prepare 50 different offensive plays. Knowing more plays does not necessarily make an offense more successful.

A coach spends a great deal of his time studying film to learn about his own team's tendencies—and more importantly—about the tendencies of future opponents. A coach knows that football players are creatures of habit, so he studies films of game to learn what those habits are. Then, the coach can teach his team to watch for those little habits that the opponent has, and take advantage of that knowledge.

First, the coach is looking for how a team reacts as a team to different formations. Then he looks to find the best matchup possibilities and to take advantage of matchups.

For instance, some young offensive linemen might have a tendency to raise their rear up a little bit higher when they are going to be blocking for a run than if they are blocking for a pass. Now, if a defensive lineman knows who has this habit, he can often read what play is coming before the snap. Little things such as this give teams a big advantage.

Here are a few other things to look for:

➤ If the quarterback walks slowly from the huddle to the LOS, it is usually a quick count, meaning that as soon as he gets under the center, the center will snap the ball on the first sound out of the quarterback's mouth.

➤ If the quarterback is in a shotgun, which means he is five yards behind the LOS, when he raises his foot you can count to two and that's when the ball will be snapped. This is used in stadiums where the noise level is such that the center cannot hear the quarterback calling signals.

➤ If the tight end is flexed, which means he is not next to the offensive tackle, but split three to five yards away, it usually means the offense wants to throw the football.

Motivation

As you learned in Chapter 1, football is a very emotional game. It really is 85 percent mental and 15 percent physical. Although coaches obviously must spend time working with players to improve physical skills, their real job is to prepare the players mentally.

Motivation is such an important factor in football that the pregame speech is often the stuff of lore. The coach's job is much more than to just get the players to know what to do on the field. It is to get the players excited to do it. The coach needs to rev up their energy level and to push the players to the utmost. Coaches are responsible for getting their players ready to play.

So, how does a coach motivate? Well, any number of ways. Coaches, in many ways, are like child psychologists, dealing with a variety of maturity and intelligence levels. The truth is, no one method works for every player. Some players need to be kicked in the butt. Some need to be stroked and coddled. Each method could backfire if used on the wrong player.

In Jacksonville, Tom Coughlin is known as a disciplinarian. Many players complained about his methods, but the team was successful, making it to the AFC championship game in his second year with the team.

In Minnesota, Bud Grant, and later Jerry Burns were much more relaxed. For a while, both coaches had great success. They would bring players into training camp only one week before the first pre-season game. Other coaches had their players in three weeks before the first pre-season game.

So what works? Well, both styles work and both don't, too.

When I first joined the NFL, I was primarily a punt returner playing for George Allen, coach of the Washington Redskins. One week, I was hurt. I had a bad thigh bruise. The coach came to me, on the trainer's table, and asked if I could play that week against the Green Bay Packers. I said, "I don't know coach." He didn't say a word. He just looked at me like he was disappointed—just like you do to your kids. He knew how to get to me, and it worked. I dressed for the game.

> **Joe's Record Book**
> Perhaps the greatest motivator of all time was Vince Lombardi, the legendary coach of the Green Bay Packers. Lombardi once said, "Coaches who can outline plays on a blackboard are a dime a dozen. The ones who win get inside their players' heads and motivate."
>
> Packer tackle Henry Jordan once said of Lombardi, "He's fair. He treats us all the same—like dogs."

> **Joe's Tips**
> A coach's relationship to the media does not have much to do with winning. It has a lot to do with ticket sales. However, if you listen closely, you will hear motivational clues. For instance, in preseason, a coach may say that one player has had a "good week of work." The other players may read this to mean that they better work harder.

Every coach has a different way of doing things, just as every parent has a different way of doing things. When I was in high school, most of my friends didn't have to be home until 11 p.m. I had to be home by 10 p.m. That didn't make my parents, or my friend's parents bad. It just meant that they had different methods. It is the same in coaching: No one method is right. Different methods work on different players in different situations.

Here are some examples of the ways coaches motivate. They offer to any defensive player $50 for any sack, $100 for an intereception. And if the coaches think you were the player of the game, you could win a television set. And one of my favorites is when the offensive line does not give up a sack, the offensive line coach usually takes them all out to dinner. Now think about this. How would you like to pay for seven 300-pound guys having dinner? If you're a quarterback or a line coach, it would be your pleasure.

Beyond individual motivation, coaches also must motivate players on a group basis. Remember, this is the ultimate team game. Some players motivate themselves. Some players have a great degree of pride in their game and work and get their mind to work to accomplish great things. But still, this is a team game and the team has to work together because a great player who is motivated can only accomplish a limited amount of success without the full support of his teammates.

Coordinators and What They Coordinate

In some ways, the head coach does not appear as important as his assistants, but he is.

Each team has an offensive coordinator and a defensive coordinator. There is also a coordinator of special teams.

Each of these assistant coaches, the coordinators, is in charge of the specific unit that his title suggests. In other words, the offensive coordinator is in charge of the offense.

Joe's Record Book
When the Chicago Bears defeated the New England Patriots 46-10 in Super Bowl XX, the Bears defense carried defensive coordinator Buddy Ryan off the field. Head coach Mike Ditka was also carried off the field. It was the only time in Super Bowl history that a team carried a coordinator off the field.

Head coaches are involved in every aspect of the team. But coordinators are specialists. The game has become so complex that it is impossible for the head coach to know everything about everything. There just isn't enough time in the day. There are some who contend that one of the primary jobs of a head coach is to hire good coordinators. Good coordinators can, in fact, make or break a team.

Coordinators, in many ways, have the same role as the head coach—except it is reduced to their specialty. They still draw up schemes. They study the personnel of their team and the opposition. And, yes, they motivate.

The coordinators spend more time with their players than the head coach can because, obviously, the head coach is in charge of all the players. But a coordinator is only in charge of one unit.

In fact, football is a game of specialization. This is true in coaching as well. Besides the coordinators who are in charge of an entire unit (i.e., offense, defense, and special teams), there are coaches who are in charge of specific positions. There are, for instance, linebacker coaches, secondary coaches, and defensive line coaches on defense. These coaches also teach schemes and use motivational techniques. But, the major job of position coaches is to teach how to do the job. The motivation is part of it, but it is not the major part of a position coach's job.

During game time, a coordinator can be along the sideline, or up in the pressbox. Some coaches feel more comfortable upstairs where they can see an overview of what's going on. Other coaches want to be down on the field with their players. In either case, the coach does not have a lot of time for one on one contact with the players. But, both can get that if they need it. How can a coach in a pressbox get one on one contact with a player? Simple. They use the telephone. Or, in the case of the quarterback on the field, he receives radio communication from his coach right into his helmet. And one other tool that teams use are photographs that are taken of actual plays during the game. The idea is to better understand what the other team is trying to do.

> **Joe's Gridiron Talk**
> When Pete Carroll was the defensive coordinator of the New York Jets, a stuffed *beaver* was given to the player who made a play that led to a fumble. The beaver, described by many as "the hardest working animal in the animal kingdom," symbolized a great play. Despite playing for millions of dollars, players took great pride in having possession of the beaver for a week.

In addition to the head coach, coordinators, and position coaches, there are strength coaches, trainers, psychologists, equipment managers, and even secretaries who contribute to the success of the team. The makeup of a football administration is quite complex, just like that of a large company.

Finally, the thing to remember about the coaching ranks is that they are a hierarchy in which position coaches hope to rise to be coordinators, and coordinators hope to rise to be head coaches. It is a logical progression.

The Various Philosophies of a Blue-Collar Game

There are a lot of ways to focus a team. Sure, as you know, there are always 11 on a side, so the ways are not infinite. But there are various philosophies that have worked to create successful teams. In fact, these same philosophies have also failed.

So, clearly, there is no one right way. But, there are ways.

For instance, on offense, there is the *grind-it-out offense* which attempts to run the ball over and over again until it wears down the opposition's defense. This philosophy relies on a powerful running game (and running backs). The justification of this philosophy is that a running game takes up time on the clock because the clock does not stop between plays. If you remember, a pass play that is incomplete (and about 50 percent of pass plays are not complete) means the clock automatically stops. Now, if a team is winning and wants the game to end, grinding the ball into the other team's gut has great appeal because you can run the clock down and keep the other team from getting another opportunity to score. When I played for the Washington Redskins, we had one of the greatest power runners in the history of the game—John Riggins. We would grind it out by giving the ball to John and he would run behind our huge offensive line we affectionately called "The Hogs." And, believe me, John made my job as quarterback infinitely easier. I have a Super Bowl championship ring to prove it.

Joe's Tips
Count how many passes versus runs that a coach calls in a game. If a team is throwing the ball a lot, the quarterback may get hit a lot. If the team is running a lot, the score will probably be low.

In recent years, a new philosophy has come into vogue—the *West-Coast offense.* This philosophy, first put together by Coach Bill Walsh of the San Francisco 49ers (it started in San Francisco, thus the name West-Coast offense) relies on using short passes to serve the same purpose as running plays in the grind-it-out offense. Short, quick passes are used in this style.

In addition, there have been teams that have almost eliminated the running game altogether and have gone with something called the *run-and-shoot offense,* in which a team uses four wide receivers, one running back, and no tight end. This is an offense in which a great majority of the plays are passes. Although it is similar in philosophy to the West-Coast offense, the run-and-shoot is even more reliant on the pass. No team using the run-and-shoot offense philosophy has won the Super Bowl. However, the West-Coast offense has won quite a few in recent years. The West-Coast offense does not have to be run on the West Coast. In fact, the Green Bay Packers, playing in probably the coldest city in the NFL, won Super Bowl XXXI using that philosophy.

Finally, there is the *air-attack offense* in which a coaching staff is so confident in its quarterback and wide receivers that they are willing to go for much longer, and riskier, passes than normally employed by either the West-Coast offense, or the run-and-shoot. The most famous proponent of the air attack offense was Don Coryell, who coached the San Diego Chargers in the late 1970s and early 1980s. Coryell had Dan Fouts as his quarterback and he let Fouts wing it to a set of great receivers, including tight end Kellen Winslow, and wide receivers Wes Chandler, John Jefferson, and Charlie Joiner. Although the Chargers never won a Super Bowl, they were one of the most exciting teams of the era and went to the AFC Championship game in 1981.

The average length of passes attempted in the various styles of offense are:

➤ West Coast   7-10 yards

➤ Run-and-shoot   7-15 yards

➤ Air-attack   15-25 yards

On defense, there are also various philosophies. Some teams are more aggressive than others. Some attack, some react. Again, there is no one style that works.

The Personality of the Coach and the Team

Teams tend to take on the personality of their coach. A fiery coach will usually have a highly emotional team, whereas a more restrained coach may have a more machine-like team.

Despite the fact that football is an emotional game, it does not require an emotional coach. One of the greatest coaches in the history of the game was Tom Landry, who coached the Dallas Cowboys. Some accused Landry of coaching "a precise, mechanical brand of football that is so efficient it is boring." Landry didn't care what others said. He believed in efficiency. "A team that has character doesn't need stimulation," he said.

The Least You Need to Know

➤ Coaches don't have lives outside of football because the job requires absolute dedication.

➤ Coaches motivate in many different ways and no one way is guaranteed to be sucessful.

➤ Teams tend to take on the personality of their coach. For example, a defensive-minded head coach will probably be more concerned with stopping a team from scoring than scoring himself. An offensive minded coach thinks just the opposite.

➤ Coordinators on offense and defense draw up the play-by-play plans.

➤ Teams rely a great deal on film study in order to learn what their opponents tend to do in games.

OH?!

Chapter 6

Understanding the Lore

In This Chapter

➤ How football began

➤ How football evolved

➤ Names and games you should know

Once upon a time in a place called America... That phrase evokes the essence of football. From the very first collegiate soccer game on November 3, 1869, when the roots of football first started to grow, the game has taken on storybook proportions.

There is a legacy to football. It has been passed down by word of mouth, newspaper clippings, and, in recent decades, on television. Ah, television. The game of football was made for television. That magic, flickering box has been a showcase for drama, comedy, news, and sports since it was born. But just as fooball was made for television, television was made for football because football is full of drama, comedy, news, and sports.

The story of football is rich. This chapter is about that history—the names, the games, the lore, and the scores. The texture of the game is deep and multi-faceted. There are more than 100 years of history. You cannot learn it all right here, but there are aspects of the history that every fan should know.

Try this experiment: Walk into a sports bar and say, "Excuse me, who is Joe Namath?"

When you do this, be sure to be carrying this book because someone is liable to say, "What are you, an idiot?" And you can say, "Not anymore."

This chapter will teach you about Joe Namath and more. Here, briefly, is the story of football and the NFL. That's this chapter, a brief history lesson, starting with the game's defining moment.

The Frozen Tundra of Lambeau Field

Every American should know that George Washington and his troops endured bitter cold at Valley Forge in order to defeat the invading British army. Every football fan should know that Bart Starr and his Green Bay Packer teammates endured bitter cold at Lambeau Field in order to defeat the invading Dallas Cowboys.

These two heroic stories obviously don't compare, except that I just compared them. See, football is what you make it, and the NFL has made football into *folklore*. Remember these words, ...*the frozen tundra of Lambeau Field*... Now say them with a deep, theatrical baritone and imagine those two football teams playing on December 31, 1967, as the temperature fell to 13 degrees below zero with a windchill factor of 50 below. Say the words to yourself, *thirteen below zero*, and imagine the two teams, the Green Bay Packers and the Dallas Cowboys, staring each other down with the championship of the NFL on the line. The winner would go on to Super Bowl II.

Joe's Record Book

The NFL underwent a metamorphosis in the late 1960s. Prior to merging with the AFL, the NFL did not have two conferences. NFL teams played each other in a championship game. The Super Bowl championship originally was not the NFL championship.

With 16 seconds left on the clock, the Packers were on Dallas' 1-yard line, one yard away from scoring. Yet, two plays in a row, the Packers tried to run, and on both plays their running back slipped. So it came down to one play.

One play.

One.

On the frozen tundra of Lambeau Field.

Bart Starr, quarterback of the Packers, walked to the line and across from him stood Bob Lilly and Jethro Pugh and the rest of the Dallas Cowboys' defense. It was the coldest day in NFL history. Brutal. It was a mean kind of cold and these two lines of large men stood, facing each other. Steam poured from their facemasks. Like animals that were exhausted and angry, they dug in. The green-and-gold of the Packers face to face against the silver-and-blue of the Cowboys. They used their cleats, and both sides actually dug in for the fight, laying it all flat for everyone to see. One last time, steam pouring out of their faces. For one play. One final burst. Just one...on the frozen tundra....

Starr took the ball and instead of handing off as expected, he was bold. He put his faith in one man, Jerry Kramer, his right guard, who caught Jethro Pugh with a block just right, so Starr could follow Kramer into the end zone. It was pure power versus power—old-time football. Facenda, the longtime voice of NFL Films, later captured the moment in that phrase because, as Facenda told it in his greatest baritone, the drama unfolded—you know where this is going—*on the frozen tundra of Lambeau Field*.

The Packers went on to win Super Bowl II, 33-14 over the Oakland Raiders.

Joe's Record Book

The first Super Bowl was not called a Super Bowl. It was called the AFL-NFL World Championship Game. In the 1960s, there was another professional league, called the American Football League—AFL. On January 15, 1967, the Green Bay Packers, NFL champions, beat the Kansas City Chiefs, AFL Champions, 35-10. Only later did the game become known as Super Bowl I.

How It Began

Before football was football, the ball game began as collegiate soccer in 1869, and then evolved into rugby. The game started changing into football when a Yale student named Walter Camp became involved. In 1876, he wrote the first rules for football. Camp, who later ran a clock factory, invented the first scoring system, and he invented the line of scrimmage (LOS), which is where a play starts.

In 1892, William (Pudge) Heffelinger earned $500 to play a game for the Allegheny Athletic Association and became the first professional football player.

Joe's Rules

In 1906, the forward pass, where the quarterback throws the ball to a receiver down field, was legalized. George (Peggy) Parratt of Massillon threw the first pass completion to Dan (Bullet) Riley.

How It Evolved

The game that Camp invented was still a kicking game. Teams originally received more points for field goals than they did for touchdowns. In 1909, a field goal dropped from 4 points to 3. In 1912, the touchdown became worth 6 points.

From there, there is so much history that I will only briefly touch on many names and places.

Jim Thorpe was the first superstar football player. He was a former football and track star at Carlisle Indian School in Pennsylvania. He was a double gold medal winner at the 1912 Olympics in Stockholm. If you ever visit the Football Hall of Fame in Canton, Ohio (and you should, it is great), you will see Thorpe's statue in the entranceway. Thorpe played for the Canton Bulldogs and is said to have possessed astonishing talent.

I didn't see him play. Neither will you. That was a long time ago, but it is a name from the lore that you absolutely must know.

In 1919, Earl (Curley) Lambeau formed the Green Bay Packers with $500 he borrowed from his employer, the Indian Packing Company. In 1921, player-coach George Halas took over the Decataur Staleys and moved them to Chicago. A year later, they became known as the Bears. These are the two oldest original teams, and both Halas and Lambeau are legends of the game.

There had been more than one league and many league names but on June 24, 1922, the American Professional Football Association changed its name to the National Football League.

In the 1920s and 30s, the league and the game evolved into, if not maturity, at least adolescence. There were stars like Thorpe, Red Grange, Ernie Nevers, and Halas himself. In a game in 1923, Thorpe fumbled on the 2-yard line and Halas picked up the fumble and ran it 98 yards for a touchdown. It was an NFL record that stood until 1972.

Grange was the first to energize the NFL up to its potential. When he joined the Chicago Bears, attendance records were shattered. Suddenly, in New York, 73,000 people turned out to watch football. And in Los Angeles, 75,000 watched the Bears defeat the Los Angeles Tigers in the Los Angeles Coliseum.

Joe's Record Book
On November 28, 1929, Ernie Nevers of the Chicago Cardinals scored 40 points, which is still the record for the most points scored in a game, against the Chicago Bears. He scored six touchdowns and he kicked four extra points.

Joe's Record Book
There have been four different American Football Leagues during the past decades. None exist now. The first AFL folded in 1926. A second AFL existed for two years, 1936 and '37, and a third was formed in 1940 and folded two years later. The fourth AFL was born in 1960, and it merged with the NFL in 1969.

The National Football League, which was born in the heartland—Ohio, Illinois, Indiana, Pennsylvania, and Wisconsin—began to move its base to the larger cities of the East in the late 1920s.

In 1930, a huge bulldozer of a man named Bronko Nagurski, a fullback, joined the Chicago Bears. Quarterback Sammy Baugh of the Washington Redskins was a star of the 1940s.

The 1930s and 1940s saw the NFL faced with rival leagues, including two versions of the American Football League, and then the more formidable All-America Football Conference in 1946.

> **Joe's Record Book**
> The most lopsided championship game in history was on December 8, 1940 when the Chicago Bears beat the Washington Redskins 73-0.

> **Joe's Rules**
>
> It wasn't until 1943 that all players were required to wear head protectors.

The AAFC began play with eight teams. The Cleveland Browns, coached by Paul Brown, won the championship of that league four years in a row. In 1950, three teams from the AAFC—the Cleveland Browns, the San Francisco 49ers, and the Baltimore Colts—joined the NFL. In the first game of the year, the Browns beat the NFL champion Philadelphia Eagles 35-10. The Browns won the NFL championship their first year in the NFL.

In 1951, the NFL Championship game was televised nationally for the first time.

In 1958, the Baltimore Colts defeated the New York Giants 23-17. Although football had been televised for a few years, this was perhaps the first televised game to really capture the nation's attention. The game ended after 8:15 of overtime when Alan Ameche of the Colts scored on a one-yard touchdown run. Colts quarterback John Unitas completed all seven of his passes on a 12-play drive that led to Ameche's run. Millions saw it on television and the myth of the game had a new technology to feed it. The game *worked* on television. Who wasn't moved by that game? Suddenly, people had heard of John Unitas.

The 1950s featured big-time stars, such as quarterbacks Otto Graham of the Browns, Unitas of the Colts, Bobby Layne of the Detroit Lions, and running back Frank Gifford of the New York Giants.

The 1960s—You Say You Want a Revolution...

Football in the 1960s became showtime. Television, money, pop culture, and the American Football League showed up at the same time like stars aligning in the sky, and suddenly it was a golden age for the sport.

The power behind football's growth was its growing partnership with television. When 33-year-old Pete Rozelle took over as commissioner in 1960, one of his first priorities was to grow football on television.

Joe's Record Book
A documentary aired on CBS television in October 1960 brought new light to the allure of the NFL. It was about the middle linebacker of the New York Giants, and it was called *The Violent World of Sam Huff.*

Joe's Record Book
The highest scoring game of all time was November 27, 1966 when the Washington Redskins beat the New York Giants 72-41.

In 1960, the fourth American Football League formed, and, although at the time it seemed to be a bad thing for the sport, the new league turned out to be a jolt of energy. From its outset, the infant league was brash. For the first few years of the AFL's existence, the two leagues didn't play each other at all. The Green Bay Packers dominated the NFL, winning five of seven championships, plus the first two Super Bowls. The Packers were the creation of Vince Lombardi, who is generally regarded as the greatest coach of all time. Lombardi, a gruff, religious man with a possessed passion to win, guided the Packers with his iron will. The Packers were a powerful football team that didn't try to fool anyone. They simply dared the other team to stop them.

The greatest running back of all time played in the late 1950s and early 1960s. Jim Brown of the Cleveland Browns was huge, fast, and overwhelmingly powerful. In his career, he gained an average of 5.22 yards every time he carried the ball. There were times he had three or four men hanging off of him and he would still be running down the field.

But the biggest hero of the 1960s was a man who was drafted out of the University of Alabama to play for the upstart American Football League in New York City. His name was Joe and he went to Broadway in 1965. Joe Namath of the New York Jets changed football. A number of positive circumstances were working for Namath and he took full advantage of his opportunity. A year after Namath joined the AFL, the two leagues announced an impending merger that was to take effect in 1969.

Until the official merger, the two leagues agreed to play a championship game at the end of the season between the champions of each league. That game eventually was called the

Super Bowl. The first two Super Bowls were won decisively by the Green Bay Packers of the NFL. Everyone assumed it would take years for the AFL to become of equal strength with the NFL.

But then came the 1968 season. The Baltimore Colts rolled through the NFL that year, winning the NFL championship 34-0 over the Cleveland Browns. The Colts were being annointed champions before they even arrived in Miami to play Super Bowl III. Some thought the Colts were even more powerful than the great Green Bay Packer teams of the previous years. Bookies in Las Vegas had the Colts favored to win by 19 points. This meant that a bet on the Colts would only win if they won by more than 19 points. (More on gambling will be covered in Chapter 23.) It was the largest point spread in Super Bowl history. The AFL champions, almost an afterthought, were the New York Jets, led by a brash young quarterback, Joe Willie Namath.

He was arrogant with a quick wit and a golden touch in his arm. In the era of The Beatles and The Rolling Stones, Namath fit in perfectly—a sort of rock-n-roll rebel with long hair, a fu manchu, and a sparkle in his eye that told he was was having *fun*. But Namath was more than a star. He was a competitor.

At the Miami Touchdown Club a few days before the game, someone asked how the Jets were going to be able to handle playing such a tough team as the Colts. Namath got angry. He thought the Colts should be worried about playing as tough a team as the Jets. He said, "We're going to beat the Colts on Sunday. I guarantee it."

The guarantee became instantly famous. He was guaranteeing that his team would pull off the biggest upset in Super Bowl history. What nerve.

Namath delivered. On January 12, 1969, the Jets beat the Colts 16-7.

Joe's Record Book

The 1960s were an era of transition for the great coaches. In 1969, Vince Lombardi left the Packers to become coach of the Washington Redskins. He died a year later of cancer. Paul Brown was fired as coach of the Browns in 1964. He emerged as coach of the new Cincinnati Bengals in 1968. In 1968, George Halas retired after 40 years of coaching the Chicago Bears.

Joe's Gridiron Talk

The *Heidi Game* took place on November 17, 1968. The New York Jets were leading the Oakland Raiders 32-29 with 50 seconds to go when the time became 7 p.m. NBC put on the scheduled children's movie, *Heidi*, right on time. In the remaining 50 seconds, the Raiders scored two touchdowns. But no one saw it because *Heidi* was on TV.

The 1970s—When Perfect Was the Standard

After Namath won Super Bowl III, the leagues merged and divided into two conferences, the National Football Conference (NFC) and the American Football Conference (AFC).

The name of the merged league remained the NFL. Three NFL teams, the Baltimore Colts, the Cleveland Browns, and the Pittsburgh Steelers, joined the AFC.

The story of the early 1970s was the dominance of the 1972 Miami Dolphins. They were more than dominant—they were perfect. The Dolphins won every game that year, going 17-0 as they won the Super Bowl with a strong defense and a powerful, multi-faceted running game featuring powerful Larry Csonka, versatile Jim Kiick, and fleet-footed Mercury Morris. This was the only team in the history of modern professional sports that has gone undefeated for an entire season.

The Pittsburgh Steelers won four Super Bowl Championships in the late 1970s and early 1980s. Led by a dominant defense nicknamed *The Steel Curtain*, Pittsurgh overpowered their opponents.

> **Joe's Gridiron Talk**
>
> The *immaculate reception* occurred at the end of the first playoff game that the 70s Steelers team ever won. The Steelers were losing to the Oakland Raiders by 1 point with five seconds to play. Steelers quarterback Terry Bradshaw threw a pass that bounced off of a Raider into the outstretched fingertips of running back Franco Harris. Harris ran the ball in for a touchdown.

The 1980s—When Guys Named Joe Went to the Show

The early 1980s were my time, and included the two Super Bowls that I quarterbacked for the Washington Redskins. My first Super Bowl, in 1983, I played well, my team was focused, and John Riggins, our big running back, ran like a bull as we beat the Miami Dolphins 27-17. Our second Super Bowl, I didn't play well, the team wasn't focused, and we were beaten 38-9 by the Los Angeles Raiders.

As the 1980s progressed, the game was dominated by two teams, the Washington Redskins, and the San Francisco 49ers. My career was shortened by a broken leg in 1985, but coach Joe Gibbs proved he could win with more than one quarterback. He next won a Super Bowl in 1988 with Doug William as his quarterback. He won again the next decade, in 1992, with Mark Rypien as his quarterback.

The San Francisco 49ers, with innovative coach Bill Walsh at the helm and the unflappable Joe Montana as quarterback, won the Super Bowl in 1982, 1985, and 1989. In 1990, George Seifert became the coach and the team won the Super Bowl again with Joe Montana. Jerry Rice, the greatest receiver of all time, played for the 1989, and 1990 teams, as well as the 1995 San Francisco 49ers that again won the Super Bowl, this time with Steve Young as the quarterback.

But in the 1980s, the most dominant single-season team was the 1985 Chicago Bears who won the Super Bowl in January 1986. That Bears team was an arrogant bully of a team that smothered its opponents. It featured the famous "46 defense" designed by defensive coordinator Buddy Ryan, the great running back Walter Payton, and a wise-acre sunglasses-wearing quarterback named Jim McMahon. The Bears beat the New England Patriots 46-10, losing only one game all season.

The 1990s—When the Teams Moved

The 1990s ushered in the new era of the Dallas Cowboys. The Cowboys, a great team of the 1970s behind legendary coach Tom Landry and the great clutch quarterback Roger Staubach, had faded by the late 1980s. In 1989, Jerry Jones bought the Cowboys and replaced Landry as coach with Jimmy Johnson, Jones' friend from college and the coach of the University of Miami. Johnson then traded the Cowboys, best player, running back Herschel Walker, to the Minnesota Vikings for draft choices that soon became some of the Cowboys' new generation of stars. The Cowboys won the championship in 1993, 1994, and 1996 behind quarterback Troy Aikman and running back Emmett Smith.

Unfortunately, there was another trend in the NFL, team movement. Movement started when the Baltimore Colts moved to Indianapolis in 1983, but it accelerated in the 1990s with the Los Angeles Raiders, who had moved from Oakland, back to Oakland. The Los Angeles Rams moved to St. Louis, the St. Louis Cardinals moved to Arizona, the Cleveland Browns moved to Baltimore and became the Baltimore Ravens, and the Houston Oilers are about to move to Nashville.

On the field, in 1997, the Green Bay Packers took Super Bowl history full circle by winning Super Bowl XXXI. The Packers have a new generation of heroes. Led by fiery, strong-armed quarterback Brett Favre and the spiritual toughness of defensive end Reggie White, the team brought a championship back to the little town in Wisconsin that is called in the lore, *Titletown*.

And the story continues…

The Least You Need to Know

➤ The Green Bay Packers beat the Dallas Cowboys in 13-below weather *on the frozen tundra of Lambeau Field.*

➤ Football evolved from soccer and rugby around the turn of the 20th century. It was a kicking game until 1912, when the value of a touchdown was raised to 6 points, making it the most rewarding way to score.

➤ Joe Namath guaranteed his AFL New York Jets would beat the heavily-favored NFL Baltimore Colts, and then he won the game 16-7.

➤ In 1969, the ALF merged with the NFL to form the present-day NFL.

➤ The only team that ever went undefeated the entire year was the 1972 Miami Dolphins.

➤ The history of football is full of historic names like coaches George Halas and Vince Lombardi, quarterbacks Joe Montana and Terry Bradshaw, and running backs Jim Brown and Walter Payton. These are names that any idiot could drop—so feel free.

Part 2
Learning the Offense and the Penalties

I was once a quarterback in the NFL. What a fantastic job. In the annals of history, I don't believe there has ever been a better way to make a living. It was more than a living, it was a life. Playing on the offensive side of a football team is challenging, exciting, fun, and rewarding.

This part of the book deals with the offense. I will go through each position, including my own, and I will give you a job description of who does what and how they do it. I will talk about the mental and physical parts of each position and I will describe different strategies that each player uses. And speaking of strategies, you'll learn how teams put together an approach to winning. I will go through the basic ways of doing it, and then I will go into details about how teams use skullduggery as a means to an end—the only end, winning.

Chapter 7

The Quarterback Is the Movie Star

In This Chapter

➤ The skills of the job

➤ The mental duties

➤ Joe's Top Five in no particular order

On the field, there is one man at the center of the action. And, no, it's not the center.

The man at the center of the action on a football field is inevitably the quarterback because all the action goes through him. Quarterback is a glamorous, dangerous, high-risk/high-reward position that is the showpiece job in the NFL.

Quarterbacks are leaders and loners, men who carry the weight of a city's hopes on their shoulders. Men with the flair of Cary Grant and the iron will of General George Patton. Quarterbacks are heroes.

This chapter is about the most complex position in football, one like no other that requires skill, passion, intelligence, and innovative savvy. You'll learn here about the mental skills the position takes, the various jobs of a quarterback, the different skills in throwing the ball, and my personal list of the five best quarterbacks of all time.

Two Choices: The Hero or the Goat

The job of quarterback is like no other in sports. When you follow the game, you have to think of the quarterback as different than the other players because, in fact, a quarterback is different. The quarterback is the focal point. Any "idiot" could see that.

You can't help but have your eyes go to where the ball is, and the ball starts with the quarterback. He is the one who calls the signals and gets to make the first decision on what to do with the ball. Sure, the center touches the ball first. But the center must always snap the ball. And, almost always, the quarterback is the one receiving the snap.

Joe's Rules

The quarterback is not allowed to throw the ball if he runs past the line of scrimmage, toward the goal. He cannot even return back behind the line of scrimmage and then throw. If the quarterback throws the ball when he is past the LOS, his team is penalized five yards and a loss of a down. If the quarterback goes past the line of scrimmage and then returns behind it and throws a pass, the penalty is a loss of a down. Chapter 13 will provide more information about penalties.

The quarterback has many responsibilities, but perhaps the biggest one is to just plain take responsibility. When things go right, the quarterback gets the credit. Quarterbacks make more money than everybody else, and they get an unfair proportion of the credit when things go right. It's true.

I always thought of a victory as a team victory. It was always *our* win. Look, the quarterback is the most dependent position on the football field, and any good quarterback recognizes that he cannot do his job without a great supporting cast.

Joe's Record Book

Bernie Kosar, who played most of his career for the Cleveland Browns, holds the record for the most consecutive passes without an interception—308. You'll learn about interceptions later in this chapter.

But every fan recognizes that the other players are exactly that—a supporting cast. The irony is that a great team cannot win with a bad quarterback, and a great quarterback cannot win with a bad team. Teams and quarterbacks are forever linked.

Despite the importance of the other positions, the fact is that quarterbacks are the ones we remember. Even Super Bowls are remembered more for a specific quarterback than for the team. Ask a football fan about the *Joe Namath*

Game and they will know which game you mean. Joe Montana (San Francisco 49ers) and Terry Bradshaw (Pittsburgh Steelers) each won four Super Bowls. Teams also are known by their quarterbacks. Football fans know the difference between the Roger Staubach Cowboys and the Troy Aikman Cowboys. Both won the Super Bowl, but in different eras, and the different teams are identified by their quarterbacks.

The statistics of a quarterback are often the product of the offensive system. For instance, an offense that throws the ball 45 times a game will help boost a quarterback's statistics, whereas a team that only throws the ball 20 times a game will not allow a quarterback to get gaudy statistics.

It is such a high-pressure, high-glamour, high-blame position that not many have the make-up it takes to handle the heat. I know both sides of the heat. I have experienced both in the biggest game in the world.

Two years in a row, I brought my team to the Super Bowl. The first time, I played well and we won. When we did, as I said above, it felt more like a *WE* experience. But when we lost, I felt it was *MY* fault.

As a quarterback, I understood that winning and losing were my legacy. I will be remembered for both, and that is why the job is so appealing and so demanding.

Joe's Record Book

Dan Marino of the Miami Dolphins holds the record for the most touchdown passes in a season—48. (When a receiver catches the ball and scores a touchdown on a play, it's called a touchdown pass.) Marino also has thrown more touchdowns than anyone else, and for more yards than anyone else. Marino holds so many quarterbacking records, he is running out of ones to break.

Joe's Record Book

Jim Hardy of the Chicago Cardinals has the record for the most interceptions in one game—eight—in a game versus the Philadelphia Eagles on September 24, 1950.

It All Starts Here

The quarterback is in charge. He runs the huddle, where details for the play are finalized, and then breaks the huddle and moves the team to the LOS where he barks out the commands that start the play. As soon as the ball is snapped, it goes into the quarterback's hands and he must decide what to do from there. That's why the quarterback is the focal point of the action.

It is a strange position in the game. The quarterback is the one player on the field (during regular play) who does not get to hit someone, but is constantly a target himself. Everybody on the defense wants to hit the quarterback. Players on the offense get to hit someone on almost every play. But the quarterback's job description includes the phrase "ability to take punishment."

The quarterback is also the person who must tell everyone else what to do. The quarterback doesn't just have to know his own job, he has to know what everyone else on his offense is supposed to do. But it is more complicated. He is also expected to know what the defense is going to try to do to stop his offense. He has to instill confidence in his team that he knows how to beat the defense and then, most importantly, he has to deliver.

As for knowing his team, he has to know the blocking assignments of his line, the routes his receivers will run, and the duties of his running backs—whether they are to block, run, or go out for a pass. On any given play, the quarterback is expected to know where all 22 men will be on the field at any time during that play. Does he always know? Of course not. The defense is doing its best to fool him. But if he doesn't know most of the time what is about to happen, he won't be an NFL quarterback for long.

There are five essential characteristics of an NFL quarterback:

1. **Be able to throw the football.** That's what the quarterback does that no one else does. Without that skill, you can't be an NFL quarterback.

2. **Be smart.** There are more than 500 plays to learn and upwards of 30 different defenses to understand.

3. **Have some athletic ability.** In order to elude pass rushers and to run the ball if necessary, a quarterback must also have some athletic skills.

4. **Have supreme confidence in his ability.** Because confidence is catchy and teammates need to believe in their quarterback, a cocky quarterback can inspire his teammates to take action.

5. **Be self-critical.** Quarterbacks need to objectively examine their own performance in order to be able to criticize others.

Quarterbacks who have these characteristics can succeed in the game. Those who don't, don't have a chance.

The rest of this chapter covers the specific skills and techniques in the quarterback's job.

Working the Pocket

The pocket is the refuge of the quarterback—an area that the offensive line tries to keep safe from defenders so the quarterback has time to evaluate the progress of the play, find a receiver downfield, and throw accurately. In theory, the more time the quarterback has in the pocket, the more accurate the passing will be.

Technically, the pocket is an area that begins two yards outside of either offensive tackle, and it includes the tight end if he drops back into pass protection. The pocket area extends all the way back to the offensive team's own goal line.

The idea of the pocket is for the quarterback to be able to find receivers and throw the ball through *throwing lanes*. If the pocket holds up, the quarterback should have time to throw the ball and will be less likely to throw *interceptions*.

Spirals

A spiral is a tight spin or rotation on a thrown football. A spiral cuts the wind, so the ball doesn't waver and the throw is more accurate. It aerodynamically works for you. If you watch a spiral go through the air, it looks like it's a still picture. It is just another part of the beauty of the game.

Joe's Gridiron Talk
An *interception* is a pass that is stolen by the defense.

Joe's Gridiron Talk
Throwing lanes are the areas between linemen that the quarterback can throw the ball through. There is a misconception about quarterbacks that they must be tall to throw the ball over linemen. In fact, offensive linemen design blocking schemes to create throwing lanes for quarterbacks to throw through.

Different quarterbacks have different ways to throw the ball, but all are trying to create a tight spin. Jeff George, now of the Oakland Raiders, and Terry Bradshaw, who won four Super Bowls with the Pittsburgh Steelers, both took their index finger and placed it directly on the back point of the ball. This is an unorthodox method and does not work for everyone. I have tried to throw the ball like this and found that, for me, it is impossible. It went end over end. But that only means it was wrong for me. Bradshaw clearly had success with this method.

Most quarterbacks grab the ball on the laces. But not Vince Evans, who played for the Oakland Raiders. When Evans was a kid growing up, he played with a ball without laces, so he learned how to throw without using the laces.

But normally, you put your middle finger on about the third lace in from the end. On about the fifth lace, the inside of your pinky finger catches. The last finger to leave the ball is your index finger, causing the ball to spin in a spiral.

There is not one right way to do it. Quarterbacks need to find the grip that is the most natural and comfortable, and then they need a fluid delivery.

Touch Passes and Bullet Passes

Quarterbacks can throw the ball many different ways. Some throws are meant to be thrown very hard, and the receiver almost needs a catcher's mitt to catch the heat of a hard throw. These are *bullet passes*.

Others are soft passes that drop into a receiver's hands and he catches the ball as if he were catching an egg. These are *touch passes*.

There isn't a right way, just different ways of throwing.

Even long passes can be thrown both ways. Some quarterbacks, such as Jeff Blake of the Cincinnati Bengals, throw the ball with a high arch. Yet others throw a long pass on a flat trajectory. Both ways work, although my belief is that a high arch on a long ball gives the receiver a better chance to catch it. If the ball is thrown flat, it must be a perfect throw or it will not be caught. A ball with a high arch gives the receiver time to adjust to the ball, and it also improves the chances that the defender will commit interference, which is a penalty that occurs when a defender illegally disrupts a pass by touching the receiver before he can get to the ball.

Reading Defenses

My first quarterback coach, Ted Marchibroda, who is now the head coach of the Baltimore Ravens, did not give me a playbook for a month. Instead, he gave me a reel of film.

The idea was that he wanted me to first learn the 11 basic defenses that were played in National Football League in the early 1970s. I had to study that film, and once I could recognize a defense, he would give me the offensive plays to run.

As I noted in the last chapter, athletes are creatures of habit. And the idea behind reading defenses is to learn those habits and recognize what they mean. For instance, if you look at a cornerback and he is lined up inside of a receiver, that usually means it is man-to-man coverage, which means one defensive man is responsible for covering one offensive player. However, if the cornerback is lined up outside of a receiver, it usually means it is zone coverage, which means the defense is in a setup where different players are responsible for defending different zones of the field.

The first thing a quarterback is trying to learn in his *read* of a defense is whether it is involved in man-to-man or zone coverage. Another way to get a read on this is by looking at the safety, who is the defensive back in the middle of the field. If the safety is lined up five to seven yards deeper than the other defensive backs, then the team is probably playing a zone defense.

If you want to boil reading defenses down to one thing, I believe it is that the quarterback is trying to read the safety first. That one player can tell a quarterback about the other 10 defensive players.

When the ball is snapped, the quarterback knows the safety has to go someplace. As quarterback, my first step and his first step tell me basically everything I need to know. Within .2 seconds, I know where I want to go with the ball. I have put my life in the hands of those five guys up front, my offensive line. Their job is to create the pocket for me, and protect me. For that reason, I don't worry about the defensive line. I worry about the safety.

The safety's actions are what concern me. His actions tell me the best chance that I have to complete a pass is on a certain side of the field. His actions could take me to a side of the field or to one specific individual. There really are two parts to reading defense. One part is to know where the defense is, another to know where your players are in relation to the defense. You not only need to know where the holes will appear in the defense, but you also want to be sure that your offensive players will find these holes. (A hole is a space between defenders.) And not just find them, but get in them and not run through them. You see, not only quarterbacks must read defenses. A good offense is one in which receivers also read defenses and know when to slow down when they reach a hole in the coverage. This doesn't happen overnight. It takes great coordination between players, and it takes an enormous amount of film study to understand the tendencies of the other team as well as of your own team.

Calling Plays, Calling Audibles

A play is a blueprint of where each player should go. The specifics of play calling will be covered in much more detail in Chapter 12. However, for our purposes here, you should know that each play (and some offenses have up to 500 plays at their disposal) tells each player exactly what he should do. The quarterback has to know what every one of them will do, and then get the ball to the player who has the best chance of success.

Joe's Gridiron Talk

A *hard count* is when the quarterback yells a signal louder than the other signals he yells in an attempt to fool the defense into thinking the play is beginning. The idea is to get the defense to jump offside, which is a penalty. The defense cannot cross the line of scrimmage before the play begins.

That's where audibles and reading defenses come in. As the quarterback approaches the line of scrimmage and begins to read the defense (in other words, study the safety), he gets an idea of what the defense is going to do on that particular play. If the play the offense has planned won't be the best one against the current defensive setup, the quarterback can call out a different play; an *audible* is simply the quarterback calling a play change at the line of scrimmage. He can also try a *hard count* to try to fool the defense into making a mistake.

> **Joe's Tips**
>
> If the quarterback, after he puts his hands under the center, backs away and gives hand signals or begins yelling to both sides of the field, it usually means he has called an audible and is switching the play at the line of scrimmage.

The idea of the audible is two-fold. First of all, the audible usually is designed to get the offense out of a play that appears destined, because of the defensive alignment, to fail. The idea is to get out of something bad. The other reason for using an audible is if the quarterback noticed a deficiency in the defense that he thinks he can exploit and have an opportunity for a big play.

An example of when to call an audible is if I have a running play set up to go to the right. Then I get up to the line and see that the defense is shifted to the right. I know that the way we have this play blocked, we cannot block all the people. I know that's a bad play. The idea then is to call an audible to run a play to go to the opposite side, or maybe to run a pass play.

> **Joe's Gridiron Talk**
>
> *Dummy audibles* are signals that are called by the quarterback at the line of scrimmage that look like an audible but are really meaningless words. The idea is to not let the other team know what you are using as your audible signal, so you call a number of signals that are known by your team to be meaningless. Just more smoke and mirrors.

You see, it's all a head game. In the example I just cited, the defense may be shifted to the right because they have seen in their film study that our team in similar situations to the one we now face, has a tendency to run to the right. Therefore, they have adjusted to our tendency. We must now adjust to their adjustment, and hope that they don't then adjust to our adjustment. It is a circle that can go on forever, and yes, it is easy to outthink yourself.

Looking Off Defenders

Quarterbacks don't want the defense to know where they are going to throw the ball. So, simply, the quarterback tries to look somewhere else until the last second. If the quarterback stares at the receiver he intends to throw to, the defense can set up and defend the play much better. Instead, the quarterback knows who he wants to throw to, where that player will be, and when he will get there. He will wait until the last second, and then turn and fire.

Pump Fake

There are times when the quarterback will fake a throw to get the defense to react. This happens when a receiver first runs a short pattern, and then takes off deep. The idea is that the quarterback dips his shoulder and reloads. The receiver runs a short pattern, the quarterback fakes the throw. If it works, the defense tries to go after the faked throw, and then the quarterback throws a pass that hopefully beats the defense. A *pump fake* is almost always followed by a real throw. It is usually a two-step motion. First the fake, and then the throw. That fast. Boom, boom—fake, throw.

Throwing It Away

There are times when a quarterback will not have an open target. Instead of taking a *sack*, which is the term used when a defense tackles the quarterback behind the line of scrimmage while attempting to pass, the quarterback will often deliberately make a bad throw. The idea is to end the play without losing any yards. Since an incomplete pass brings the ball back to the line of scrimmage, there are times when an incomplete pass is a good thing.

Joe's Rules

Intentional grounding is a penalty given to the quarterback if he throws a pass that he does not really attempt to complete. If the quarterback is in the pocket and is pressured by the defense, he is guilty of intentional grounding if he throws a pass he does not have a realistic chance of completing. However, if he is out of the pocket, it is NOT intentional grounding if he throws the ball past the line of scrimmage, even if an offensive player has no chance of catching it. The penalty for intentional grounding is:

➤ Loss of down and 10 yards from the previous spot if the passer is in the field of play,

➤ Loss of down at the spot of foul if it occurs more than 10 yards behind line, or

➤ Safety if the passer is in his own end zone when the ball is released

Throwing away is to throw the ball away to avoid a sack and you are not penalized because you throw near an eligible receiver. Intentional grounding involves a pass that is not thrown near an eligible receiver.

The Bomb

The *bomb* is a long pass. It is one of the most exciting plays in football, but it is also a low-percentage play. Bombs are not often successful, but when they are, they are a thing of beauty.

From a strategic standpoint, the bomb does a couple of things. First, it keeps defenses from crowding your receivers. In essence, it stretches out the field because it lets the defense know that the offense is not afraid to go for a big play. The defense is put on alert that the offense can and will go for it all in one play. This can then open up the short-yardage plays by making the defense back up a bit.

As a quarterback, there is no greater feeling than completing a bomb. I can remember getting hit and laying on the ground watching the play unfold. I would be on the ground and the ball would still be in the air and it seemed like it all took place in slow motion in front of me. You can almost see the laces spinning as the ball falls into the receiver's hands. It is beautiful.

The Hail Mary

Joe's Record Book
On September 22, 1996, at Foxboro Stadium, Mark Brunell of the Jacksonville Jaguars completed three Hail Mary passes—one at the end of the half, and two at the end of the game. The third, which would have won the game, ended on the 1-yard line. The Patriots won on a field goal in overtime.

This is a desperation pass that got its name because it is usually thrown at the end of a half or the game. Simply put, it is a prayer.

These are thrown by teams that are far away from the End Zone and need a touchdown to win. It is usually the last play or one of the last plays of a game or a half. The quarterback backs up and throws the ball to an area on the field. Most NFL quarterbacks can throw the ball about 65 yards.

A Hail Mary pass is pure chaos. Usually, the offense has three players waiting for the ball, and the defense has at least five players. The offensive players first want to try and catch it. If they can't, the next thing to do is to try to get a hand on the ball to keep it up in the air and hope for a lucky bounce. It happens.

Running with the Ball

Occasionally, the quarterback will need to run with the ball. Sometimes, on a short-yardage play, the quarterback will take the snap and immediately push forward to try to get enough for a first down. This is called a *quarterback sneak*.

Other times, he may find that his receivers are all covered and he will run with the ball. This is called a *scramble.*

Quarterbacks are allowed to slide with their feet forward. When they do, they are not allowed to be hit by the defense. As soon as they begin the slide, the ball is down.

Joe's Record Book
Fran Tarkenton, a quarterback with the Minnesota Vikings and New York Giants who was known as one of the greatest scrambling quarterbacks of all time, was also caught a few times behind the LOS. In fact, in his career, Tarkenton was sacked more times than any other quarterback—483.

Joe's Top Five Quarterbacks

Keeping in mind that although the game has changed over the years, each of these quarterbacks would have been a star in any era. Here are the top five quarterbacks to play in the NFL in no particular order, in my opinion.

➤ **Otto Graham**—QB of the Cleveland Browns in the '40s and '50s. He won four championships of the old All-America Football Conference, and three NFL championships.

➤ **Joe Namath**—QB of the New York Jets who won Super Bowl III, the first time the AFL beat the NFL. Namath guaranteed the victory.

➤ **Terry Bradshaw**—QB of the Pittsburgh Steelers who won four Super Bowls in the 1970s and 1980s.

➤ **Joe Montana**—QB of San Francisco 49ers who won four Super Bowls in the 1980s and 1990s.

➤ **Dan Marino**—QB of the Miami Dolphins who holds most all-time quarterback records, including most yards and most touchdowns.

Statistics to Look for in a Great Quarterback

➤ Touchdowns versus interceptions. If a quarterback throws twice as many touchdowns as interceptions, he is doing a good job.

➤ Pass-completion percentage. If a quarterback completes more than 60 percent of his passes, he is doing a good job.

➤ Sacks. If a quarterback only gets sacked 15 to 20 times in more than 400 pass attempts, he is making good, quick decisions and his offensive line is doing a great job protecting him.

The Least You Need to Know

➤ Quarterbacks get blame and credit because they play the most visible and important position on the field.

➤ Quarterbacks must be able to throw because that is their primary skill. It is the quickest and easiest way to advance the ball down the field.

➤ Quarterbacks read defenses because they want to figure out what the defense is going to try to do. They do this by looking at the safety first. The safety's actions will tell the quarterback whether it is a zone or a man-to-man coverage and which side of the field he should throw to. Zone and man-to-man will be explained in Chapter 14.

➤ Quarterbacks can change the play call at the LOS by calling an audible, which is usually a color, some numbers, words, or series of words that signal the play has been changed.

Chapter 8

The Offensive Line: They Called Mine "The Hogs"

In This Chapter

➤ Who were the Hogs?

➤ Room to run and throw; what these heavy hitters accomplish

➤ Blocking schemes—Different ways to do different things

An offensive lineman once said to me, "My job is to make heroes."

Offensive linemen are the guys who do the dirty work so others can get the glory. They get their noses bloodied, their faces battered, and their bodies smashed and smacked on every play. But they also get to do a bit of the bloodying, battering, smashing, and smacking. Offensive linemen are blue collar guys who thrive on repetitive physical contact. And that is exactly what they get.

This chapter is about the guys who have one of the toughest physical jobs on the football field. Every play they are supposed to hit and get hit. But their job is more than just physical—these guys also have one of the toughest mental jobs in the game. You see, despite the fact that these guys make their living from their brute force, there is incredible coordination that goes into being an offensive lineman, which will probably surprise the novice fan.

Take, for instance, a guard and a tackle (you'll learn more about these positions later). If the two guys they are facing try to do something, the guard and tackle need to know whether to zone block, block man-to-man, or double team—and they need to communicate quickly. The area on the football field where there is the most communication is the offensive line.

An offensive line position, as all in football, requires skill, yet it is the one position in which work ethic can make up for limited skills. Offensive linemen can outwork people, and often do.

This chapter will cover my offensive linemen, and how they became one of the first groups at that position to ever get some prestige. It will cover different offensive line blocking schemes, the difference between pass blocking and run blocking, and the importance of the initial push off the line. This chapter is about the guys on the offense who make their living in the trenches.

Hogs and Such

For decades in football, offensive linemen were the invisible men. Their job was to block so the quarterback could pass and the runners could run. A *block* is when offensive player runs interference for the man with the ball. He is trying to "block" the opposing team's effort to stop the ball carrier. No glory there. Just as a reference, the difference between a block and a tackle, a player executing a block is trying to help his teammate advance the football. A *tackle* is when a player on one team wants to stop a player on the other team from advancing the football. A simple example of a tackle: wrap your arms around a friend and throw that person to the ground. You've just tackled him or her.

Joe's Record Book
They are getting bigger. In 1996, the average weight of the Dallas Cowboys' offensive linemen, generally regarded as the best in football, was 324 pounds. Twenty years ago, the average weight of the Cowboys' offensive linemen was 254 pounds.

The only people who ever knew anything about the offensive line were their coaches, quarterbacks, and ball carriers because those were the people who understood very clearly the importance of the job. But to everybody else, offensive linemen were just big guys.

The truth is that offensive linemen hold a very complex job. Only recently have those outside the game begun to notice.

In 1982, George Stark, a teammate of mine on the Washington Redskins, decided that offensive linemen deserved some glory. He came up with an idea to give the offensive line of the Redskins an identity. He decided the unit should be called "The Hogs." It was brilliant.

He came up with the name because offensive linemen seem to always be the ones in the dirt. The other offensive linemen, tackle Joe Jacoby, guards Russ Grimm and Mark May, and center Jeff Bostic, posed with Bostic sitting on a bale of hay and they put out a poster. For the first time ever, the least glamorous position in football finally began to receive some recognition.

Of course, it didn't hurt that over time, the Redskins—my team, *our* team—became a dominating power football team. The Hogs could have an identity because they were good. They were really good. Add to that the fact that we had a running back, John Riggins, who ran with such overwhelming power behind that huge line that the entire thing became something of a myth in Washington.

It was a good thing to be a Hog. Riggins was eventually honored by the Hogs and named a Hog himself. And, I am honored to say that, after one game against the New York Giants in which I threw a block, the Hogs made me their piglet. I look at it this way: I accomplished many things in my NFL career that make me proud. Among other things, I won a Super Bowl and I was MVP of the League. However, other guys have won Super Bowls and every year, somebody has to win the MVP. But I am the only player in the history of the NFL to become a piglet. Now *that's* something.

Who Are Those Five Big Guys?

The five offensive linemen line up next to each other at the beginning of the play, just along the line of scrimmage (LOS). The one in the center is called, get this, the *center*. The center is the one who snaps the ball between his legs to the quarterback, whose hands are under the center's butt. The center is also the one who calls most of the signals for the line and who coordinates the blocking schemes. What is a blocking scheme? Just keep reading.

On each side of the center is a guard. Although all offensive linemen are powerful, guards are perhaps the most powerful—they push open holes for running backs and they fight off defensive tackles, who tend to be the largest defensive players on the field.

On the outside of each guard is a tackle. As offensive linemen go, tackle is the prestige position. The reason is because tackles are on the outside of the line and are called upon to stop defensive ends and outside linebackers, who tend to be quick, strong, and mean and really like to hit quarterbacks. The most prestigious position is usually left tackle

Joe's Gridiron Talk
The *neutral zone* is the area between the offensive and defensive lines. It is the length of the ball in width. No player except the center may enter the neutral zone until the ball is snapped.

because most quarterbacks are right-handed. When a right-handed quarterback drops back to pass, his back is facing the left. Therefore, the left is his *blind side*, and protecting a quarterback's blind side is of utmost importance. Obviously, a quarterback doesn't want to get hit by a 300 pound defensive lineman. But, if he gets hit from behind when he doesn't even know the guy is coming at him, it can really ruin his day—or career, as in my case. And that's why quarterbacks like their left tackles so much.

One Line, Two Jobs

The offense is going to pass or it is going to run. That means offensive linemen are going to pass-block or run-block, and these two jobs are different.

Both, however, involve the simple concept of blocking. The easiest way to describe a clean, legal block is to position yourself somewhere on the front part of your opponent's body. If you grab him, hit him from behind, or chop at his knees from the side, you have committed a violation. A *holding* penalty is 10 yards. A *clipping*, (hitting from behind, or a chop at the knees) is a personal foul and a 15-yard penalty from the spot of the infraction.

Run-blocking is an aggressive type of blocking that offensive linemen like to use when creating holes for running backs to run through. When an offensive lineman run-blocks, he comes off the ball, making contact with the defensive player and pushing him in a certain direction. He continues to do that until the whistle blows, stopping the play. One very important difference between run-blocking and pass-blocking is that offensive linemen can continue to block downfield while a play is in progress when they are run-blocking.

Pass-blocking, although it can be aggressive, is usually more reactive. Usually, pass-blockers back up and take the hits from the defense instead of moving forward and giving the hits as they would on a run-block. However, as was mentioned in Chapter 7, offensive linemen on passing downs are doing more than just protecting the quarterback from punishment. Remember, the guys who are coming after the quarterback are often huge. So offensive linemen are trying to create *throwing lanes* for the quarterback. The idea is to give the quarterback an open slot of air to throw through as well as to see through. But most important of all is to stop the quarterback from getting *sacked*.

Joe's Gridiron Talk

A *sack* occurs when a quarterback is tackled behind the line of scrimmage while he is trying to pass.

There are times when pass-blocking is aggressive. Those times are when the offense wants to fool the defense in what is called *play action*. In play-action plays, the offensive line will push forward as if it is blocking for a run, a running back will pretend to take a hand-off from the quarterback, and the hope is that the defense will try to tackle the running back. If it works, the defense is fooled and the quarterback should have time to throw—and should have a wide-open receiver as well.

They Get Noticed When Something Goes Wrong

Although they are finally beginning to get some acclaim, offensive linemen still lead rather anonymous lives on the field. The truth is, about the only time they get noticed is when they do something wrong.

So, when you hear an offensive lineman's name or number called during the game, chances are he did one of the following things:

➤ **Holding.** When an offensive player grabs a defensive player, or wraps his arms around a defensive player. Ten-yard penalty.

➤ **Encroachment.** When an offensive player enters the neutral zone and makes illegal contact with the defense. Five-yard penalty.

➤ **False Start.** When an offensive lineman moves after assuming a set position. Five-yard penalty.

➤ **Ineligible Receiver Downfield During Passing Down.** When an offensive lineman advances after losing contact with his opponent at the line of scrimmage. This is an arbitrary decision by the official. Usually, if an offensive lineman is three to five yards down the field without being in contact with a defensive lineman, he is considered an ineligible receiver. Five-yard penalty.

➤ **Chop Block.** When an offensive lineman hits a defender at the thigh or lower while another offensive player has engaged the defender. Fifteen-yard penalty.

➤ **Clipping.** Hitting a defensive player in the back of the legs. (There is a legal clipping zone—called *close-line play*. This is the area between where the offensive tackles line up and extends three yards in each direction from the line of scrimmage.) Fifteen-yard penalty.

Joe's Gridiron Talk

Prior to the snap, all offensive linemen must assume a *set position* without moving their feet, head, or arms, and without swaying their body.

Joe's Record Book

Fran Tarkenton of the Minnesota Vikings and New York Giants was sacked the most times in his career—483.

Randall Cunningham of the Philadelphia Eagles was sacked the most times in one season—72 times in 1986.

Bert Jones of the Baltimore Colts and Warren Moon of the Houston Oilers were sacked the most times in one game—12.

Or, of course, the other way that offensive linemen get noticed is when they give up sacks. Then, everyone knows their names.

Blocking Schemes

There are a lot of different ways for five big guys to act as a unit and push the big guys on defense out of the way. The first part to understand is the math. Usually, the five guys on the offensive line are blocking four guys on the defensive line, or they may *swoop* by the guys up front to get to the players behind them. Or, almost as often, there are three guys on the defensive line. But wait, there could be only two guys on the defensive line, or, there could be eight. It can make for some complicated, quick-thinking math. That's why they rely on *Coach Einstein* to develop good blocking schemes.

Okay, it's not really so complicated that coaches need a nuclear physicist to design schemes. In fact, usually it is big guys hitting big guys. But the math is a factor. The offense must have five offensive linemen. The defense, however, can do whatever it wants. And it doesn't have to tell the offense.

Joe's Gridiron Talk
A *swoop* is a block where a lineman goes by (swoops by) the defensive line to get to the next level of the defense, the linebackers.

Of course, the way a defense lines up on the field or the particular players it puts on the field does tell the offense quite a bit about its approach. However, as I explained before, it's a head game. The defensive players may not do what they look like they are going to do.

Nevertheless, the offensive line has a few basic blocking schemes used to attack the defense.

Trap Block

The *trap* block is used on a sweep (see Chapter 10 for a more detailed explanation of the sweep). The idea is to get the guard to back away from the line and then run outside to lead the way for a running back carrying the ball. For instance, if a play is designed to go right, the center would hit the man in front of the left guard. Simultaneously, the left guard backs away from the line, runs behind the center and off to the right. The guard who does this is called the *pulling guard*. See the following diagram of this blocking scheme.

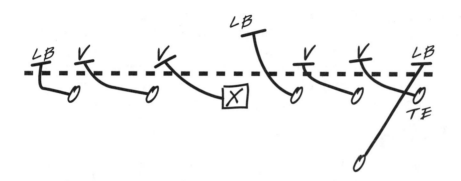

In a trap block, the left guard drops back, runs to the right, and blocks to clear a path for the running back.

Reach Block

The *reach* block occurs when an offensive lineman doesn't hit the player directly in front of him, but rather reaches to hit the player in front of another lineman. This scheme is usually for running plays. See the following illustration.

The reach block is when each of the offensive linemen reaches forward and to one side to try and block the man diagonally across from him.

Double Team

The *double team* really is as simple as it sounds. A double team occurs when two offensive linemen take on one defensive player. Quite simply, it is two on one. This could be used on running plays in which both offensive linemen attack the defender, or it could occur on passing plays in which two offensive linemen get in the way of a defender.

Slide Block

The *slide* block is a coordinated effort by the entire line to *slide* down the line. Basically, at the snap, each lineman pushes off the line in one direction. Either they all go right, or they all go left. This blocking scheme is used in passing plays. For instance, if the quarterback is planning to run a few steps to the right before he passes the ball, the offensive line may slide to the right. See the following illustration. When this happens, there has to be great coordination. For instance, on a slide block to the right, the running back may need to cover the left side.

The slide block is when the offensive linemen slide laterally—to stop penetration expected from a particular side.

Cutoff Block

A *cutoff* block requires an offensive lineman to get in the way of a defensive player and cut off his angle of pursuit. This technique is most often used for running plays.

Zone Block

Zone blocking requires an offensive lineman to protect a *zone,* or an area of the field. No matter who comes into that area, the offensive lineman is responsible. If the player across from a lineman goes into another zone, the offensive lineman still stays in his zone. If the zone gets "flooded," meaning more than one player comes into that zone, the lineman's teammates (whether a running back or the extra lineman who does not have a zone) has to come and help. If not, the quarterback is not going to be happy.

Man-On-Man Blocking

This means exactly what it sounds like—one man is responsible for one man. No matter where the defensive man goes, the offensive lineman is responsible. But, if the defensive lineman runs to the other side of the field, the offensive lineman responsible for him won't be too worried. By the time the defensive lineman reaches the other side of the field, the chances are that the play has run its course.

The Push Off of the Line

Television announcers like to talk about who is *controlling the line of scrimmage*. They usually mean that if one team's big guys are pushing the other team's big guys forward, the pushing team has a better chance (on offense or defense) to do well on any particular play. If a pattern develops and one team continually controls the line of scrimmage, chances are you will see a pattern develop on the scoreboard as well.

On the line, different players have different stances, and the stance can affect which player gets the advantage of movement. Some linemen drop one foot back, others have their feet parallel. Usually, players on the left will have their left (the outside) hand down, while players on the right will have their right hand down. The idea always is to gain any advantage possible.

As far as technique, a key for linemen is not so much speed as it is quick feet and balance. Quick feet allow him to drive more quickly at the defender and enable him to get in the best position in which to engage the defender. While his balance allows the lineman to remain standing, without getting bowled over by the defensive player.

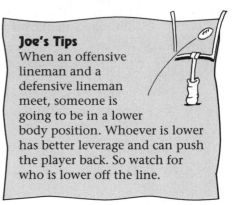

Joe's Tips
When an offensive lineman and a defensive lineman meet, someone is going to be in a lower body position. Whoever is lower has better leverage and can push the player back. So watch for who is lower off the line.

Joe's Top Five Offensive Linemen

Although offensive linemen have gotten bigger over the years, these players had such determination and skill that they would have been a star in any era. These are the top five offensive linemen to play in the NFL, in no particular order.

➤ **John Hannah**, guard with the New England Patriots. Great leverage player who played low and hit like a Mack truck.

➤ **Russ Grimm**, guard with the Washington Redskins. Could have been an All-Pro at tackle, guard, or center. He was extremely versatile.

➤ **Anthony Munoz**, tackle with the Cincinnati Bengals. He had a combination of great size and quickness.

➤ **Jackie Slater**, tackle with the Los Angeles Rams. He used his body and hands better than anyone.

➤ **Mike Webster**, center with the Pittsburgh Steelers. He was a like a pit bull—an extremely hard worker—and it paid off.

The Least You Need to Know

➤ The 1982 Washington Redskins, offensive line was the first to bring public acclaim to the offensive lineman position. They did it with the glamorous nickname, "The Hogs."

➤ The offensive line's job is to block defenders to keep them away from the quarterback so he has time to pass, and to block defenders out of the way of the running back.

➤ Run-blocking is usually agressive, and pass-blocking is usually reactive.

➤ If an offensive line pushes a defensive line more often than vice versa, that team has a much better chance to win.

➤ Teams use a number of different blocking schemes, including trap blocks, slide blocks, reach blocks, and zone blocks.

Chapter 9

The Receivers: Glue on Their Fingers and Rockets in Their Shoes

In This Chapter

➤ What receivers do: Catch the ball and run like heck

➤ The difference between a split end, flanker, and tight end

➤ Pass patterns and the passing tree

➤ A look at *YAC* and end arounds

Receivers are the acrobats of football. No, that doesn't mean they are on a flying trapeze. They don't need a trapeze.

What they do need is great hands and a ton of courage. Oh, and did I mention speed? Receivers have one of the most glamorous jobs in the game, and perhaps the most dangerous. The reason for the glamor is the nature of the position. They catch passes.

When they do, their pure athleticism, their body control, their speed, and their agility are on display at such a high level, fans cannot help but be amazed that human beings can actually do this stuff and still hold a football. They look really pretty doing it, but what is really on display is their focus.

It is a dangerous position for the same reason. Think of it this way: Receivers are trying to catch something in the middle of a group of guys who don't want them to catch it. I mean the other team's members *really* don't want them to catch it.

This chapter covers the position of receiver, the various roles receivers have, and the different types of receivers. It describes speed guys, possession guys, and tight ends. It also details different pass patterns, the importance of running after the catch, and how and why to use the end around. All that, and no flying trapeze.

Who Are They?

Receivers catch the ball. They *receive* passes. In a standard offense, there are usually three receivers. Two are *wide receivers*, called so because they line up away from the offensive line, also called wide of the line. The third receiver is a *tight end*, who usually lines up next to the offensive tackle at the end of the line.

Wide receivers come in two types, *speed guys* and *possession guys*. The truth is, they both do the same things, only in different volumes. Speed guys, known for their speed, can also catch. Possession guys, known for their ability to catch, can also run—especially *between* defenders. Each one serves a different role.

Let's talk more about how receivers line up. Remember that only seven offensive men are allowed on the line of scrimmage. Automatically, five of those men are linemen. If you

Joe's Gridiron Talk
Wide receivers also go under the name of *flanker* and *split end*.

have a tight end, that leaves only one more player that can go on the line of scrimmage. The wide receiver, who's also called the *split end*, lines up on the line of scrimmage on the side away from the tight end. He is on the side away from the tight end because only the outside players on the line of scrimmage are eligible to receive a pass. The outside two players are called the tight end and the split end. One because he is in tight to the offensive line, the other because he is split out from the line.

Joe's Rules

The two outside offensive players on the line of scrimmage are *eligible receivers*.

The other wide receiver, who usually lines up on the same side as the tight end, is called the flanker. The flanker lines up *one* yard off the line of scrimmage.

If the flanker were to line up on the line of scrimmage (first of all, he wouldn't be called the flanker), the tight end would become ineligible to catch a pass because he would no longer be one of the two outside men on the line of scrimmage. See the following illustration, which shows the correct line-up for the three receivers: tight end, split end (wide receiver), and flanker (wide receiver).

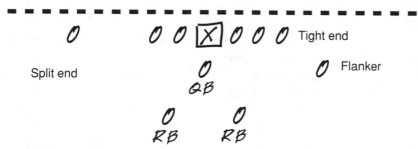

Standard offense showing the split end, tight end, and flanker.

Speed Guys

A receiver's job is to catch the football and advance it toward the end zone, preferably in large chunks of yardage. The best chance to advance it quickly is with speed.

You have to understand, nobody in football is really slow. But some guys are *fast*. I don't mean sort of fast. I mean blistering fast like a jaguar, and no, not a Jacksonville Jaguar. I mean a real jaguar—you know, one of the fastest animals on earth. These are usually the guys with the best *40 time* on the field.

When a team has a receiver who can run like the wind during hurricane season, it has a high-caliber weapon. From a quarterback's perspective, speed is a beautiful thing. There is nothing in the world like seeing one of your guys blazing down the field past the defense.

Of course, the defense is aware of the weapon and won't often let the speed guy shoot right by them. In football, perception is reality. If they think a receiver is fast, they will back up some so that the speed guy just doesn't have enough time to run past them. We are not talking about the tortoise and the hare. Not

> **Joe's Gridiron Talk**
> The *40 time* is how long it takes for a player to run 40 yards. It is the standard measurement of speed in football. It also seems to be the distance most guys run on any given play since everything is run in short bursts. The fastest times are now about 4.1 seconds; 4.5 is average for the NFL, and 5.2 is average for big linemen.

at all. Everybody's fast. Some guys are just faster than others. The guys who are really fast, the ones who can *clear it out*, are called speed guys.

As great as speed is to a team, it is not the most important thing. A lot of people have speed, particularly track guys who play football. There have been a few. Some are successful, but most are not.

Renaldo Nemehiah, who once held the world record for the 100-meter hurdles, played in the middle 1980s for the San Francisco 49ers. He couldn't make it for long. It didn't work. Part of his problem was he trained as a track athlete, but football is a team game. It's a different mentality. One of his bigger problems was that he didn't have good hands. This guy had all the speed in the world, but he learned that even if you are a speed guy you still have to catch the ball. You can't just run down the field and expect people to worry about you. The quarterback has to throw the ball to each receiver sometimes, just to let the defense know the receiver is a legitimate threat. Nemehiah never became a legitimate threat.

> **Joe's Gridiron Talk**
>
> *Clearing it out* is what a speed guy is often asked to do. This means he is asked to take off down the field in an attempt to get open for a long pass. Even if he doesn't get open, he clears out some defensive players from where a shorter pass or run might go. This is also called *stretching the defense* or *stretching the field*.

Two decades earlier, Bob Hayes, who was the world's fastest man in the 100-meter dash in the 1964 Olympics, became a very legitimate threat. Bullet Bob Hayes. The name says it all—and he could catch.

There are two main reasons why some track runners fail in football. One is they bounce their head when they run. I have seen speed guys who look like one of those dolls with the bobbing head you see in the backs of cars when they run. When they do this and try to lock a football into their hands, it is very difficult to focus. Thus, they often drop the ball. Another big reason fast guys fail is because they don't know how to stop. Really. They can all run fast, but football is a game of running fast and stopping quick as well. Two more things differ between football and track: Football players need the ability to turn quickly, and in track, people don't hit you.

Good speed guys serve a few functions on offense. Like all wide receivers, they are first called upon to catch passes. They are also called upon to do some blocking. In fact, whenever you see a big running play in football, there is a good chance it happened because the wide receiver did a good job of blocking.

Here is what speed guys do:

➤ Go deep to catch bombs (long passes), usually 30 to 50 yards downfield.

➤ Go deep to be a decoy for runs or short passes.

➤ Run short patterns and outs (patterns to the outside of the field).

➤ Go for passes over the middle.

➤ Block.

➤ Participate in trick plays (such as an end around, which I'll describe later in this chapter).

Possession Guys

These are the good-hands people. They are also blockers, but they are known for their ability to catch. If you put a dot on their chest and you draw a big circle around the dot at the width of their outstretched hands, that's the kind of catching range they have—that's the margin of error that you have when you throw a possession guy a football.

For other guys (some speed guys), you have to throw the ball right at their numbers to make it easy to catch. But for possession guys, it's like throwing a dart at a dartboard. They sometimes make it easier for themselves by enhancing their chances with gloves. These gloves usually have sticky palms so that when a leather ball on a dry day hits them, the ball sticks on the glove making it easier to catch. In the past, players used to use a substance called *Stick-Em,* which is a sappy substance that a player could literally catch the ball one-handed with. It is now illegal. As long as you keep it within that dartboard, they should catch it. You can throw it real high and they catch it; real low, same thing. You (if you are a quarterback, and I was one) can gain a lot of confidence throwing to possession receivers.

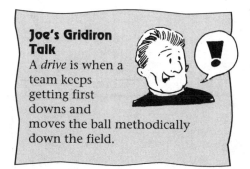

Joe's Gridiron Talk

A *drive* is when a team keeps getting first downs and moves the ball methodically down the field.

Joe's Rules

For a catch to be a legal reception, the receiver must have control of the ball and land both of his feet in bounds. If even a toe lands out of bounds, the catch is ruled incomplete. This means the down is over and the next play begins at the previous line of scrimmage.

Possession receivers do everything speed guys do, but mostly they work the field from the line of scrimmage to 15 yards down the field. They are used to basically getting first downs for you. Possession guys also help the offense maintain possession of the ball, because a guy who catches the ball keeps a drive going for you.

Even though they may not be the fastest guys on the field, possession receivers have the ability to get away from defensive backs and linebackers and find holes in defense. Finding those holes is hard to teach. It's a natural instinct, a knack.

But not every pass is catchable, even by possession receivers. Some quarterbacks throw the ball so hard that a receiver needs a catcher's mitt to catch it. Some guys throw it so hard, two catcher's mitts won't do the job.

Tight Ends, Like Hogs with Hands

As I showed you earlier, tight ends line up next to the offensive line. Although tight ends are not as big as offensive linemen, they can be pretty darn close. They generally range from about 6'2", 235 pounds to 6'5", 285 pounds. They have similar responsibilities to wide receivers, except their priorities are reversed.

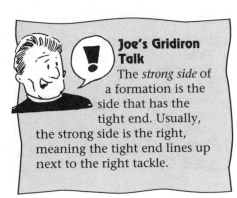

Joe's Gridiron Talk
The *strong side* of a formation is the side that has the tight end. Usually, the strong side is the right, meaning the tight end lines up next to the right tackle.

Whereas wide receivers are mostly responsible for catching passes, but also block, tight ends are mostly responsible for blocking, but also catch some passes—usually shorter passes than those caught by wide receivers. Same sort of job, different priorities. It is also a little different workplace for the tight end. They are not out on the outside running and rambling with 200-pound defensive backs. No. Tight ends live at the mouth of the trenches. Three hundred-some-pound guys are his neighbors. It's a mean neighborhood right from the get-go. And then when the tight end leaves there, he enters the middle of the field. Read on to find out about the middle of the field—talk about mean neighborhoods.

Different teams have different types of tight ends. Which type depends on the offensive philosophy. Some teams want a really big tight end who is a tremendous blocker. Other teams use their tight end more in the passing scheme, so the blocking skills aren't as important. Still, blocking skills are always important for a tight end, by the simple nature of where they line up.

Some teams use two tight ends, one on each side of the offensive line. The second tight end, taking the place of the second running back, lines up a yard behind the line of scrimmage and is known as the *h-back*. His job is more of a pass catcher than a blocker, but, anyone in close to the line better know how to block.

The Patterns

Comedian Bill Cosby used to have a bit that he did talking about playing football as a kid on the street. In it, he talked about sending receivers out past something like the blue Chevy, or around the fire hydrant, or past the third telephone pole on the right. In the NFL, it is even more complex.

Actually, it is precise. For instance, wide receivers know on every play where they are supposed to go. A receiver's running course on a play is called a *route* or *pattern*. Each different pattern is given a number, and the receiver has to know, for instance, what is a 7 pattern, a 4 pattern, or a 9 pattern. Wide receivers memorize what is known as a *passing tree*. An illustration of a passing tree for a wide receiver (in this case, a split end) appears next.

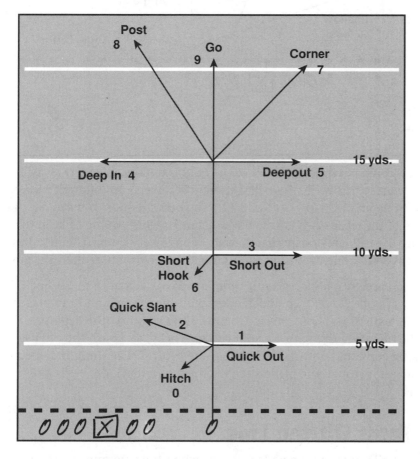

This passing tree shows patterns for the right wide receiver (split end).

Tight ends and running backs (see Chapter 10) also have a passing tree. The following figure is a tight end passing tree.

This passing tree shows patterns for tight ends. They are a very integral part of a pass offense.

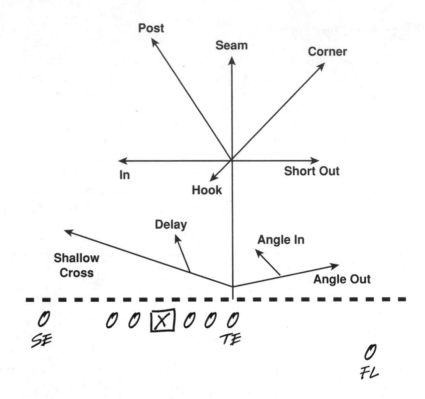

The point of sending receivers to different areas of the field is to take defenders away from places that you want to throw the football. Different receivers run different routes. (This will be covered in depth in Chapters 11 and 12.) The best situation you can get in football is when none of the receivers is covered by a defender who's trying to keep the receiver from catching the ball. Obviously that doesn't happen very often. The next best thing is one-on-one coverage—one defensive guy trying to cover your one offensive guy.

The idea is to run *complimentary routes* to give the *primary receiver* a chance to get open. This means that you want one player to pull defenders with him so that another player will be open. (You will learn more about this in Chapter 12.) Of course, the defense knows this is what the offense is trying to do, so it can get tricky, and both the offense and defense are making constant adjustments as the game evolves. The thing to remember is that patterns are set up for all the players to give the quarterback the best chance to complete a pass.

The First Five Yards Off the Line

Defensive backs are not allowed to touch wide receivers when they are running their pattern. However, that rule does not apply in the first five yards from the line of scrimmage.

From the line of scrimmage to five yards down the field, the defense *is* allowed to make physical contact with the receiver. This is usually called a bump-and-run technique, in which the receiver is bumped while he is running in the first five yards off the LOS. As a matter of fact, they can downright mug him. But after those five yards, they have to eliminate all contact. Thus, those first five yards are often the key to the pass pattern.

The passing game is all timing. Receivers are expected to be at a specific part of the field at a specific time. That's why you will see receivers do an assortment of tricky moves in those first five yards. They have to get past the possible contact. Some guys use quick little stutter steps to try to fake out the defender. Other guys use what is called a *swim over move.* This means they run to the defender and then as the defender tries to initiate contact, the receiver rolls his arm over the back of the defender (as in a swimming stroke) and then takes off running.

But defenders don't always attack in those first five yards for a very simple reason—if they miss they are in big trouble.

Joe's Rules

Interference is when a defender hits a receiver as the ball is on its way to him. It is an automatic first down at the point of the penalty. *Offensive interference* is when the receiver hits the defender in an effort to not allow him to intercept. It is a 10-yard penalty against the offense.

Going Over the Middle, Leave Your Sanity on the Bench

A wide receiver is usually dealing with a cornerback and a safety. But if the receiver runs to the middle of the field, he is dealing with a lot more defenders.

Not only does he attract the cornerback, who normally would be covering him and the safety on his side of the field, but suddenly there are two, maybe three linebackers in the area. And there may be the other safety as well. The receiver who goes to the outside of the field is dealing with two defenders. In the middle of the field, there are five or six defenders. The middle is crazy. Think of it this way: In your life, is it easier to get something that only two people want, or to try and get the same thing when six others want it? Now think about it in terms of the physical nature of professional football, where the best athletes in the world can see millions of dollars stuffed inside that ball.

The middle of the field is a very exciting place, to put it mildly. It is where some of the best acrobatics occur. Going across the middle takes great discipline, focus, and body control. First, the receiver is avoiding defenders. He is trying to find a hole, an area on the field where there are no apparent defenders. But he doesn't really know where those defenders are located. He may have an idea, but there is no guarantee that they will be where they are supposed to be. Even if the receiver gets open and catches the ball, he has to know that that ball is instantly going to attract a crowd. Once he catches the ball, he knows he is in the middle of at least five guys—and they are all going to try to hit him. But from where?

Using the Clock

The passing game can be used very effectively to control the clock. Remember, when a pass is incomplete (not legally caught) the clock stops. Sometimes, teams will deliberately throw incomplete passes to stop the clock. Also, if a receiver (or any ballcarrier) catches the ball and runs out of bounds, the clock stops. Thus, sideline patterns are popular when time is winding down.

Yards After Catch—Also Called YAC

Joe's Tips
Watch how a receiver catches the ball. The most exciting receivers use their hands only to catch the ball because they control the ball immediately and have a bit more time to figure out where to go next. Receivers who trap the ball in their hands, forearms, and chest usually need to take a little longer to get the ball in position to run with it.

There is a statistic that football people like to know about receivers: How many yards do they gain after they catch the ball? The acronymn for this is YAC. For instance, if the quarterback throws a 10-yard pass to a receiver and then the receiver gains an additional seven yards before he is tackled, his YAC yardage is seven.

Other statistics to keep an eye on include average receptions per game, touchdown receptions, and yards per reception.

Some guys are so concerned with catching the football that they can't do anything else and don't end up with much YAC yardage. Other guys have the ability to run with the ball once they get it. These are special YACers.

End Around—It's a Trick Play

Wide receivers (and even tight ends on occasion) are sometimes called upon to take a hand-off. It is not part of their job description, and that's why when it happens it is considered a *trick play*. This means that the offense wants to trick the defense. Sometimes it works, but the stage for a trick play has to be set up over a period of time.

An end around is a hand-off that is given to a receiver. It is a running play for a receiver and it works by having the receiver run from one side of the field, behind the offensive line where he takes a hand-off and then runs around the other side circling the entire defense.

The offense leads up to an end around by first running a few plays in one direction, say the right. This gets the defense moving that way, flowing that way. If you can get a whole defense to begin flowing one direction, you have set up an end around.

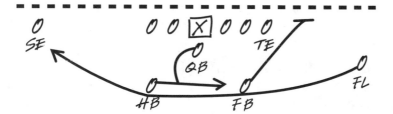

Joe's Gridiron Talk
The *front side* of the play is the direction the ball carrier runs to start. The *back side* is opposite where he is going.

So if you have the defense flowing toward your right, the end around works this way: The quarterback hands the ball to the running back who heads toward the right. Then, the receiver on the right, probably the flanker, heads left and takes a hand-off from the running back. Hopefully, the entire defense is chasing the running back and the wide receiver can run around the back of the defense for a big gain. This play has recently been dubbed the *reverse*, because the receiver reverses the direction of the play suddenly. See the following illustration of how the end around play works.

The standard end around.

Sometimes, the quarterback will give the hand-off himself to the wide receiver, or sometimes there will be a double end around where one receiver hands the ball to another receiver going around yet the other way. But the more hand-offs there are, the more interesting it gets.

Joe's Top Five Receivers, Starting with Jerry Rice

In the history of football, there are two players who have dominated their position like no others. One of those is Jerry Rice. The other you will read about in the next chapter.

Jerry Rice of the San Francisco 49ers is the greatest receiver of all time. He holds many receiving records, including most seasons with 1,000 or more yards pass receiving, most pass receptions in a career, and most yards gained in a career. And as of 1997, his career wasn't even close to over. He also holds the record for most yards gained in season. And, get this, he holds the record for all players—not just wide receivers—for most touchdowns scored in a career. It has been and it remains, some career. There are five main reasons for Jerry Rice's success.

1. He is both a speed receiver and a possession receiver.

2. He plays in a system that uses the West-Coast offense, an offense that relies on a short passing attack.

3. Jerry has great ability to get open.

4. He catches everything.

5. Nobody has ever been able to run after the catch like Jerry Rice. Check the record book under *touchdowns*.

Here is the rest of my top five, in no particular order:

➤ **Raymond Berry**, sure-handed precise receiver for the Baltimore Colts, had 12 catches for 178 yards in the NFL title game in 1958.

➤ **Mike Ditka**, a tight end with the Chicago Bears, not only had great hands but was real nasty as a runner. He would just as soon run over someone as try to run away.

➤ **Paul Warfield**, a wide receiver for the Cleveland Browns and the Miami Dolphins, was an amazing athlete who could catch anything at any angle. A key member of the 1972 perfect 17-0 Dolphins.

➤ **Art Monk**, a wide receiver for the Washington Redskins, could do it all. He never missed a day of work, he could run right by defensive backs, run over them, or take their heads off with devastating blocks.

The Least You Need to Know

➤ Receivers catch passes using a combination of speed and great hands.

➤ Receivers run patterns that test their ability to stop and turn. The three receivers on the field run complimentary patterns that help draw defenders off one receiver, who is then free to catch the ball.

➤ There are two types of receivers, speed receivers who are known for their speed, and possession receivers who are known for their ability to catch *everything*.

➤ The tight end lines up on the LOS next to the offensive line, usually on the right side. The flanker is on the same side (usually right) as the tight end but is lined up off the LOS. The split end lines up on the LOS on the side (usually left) opposite the tight end.

➤ Jerry Rice was/is the best receiver to ever play the game.

Chapter 10

The Running Backs: Great Ones Control Games

In This Chapter

➤ Why great teams run

➤ The role of the fullback and the halfback

➤ Some guys are powerful, some elusive—the great ones are both

➤ How they line up

Behind the quarterback are the play-by-play heroes, the man or men who are counted on to bring the ball forward a few yards at a time. They are expected to do it over and over again. Bang, get up and do it again. Bang. A running back takes the ball and sees how far he can get before the guys wearing other colors stop him. It's simple: take the ball and bang into the defensive line.

Of course, it is not that simple. Like everything in football, there is a method to the madness. This is a chapter about running backs, the running game, and how and why a great running back is able to take over a game. I will discuss the various types of running backs—fullbacks, halfbacks, and R backs—as well as talk about different formations; a few select plays, such as the sweep and the draw play; and the importance of vision. Finally, the chapter lists my top five running backs of all time, starting with Jim Brown.

The Importance of the Running Game

Great teams run the ball. When great teams want to run the ball, they are successful. They do what they want. They will not be denied, and that is painful to a defense. More importantly, it is painful to the defense's psyche.

A running team pushes and punishes a defense with a ball control offense, meaning that they run the ball and then let the play clock tick down to almost zero before starting a new play. The entire time the play clock is ticking, so is the game clock. In a running play, which is also called a rushing play (and a run is also called a rush), if the ball stays inbounds, the game clock continues to run. The play is over when the ball is *down*, which means the ballcarrier has been tackled or has gone out of bounds. The play is also over in a passing play if the ball is not caught. When the ball is not caught (incomplete), the game clock stops until the next play starts.

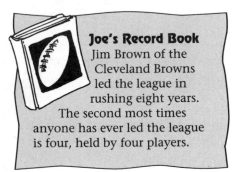

Joe's Record Book
Jim Brown of the Cleveland Browns led the league in rushing eight years. The second most times anyone has ever led the league is four, held by four players.

Ball control wears down a defense as it runs down the clock. When a team has a good offensive line and a top-flight running back, the chances are that at some point in the game it will call upon its running game to take over. Especially if it already has the lead.

If you can average four yards per running play, you will get 12 yards every three downs. You only need 10 yards to earn a new set of downs. A good series of running plays can eat up time on the clock by grinding out yards down the field. In theory, a good drive ends with a three-yard touchdown run. It is primitive football. *Here we come—stop us.*

Fullbacks, Leading the Way

Fullback is a job for a titan, a warrior, a *Moose*. The fullback's primary job is to lead the way on running plays. The fullback is the lead blocker.

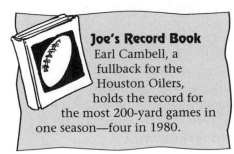

Joe's Record Book
Earl Cambell, a fullback for the Houston Oilers, holds the record for the most 200-yard games in one season—four in 1980.

Although fullbacks do run the ball and even catch passes, the main job of a fullback is to lead the way for the halfback. A classic example of the optimal fullback-halfback relationship is in recent years with the Dallas Cowboys. Fullback Daryl Johnston, nicknamed "Moose," primarily blocks for running back Emmitt Smith. Smith has been generally considered the top running back in the NFL, and the Cowboys have won three Super Bowls with Smith as the running back, following Johnston.

When fullbacks do run with the ball, there is usually not much in the way of finesse. The normal NFL fullback is a straight-ahead I-dare-you-to-stop-me type of runner. Big backs normally are about as subtle as a bulldozer. However, Natrone Means of the Jacksonville Jaguars is a big back who has great feet. I mean quick, not pretty. So there are exceptions to the rule. But the rule is that fullbacks are mostly straight-ahead power runners and blockers. And it helps to have a fullback named Moose.

Halfbacks, Ball Carriers

More than a ton of linemen (offensive and defensive) meet at the line of scrimmage on each play. The fullback usually meets a linebacker there too. On running plays, halfbacks carry the ball through the middle of all of that. The ball attracts attention, thus halfbacks attract attention. Running with the ball is a guaranteed way to get noticed—by the fans, by the coaches, and especially by the other team.

Runners make their living by getting hit. They get hit because the defense notices them with the ball. Everybody notices. Just watch. Carrying the football is like putting a sign on one's uniform that reads, "Hit me."

Playing running back means living with the pain. In fact, coaches even talk about the wear-and-tear on a runner's body as he goes through a season, or several seasons.

Ball carriers are tough. There is no other way to be in such a profession. Although all football players are tough, ball carriers are asked to prove their readiness for battle on every play. Ball carriers carry what everyone else on the field wants.

Halfbacks are generally smaller than fullbacks, but not by much. In a standard offense, a halfback carries the ball and the fullback leads the way blocking. Halfbacks also catch passes and block. Although the halfback position relies heavily on natural skill, it is not at first a measurable natural skill. In other words, running 40 yards faster than anyone else does not make one a great running back. Neither does lifting more weight than anyone else. The important measurables for running backs (those who carry the ball, whether they are halfbacks or fullbacks or R backs, are called running backs) are yards gained and touchdowns scored.

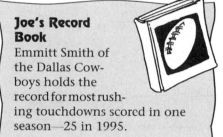

Joe's Record Book
Emmitt Smith of the Dallas Cowboys holds the record for most rushing touchdowns scored in one season—25 in 1995.

Joe's Gridiron Talk
You may wonder about the names *fullback* and *halfback*—especially since the halfback usually lines up farther back than the fullback. Here's my guess: Consider the fullback a full-sized football player, and the halfback less than that—maybe even half-sized.

The R Back

The R back is used by teams that only use one running back. They can call their back a halfback or a fullback, or whatever, but the real name for the one back in a one-back offense is the R back, which stands for "remaining."

Halfbacks and Fullbacks, a Great Tag-Team

Football is a game of great choreography. Everything must work together. The philosophy of a running play is simple: Give the ball carrier the best possible chance to advance the football.

That best chance for the halfback comes when his fullback is in front, leading the way. They are both running backs. The fullback's and halfback's work must compliment each other. They really are complimentary roles when it works right. When a halfback knows the way a fullback blocks, it helps the halfback run. For example, if the ball carrier is following the fullback, who is going to block somebody, and the halfback knows that the fullback likes to hit a defender's outside shoulder, the halfback can get ready to run outside. The knowledge of the fullback's habits gives the halfback a little bit of an anticipated edge. Likewise, fullbacks know how their halfbacks like to run, and they make adjustments. Great choreography is often also improvised. But improvisation only works if it ends up looking choreographed. That's why it is so important for a fullback and halfback to work together and learn each other.

The two positions have the same roles, but with different priorities:

Fullback	Halfback
Block	Run
Run	Catch
Catch	Block

Vision and Quickness

Great running backs have great quickness and vision. Speed is not as important as quickness. There is beauty to the short burst in football. Sometimes, it is the difference between nine inches and 99 yards. A short burst of speed can break through the very first hole, past the first group of would-be tacklers. At worst, running backs need to get through an area with five to seven defensive linemen and linebackers and not get piled on every time. From there, anything can happen.

Some backs have great instincts. I don't know why. It's a quirk of nature, I suppose. Who can say? I don't know a genetic answer, yet I do think there is more than genetics involved. I think some of it can come from playing the game at a young age and being exposed early to good coaching. Learning where to look and what to look for are key skills necessary for a ball carrier. But still, in the end, it comes down to some guys have it, and some guys never will.

Speed and quickness can come from many areas as well, but one area that should not be overlooked in pro football is the game surface. Remember, artificial turf is faster, and that especially affects running backs who can cut and grip much better than on grass.

Finding that hole and getting through it requires vision and instincts. A back looks at a defense and has an idea where the defense is going to go. But it happens so fast. In .2 of a second decisions are made that make or break a run. A lot of things in football are an idea or anticipated movement. If a runner *thinks* the defense is going to do something, he will do something to counteract it. This is not a hard science, it is a game of actions and reactions. There is not a thought process that a runner goes through as he approaches the line with the ball under his arm. The coaches have done the thinking and the teaching. The players do the reacting.

The runner sees the defense, he pictures the way the offensive line is going to block that defense. As he gets the ball, he sees the position of the offensive line and of the defense, and he makes his adjustments accordingly. He doesn't think about putting his left foot in front of his right, but he just sees where he wants to go and he gets there.

North-South Runners and East-West Runners

Take out your compass. The offense is always going North or South on the field—toward the end zone. That is just the way it works. Once you know that, you can understand the term *North-South runner*. This is a player who doesn't try a lot of fancy footwork to fool the defense into missing. Instead, a North-South runner goes straight ahead.

Emmitt Smith of the Dallas Cowboys is an example of a North-South runner. He doesn't waste a lot of time trying to make people miss. He heads right to the hole. He has subtle moves. The slightest shifting of foot, just a slide of three or four inches where you can't hit him really solid. Emmitt Smith is elusive like all North-South runners. He just makes his moves in a very confined area, and then he dares the defense to bring him down.

Joe's Tips
The runners who end up with the most yards are usually the ones who run straight ahead—the North-South runners.

An *East-West runner* is always trying to juke his way out of trouble, back and forth. It is not a compliment to be called an East-West runner. Watch any football game and you will see one of these guys tap-dancing outside the hashmarks. That's where they usually end up—outside, away from the heavy traffic of the trenches.

Joe's Gridiron Talk
A *scatback* is a small, swift running back with elusive moves. They are used a lot in third down situations where they are counted on for their ability to scat here and there, making tacklers miss.

And although these guys have the potential to turn a short run into a long run, they are just as likely to get caught behind the line of scrimmage.

But that elusiveness is exciting. There is a term that goes back to the days of Elvis Presley in rock 'n' roll—*swivel hips*. That is an apt term to describe some running backs. It also explains the elusiveness because defensive players are taught to focus on the hips as they go for the tackle. A good set of swivel hips can really throw that off.

There is one player of recent years who has the ultimate swivel hips, and yet he defies description on the compass. That player is Barry Sanders, running back with the Detroit Lions. He is a North-South-East-West runner.

Sanders goes every direction on the compass, but he always ends up going towards the goal line. He just takes a circuitous route. When Sanders plays, there are ballet-like moves—leaps, turns, things that you don't think are physically possible. Barry Sanders makes the kind of moves that were made for slow motion, to watch over again in awe.

Catching Passes—a Safety Valve and More

Running backs catch passes. They are usually, but not always, a *safety valve* receiver, meaning they are a last resort type of receiver. If the first choice and second choice of the quarterback are covered, he may start to look at his running backs. If the offense hasn't thought of him first, in all likelihood neither has the defense. A safety valve is like a spout on a tea kettle—when it whistles, it lets the steam out. A safety valve receiver gives the quarterback a chance to escape a situation that may be overheating.

A running back is not always a mere safety valve receiver. Sometimes he is the primary receiver. Here is a passing tree of patterns for running backs. In this tree, these patterns are called by names, not numbers.

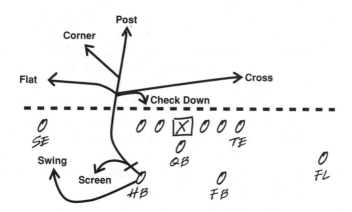

The passing tree for running backs is a descriptive way to tell the running back exactly what pattern he should run.

Formations for Running Backs

There are several basic ways to line up running backs. The idea is to give the running backs a chance to get to the line, see the blocks on the line, run through the line, or go out for pass patterns. Oh, and of course, to also be ready to block defenders at every turn. Each lineup is called a formation and the coach chooses different formations based on the strengths/weaknesses of his offensive players, plus the strengths/weaknesses of the defensive opponent for the week. Let's take a look at each formation now.

Split "T"

The split "T" formation is when both backs are split behind the quarterback. Neither one is directly behind the quarterback. This is more of a passing formation than a running formation because the backs are closer to the line of scrimmage. Each is behind the tackle or in the gap behind the tackle and guard. See the following illustration.

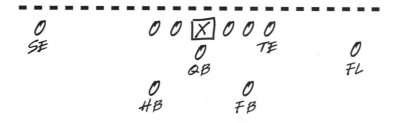

The split "T" formation is a passing formation that has the fullback and halfback split evenly behind the quarterback.

"I" Formation

In the "I" formation, called such because it looks like an "I," the quarterback is behind the center and the running backs are in a line behind the quarterback. The fullback is about five yards deep of the line of scrimmage. The halfback is seven yards deep. The fullback lines up in a three-point stance, meaning both of his feet and one of his hands are on the ground. The reason is simple. The halfback needs to see over his back to the line, and to the defense. The halfback takes a two-point stance, meaning only his feet are on the ground. His hands are on the front of his thighs and his eyes look over the back of his fullback. In the time it takes for the halfback to the get to the line, the blocks should have developed. See the following illustration of the "I" formation.

The "I" formation sets the running backs in a line behind the quarterback.

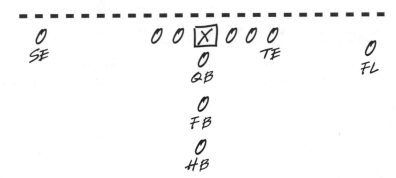

Offset "I" Formation

This is almost like the "I," except the fullback is moved over slightly to one side. He is lined behind the tackle. The halfback, however, remains directly behind the quarterback. See the following illustration.

Offset "I" formation sets the running backs so that one is behind the quarterback and the other is off to one side.

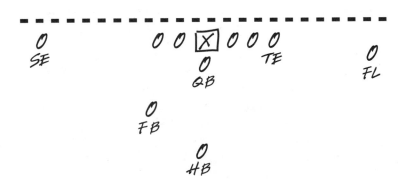

Two Tight Ends with an R Back (Ace Formation)

This is a power formation because you are lining up an extra huge body closer to the offensive line. See the following illustration.

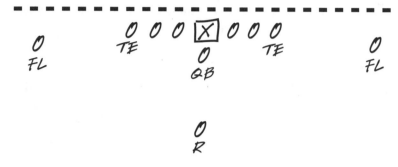

Two tight ends with an R back (also called an Ace formation) is when there is only one back in the backfield.

Between the Tackles—the Meat and Potatoes of the Running Game

When an offensive team can run at the gut of a defense and find success, it has made a statement. It has said, "You cannot stop us."

There are different ways to run the ball, but the most demoralizing way to hurt a defense is to stuff the ball right down their throat. A common name for this type of play is an *off-tackle*. When teams run off-tackle consistently, it shows that they can control the ball with a power running game.

The Sweep

There is an old, rare art form in football that is still pulled out from time to time. It is called the *Sweep* and it is one of the most basic—and classic—plays in the game. The idea is simple, to run the ball to the outside of the field.

The halfback takes the hand-off and then heads outside. When it works right, he has blockers in front of him, leading the way. On the Classic Sweep, both guards back up a step and then *pull* behind the line and lead the way. The fullback also leads the way. The center and tackle try to cut off the pursuit at the line, and then it all swings around the end.

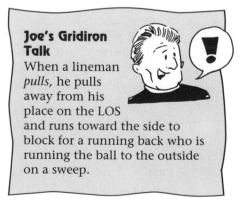

Joe's Gridiron Talk

When a lineman *pulls*, he pulls away from his place on the LOS and runs toward the side to block for a running back who is running the ball to the outside on a sweep.

Vince Lombardi built a dynasty in Green Bay in the 1960s using this play as his primary weapon. It was one of those macho things—*"You know what we're going to do, so stop us."*

In recent years, the sweep has not been used as much. One reason is simply that the athletes on defense are much faster now. Even if the blockers get out front, there are often defensive players fast enough to get to the play from the opposite side of the field. So, like everything else, the sweep often must be set up.

Here is an illustration of a Classic Sweep.

The Sweep is when the ball carrier runs parallel to the line of scrimmage until he gets outside when he turns upfield.

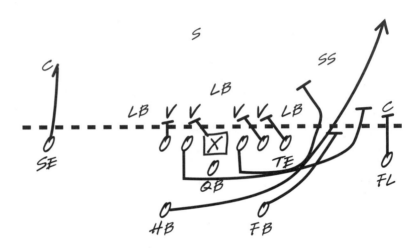

The Draw Play

The draw play is a trick play but it's not—say what? It is designed to trick the defense, so technically it could be called a trick play. Except it is used a lot in games, so that automatically disqualifies it from trick play status.

But you will learn more about trick plays in the next chapter. The draw play is designed to make the defense think that a pass is coming. The quarterback drops back from the line as if he was dropping back to pass. But when he gets a few steps back, he gives the ball to the running back, who just stood there waiting.

The offense wants the defense to commit to come after the quarterback. When they do, spacing is created between linemen. Spacing means holes—holes for the back to run through.

Finally, there is one more bonus when a draw play works well. The linebackers drop back into pass coverage. So, if the running back gets past the linemen, he should have a cushion before he reaches the next level of the defense, the linebackers.

There is yet one more layer to the strategy of the draw play—the *fake draw play*. Yes, teams can—and do—fake that they are faking a pass, and then really pass. Anytime an offense can create hesitation in a defense, it has an advantage.

Some key statistics to look for when evaluating running backs include average yards per carry (4.5 is a good average), total yards per game (100 is a benchmark), and yards per season (1,300 is a benchmark—it used to be 1,000 yards but that was when the season was 14 games).

Joe's Top Five Running Backs, Starting with Jim Brown

Some running backs have speed. Some have power. Some are elusive, and some run right over people. Jim Brown of the Cleveland Browns could do it all.

In eight of his nine years in the NFL, Brown led the league in rushing. He averaged an astonishing 5.22 yards per carry. Although many of Brown's records have since been eclipsed by the great Walter Payton of the Chicago Bears, Brown is still considered the best of all time by the mere fact of his rushing average. And anyone who ever saw Jim Brown carrying defenders down the field as if he were giving them rides in an amusement park knows for a fact that there will never be another Jim Brown.

Here is the rest of my top five, in no particular order:

➤ **Walter Payton** of the Chicago Bears in the 1970s and 1980s. He holds the record for most yards in a career—16,726. Nicknamed "Sweetness" because he had such a sweet running style.

➤ **Gale Sayers** of the Chicago Bears in the 1960s. He was the most exciting open field runner of all time. Once, he scored six touchdowns in a game. His career was cut short by a knee injury.

➤ **Emmitt Smith**, a halfback with the Dallas Cowboys, who holds the record for the most rushing touchdowns scored in a season—25.

➤ **John Riggins**, an R back of the Washington Redskins in the 1970s and 1980s. He was a combination of a halfback and a fullback who ran with overwhelming power and tremendous speed. John was my teammate; the MVP of Super Bowl XVII, which we won; and one of the most powerful runners to ever play in the NFL.

The Least You Need to Know

➤ Great teams run the ball because ball control is directly related to clock control and clock control is directly related to controlling the game.

➤ Fullbacks usually lead the way for halfbacks, who must be quick, elusive, and powerful.

➤ There are a number of backfield formations (Split "T", "I", Offset "I") that running backs line up in for different reasons.

➤ The Sweep is a classic old-time running play that is built on the concept of power around the end of the formation.

➤ Jim Brown was the best running back of all time and he quit at the top of his game.

Chapter 11

Strategies: A Lot of Ways to Go 80 Yards or One

In This Chapter

➤ Different philosophies, running or throwing

➤ Learn the standard formations

➤ Smashmouth, Air-it-out, and other funny names

➤ Making the most of the two-minute drill

The idea of football is to create opportunities. The strategy of the offense is to move the ball down the field and score touchdowns. See, it's an easy game.

Okay, it's not really that easy. In fact, the game offers almost unlimited possibilities for how to move the ball down the field. Of course, there are only two major possibilities—pass or run.

But there are different ways—philosophies really—to approach putting together an offense. A basic rule that most teams, not all, follow is that teams must be able to run the ball on offense and stop the run on defense. From there, things get complicated.

Some teams like to throw the ball more. Some like to run. Some like to run to set up the passing game, and some like to pass to set up the running game. Nothing is etched in stone, except that all these philosophies have as their main goal putting points on the scoreboard.

This chapter will cover basic offensive philosophies and it will present some of the basic formations. It will discuss the difference between smashmouth football, air-it-out football, the West-Coast offense, and the run-and-shoot. There are a lot of ways to go 80 yards or one yard. This chapter will show you a few of the basic ways.

Run, Throw, or Mix It Up

What to do with the ball? That is the question and there is no easy answer. Look around at the end of any NFL season and ask all the fired coaches if there is an easy answer. There are always fired coaches. If you can get past the colorful language, they will surely tell you that there are no easy answers. Instead, there are great athletes and an 11-inch long football that bounces funny.

So go ahead, devise a strategy.

So, what to do? To start with, there is the basic chicken-and-the-egg question. Each coach comes to a team with a philosophy. Some coaches like to run, some like to pass, some coaches like a good mix. The truth is, all would prefer a good mix because they all know that champions are the ones that can do everything.

Still, the question comes: Should coaches force their players to conform to their philosophy, or should coaches conform their philosophy to the talents of the players? It's tough to say with a blanket statement. But generally, good coaches adapt to the personnel, and the bad ones try to force their system on their people.

All offensive strategy starts with the question: *What do we do best?* Essentially, teams want to do what they do best because clearly that gives them the best chance to score and win.

A lot of factors dictate what a team does best. The first factor is always the talent of the players. All good offenses have two main factors—a great quarterback and a great halfback. Look back on the last few Super Bowl champions. The Dallas Cowboys have had quarterback Troy Aikman and halfback Emmitt Smith. The Green Bay Packers have had quarterback Brett Farve and a combination of running backs, Edgar Bennett and Dorsey Levens. And the San Francisco 49ers had a combination of quarterback Steve Young and running back Rickey Watters. Before that, the 49ers had quarterback Joe Montana and running back Roger Craig.

The success of these tandems is not a coincidence. Teams need to run and pass. Teams that can do both, win.

There is more to figuring an offense than taking into account personnel. There is location. In what city is a team located? What is the weather like in November and December? And, who are the opponents in their division. In the NFL, each team plays teams that are in its division twice a year—once at home and once away. Divisions tend to take on personalities and coaches need to be aware of the personalities of its opponents before trying to put together a philosophy.

There are many considerations. Teams that play in colder weather, for instance, will need to rely on the running game more because it will be much more difficult to have a passing attack in brutal weather. Teams that play in a dome on artificial turf will want faster players.

Don't Make Mistakes

Discipline is a big word in football. Teams that don't turn the ball over (losing a fumble or throwing an interception) win much more often than teams that are turnover prone. Turnovers are a huge part of the game.

So, the most basic philosophy in the game is *don't make mistakes. Don't commit penalties* can also be considered part of it because no team can be good if it is constantly being punished and made to work harder. The game is already hard enough.

But the biggest mistake and the hardest to overcome is the turnover. A turnover is an interception (stolen pass) or fumble (a dropped ball that was once possessed by the offense that is then recovered by the defense). When a turnover occurs, it gives a team an opportunity it wouldn't have had, and it gives the team the ball much closer than they would get it if they had to wait for a punt. Or, perhaps a turnover occurred as the offense was moving close to scoring. Sometimes a turnover can be thought of as accounting for a two-touchdown turnaround. Suppose the

Joe's Record Book
The Chicago Bears of 1938 and the San Franciso 49ers of 1978 share the record for the most fumbles in a season—56.

offense was near the end zone when the turnover occurred. That's 7 points it didn't get. Then, if the other team scores, that's 7 points given up—it all adds up to a 14-point turnover.

Turnovers change momentum, and they change the mental approach of both teams. The team that gets the ball is suddenly given a gift. The team that loses the ball suddenly gets coal in their Christmas stocking.

The statistics on the effect of turnovers are amazing. Check out these statistics from the 1996 season, compiled by Stats Inc. of Skokie, Illinois.

Table 11.1 How Often Teams Won in 1996 When They Turned the Ball Over

Turnovers Per Game	Wins	Losses	Winning Percentage
0	69	16	.812 (81.2%)
1	75	48	.610 (61.0%)
2	58	69	.457 (45.7%)
3 or more	38	107	.262 (26.2%)

Formations, Playing Chess with Giants

A football game is a constant fact-finding mission, and a lot of the strategy has to do with formations. Sure the game has some general rules about where the players must line up. There have to be seven offensive men on the line of scrimmage and five of them must be linemen who are ineligible to catch passes. After that, there is a lot of leeway.

Each play is a fact-finding mission because the other team always does things for a reason, but the reason may not always be as it first seems. In fact, failure of a play is sometimes as good as success because the failure of that play teaches you about the other team.

The first goal of a formation is to allow a team to do what it does best. The next goal is to find out how the opposition will line up when it sees a particular formation. The first time the offense uses a particular formation is a test run. Sure, the offense wants the play to work, but if it doesn't, that's okay as long as they learned something. If the defense does the same thing the next time the offense comes out with the same formation, the offense has learned about a *tendency* of the defense. The next step is the important one—taking advantage of the tendency.

Everything in a football game is built upon what came before. What teams learn in the first quarter helps them decide what to do in the fourth. But it all starts with formations.

The Split "T" Formation

This formation, illustrated in the previous chapter, is primarily a passing formation. But this formation has advantages because it is balanced. There is a back on either side of the quarterback who can get out into pass patterns fast. It can also be used for runs. It is balanced; it allows for runs or passes to both sides of the field.

Two-Tight-End Formation

This formation, also illustrated in the previous chapter, is primarily a running formation that allows for power runs to either side of the line.

Three Wide Receivers

This is a passing formation. Three wide receivers gives the quarterback more options to throw the ball, and, just as importantly, it forces the defense to react. When a team has three wide receivers and a tight end, it can do a number of things, including put two of the wide receivers on one side with the tight end, or to only put one on the same side as the tight end. Here is an illustration of a three-wide-receiver offense, *trips right*, meaning two of the wide receivers and the tight end all line up on the same side.

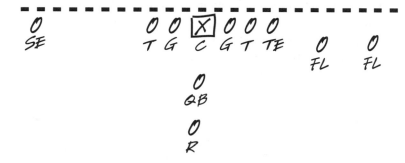

This is the three-wide-receiver, trips right formation. This is when two of the wide receivers and the tight end all line up on the same side.

Four Wide Receivers

Sometimes teams need to pass. It can be because of time or the scoreboard or a combination of both, which is usually the case. But there are times when it is silly to even give a pretense that you might run (although you *really* might). In those cases, teams like to line up with four wide receivers. This is where they may use a shotgun formation, in which the quarterback does not line up directly underneath the center, but instead lines up five yards back.

There are two ways to do it. One way is to line up balanced, with two wide receivers on each side. See the next illustration for a look at this lineup.

This is the four-wide-receiver, balanced formation. This is when there are four wide receivers on the field—with two on either side of the formation.

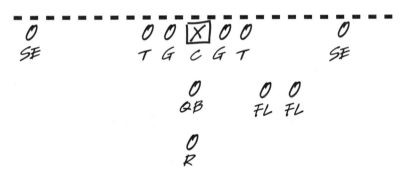

But sometimes, teams will want to line up three of the wide receivers on one side, called trips right. In this case, the idea is two-fold. First, to try to make the defense react to the formation. For instance, a team may want to put three wide receivers on the right in order to get the one receiver on the left room to work. By pulling the defense to the right, the formation frees up the receiver on the left to hopefully work one-on-one. If the defense doesn't bite and react to the formation, you have an automatic advantage by putting so many people on the right. The key is to make the right decision. See the illustration below of a four-wide-receiver set (*set* is another term for formation), trips right.

This is the four-wide-receiver set, trips right formations, in which three receivers line up on the right side.

The Shotgun

Sometimes, the quarterback will line up five yards behind the center and wait for the snap through the air. This is called the *shotgun*. The name only refers to the placement of the quarterback. It does not refer to the placement of any receivers. This is used primarily in passing situations to give the quarterback a better perspective to see the field; it also gives him an advantage not having to backpeddle before throwing.

Smashmouth Football

Smashmouth football is a simple philosophy—run the ball and then run it again. And then after that, run it again. There are usually about 65 offensive plays in a football game. If 40 of them are runs, the team is playing *smashmouth* football.

Smashmouth football is pure power. Woody Hayes, the legendary coach of Ohio State, compared power football to getting "three yards and a cloud of dust." It is a challenge to the defense that says, *"You cannot stop us. We will get those three yards. Maybe more."*

When a team has a lead, smashmouth football is beautiful because it demoralizes its opponent while taking time off the clock.

Another reason to play smashmouth football is to hide a quarterback who may not be the most gifted. If you run and run and run, the quarterback obviously doesn't have to throw. If a team can get away with just running the ball, it makes the quarterback's job easy. Hand off the ball. Hey, I could do that.

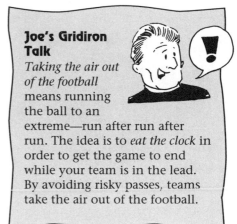

Joe's Gridiron Talk

Taking the air out of the football means running the ball to an extreme—run after run after run. The idea is to *eat the clock* in order to get the game to end while your team is in the lead. By avoiding risky passes, teams take the air out of the football.

Air-It-Out Football

Sometimes teams have such a good quarterback that they can't resist letting him take charge of a game. This is certainly the most exciting brand of football. As I just said, there are usually 65 offensive plays in football. If a team passes 40 times, they are playing *air-it-out* football.

Give a gunslinger the ball and see what he can do with it. The passing game is fun to watch. It produces quick results. The ball flies in the air, receivers are constantly being asked to do great things, and the defense is ultimately challenged. The only problem is that things can go wrong. When an air-it-out offense plays a great defense, the defense can usually stop it because they really only need to focus on stopping the pass. But, if the offense also has a running game that it can make the defense think about, it has a much better chance of succeeding. Balance is always the best policy because it forces the defense to be prepared for everything.

Big-Play Football

The Pittsburgh Steelers of the 1970s played mostly smashmouth football. They banged their big running back, Franco Harris, into the line over and over. Of course, the signature of the Steelers was their great Steel Curtain defense, but you don't win Super Bowls on defense alone. The Steelers won four Super Bowls. Clearly, they had a great offense too.

And the thing about that Steelers offense was that despite its ability to pound the ball into the heart of any defense, it had something more. That Steelers team could strike big at any moment. It had a great, strong-armed quarterback in Terry Bradshaw and two big-play wide receivers in John Stallworth and Lynn Swann. Defenses knew that if they worried too much about the run, bombs would be flying over their heads.

Joe's Record Book
Eight players in NFL history have caught a 99-yard pass (the longest ever). The most recent was Robert Brooks (from Brett Farve) of the Green Bay Packers on September 11, 1995 against the Chicago Bears.

Big-play football is simply a willingness to go for it all at any given time in a game. I believe teams need to call at least six long passes in every game. You need the long passes to keep the defense from crowding the line of scrimmage. And, most importantly, you need to complete at least half of those long throws. If you throw six bombs and none of them are complete, you don't have a big-play offense. Instead, you have a busy punter.

The West-Coast Offense

Your football team does not have to be on the West Coast to play this offense. It doesn't even necessarily work better on the West Coast. In fact, the Green Bay Packers, playing in a place that no one will ever mistake for the West Coast, won Super Bowl XXXI using the West-Coast offense.

You need a good quarterback and receivers. The idea of the West-Coast offense is simply to use short passes instead of runs for the ball control aspect of the game. Most passes are short—usually the quarterback will drop back three-to-five steps and the receiver will run 5-10 yards. The entire offense is based on timing. And it has been quite successful in recent years. But there are a couple of drawbacks. First of all, because the quarterback takes such a short drop, he gets hit quite a bit. More so than in other offensive sets. And also, the West-Coast offense relies on a decent running game. You cannot live by the pass alone. Although it has been very successful of late, it still requires execution and athletes.

The Run-and-Shoot

There are trends in football. Everyone wants to be an innovator and folks follow success. When things don't succeed, they become dinosaurs. A dinosaur of recent vintage is an offense called the *run-and-shoot*.

The setup is a basic four-receiver formation. The only difference that the run-and-shoot brings to the equation is that on every play the quarterback does a slight *roll out,* meaning that he takes the snap and instead of dropping straight back a few steps, he runs back and to one side—usually the side of his throwing arm. So, if the quarterback is right-handed, he will roll a few steps to the right before setting and throwing. The idea of the run-and-shoot is to replace the run with a short pass.

One of the biggest problems with the run-and-shoot was that it actually was too successful. Here's why. If a team took eight minutes to drive down the field and score a touchdown, the defense that gave up that touchdown was tired. Then, if the other offense—a run-and-shoot offense, let's say—scored in 30 seconds, the score was tied. But the problem was that the run-and-shoot team's defense ended up playing a lot more time. And for some reason, defenses get more tired than offenses. In the course of a game, those quick scores by an offense began to hurt their own defense.

The run-and-shoot offense sometimes had trouble scoring in tight field situations such as near the goal line. Without a tight end, it was difficult to run the ball with power, and the smaller field made it easier for defenses to cover receivers.

But for a while, the run-and-shoot had great regular-season success. The Houston Oilers made the playoffs a number of times using the offense, but were unable to win big games. Over time, coaches figured out how to stop it, or at least slow it down. Every year, the average yards per play went down for the Oilers. A number of teams used to use the run-and-shoot. Today, it has become a part of football's past.

The Two-Minute Drill

At the end of each half, there is a time-out with two minutes left on the clock. And then, everything changes. It looks like panic sets in. Teams go into a quicker mode because they know that there are only two minutes left.

In the final two minutes, teams are trying to score quickly. Everything is accelerated. Teams almost always pass and the clock is the major consideration. Seconds become like treasures to hoard. Sometimes, teams will call more than one play at once so that everybody can come and line up without a huddle. The idea is to run plays quickly, get the ball out of bounds to stop the clock, and move the ball down the field as fast as possible.

Joe's Gridiron Talk

The *hurry-up offense* is one that is usually used with two minutes to go in the half. Almost all plays are passing plays designed to get as much yardage as possible and still stop the clock by going out of bounds. Short passes to the sidelines work best. Runs, because the clock continues to tick, are not used often in the hurry-up offense.

Joe's Tips
All football games inevitably come down to five or six plays. A fumble, an interception, a big run, or a big pass. You never know *which* five plays, but you can count on it—it comes down to five big plays. So pay attention.

Often it works. The reason is odd. Defenses, knowing what teams are trying to do in the final two minutes, play a *prevent defense*, meaning that it puts more defensive backs on the field and it pulls them far back. The last thing in the world the defense wants to do is give up a big play like a bomb. So instead, it is willing to give up shorter plays. The thing is, most two-minute offenses are quite happy to take the shorter plays. At least at first. But in the end, it usually comes down to a showdown where one team or the other makes a stand.

The Size of the Field

Sure, all football fields are the same. But, field position changes constantly, and that directly affects the offensive strategy. If a team is on its own 5-yard line, it has 95 yards to get to the end zone. There are dangers there of throwing a short pass and maybe having it intercepted for a touchdown (I know, I did this in Super Bowl XVIII). But there are also opportunities. Ninety five yards gives the offense a lot of field to cover.

On the contrary, if a team reaches the red zone (inside the 20-yard line of the defense), the field becomes shorter. There is much less room to work. This brings a new meaning to the term accuracy. Normally, a quarterback may have about a three-yard window to throw the ball into in the middle of the field. But nearing the end zone in the red zone, that window is usually reduced to about one yard. That's why quarterbacks make their money in the red zone.

Plays are also called for the length of the field that teams have to work. In a nutshell, a shorter field requires more accuracy.

When to Go on Fourth Down

Teams almost always try three plays to get 10 yards and a first down. If they don't get that far in three plays, they usually punt. But not always.

There are times that teams will use their offense on fourth down. The usual rule is that they will go on fourth down if they don't have a choice—in other words time is running out and they need to score so they are willing to take their last chance *right now*. But sometimes, coaches will decide to go for it on fourth down early in the game. They may think they have a great opportunity *right now*, and they also may think that they have time to recover if they fail.

The problem, of course, is what if they do fail? Well, the other team gets the ball. Right there. No punting 40 or so yards. The ball changes hands when a team fails to reach the first-down line within four downs. Going for it on fourth down is a very risky proposition.

The Least You Need to Know

➤ Good teams do what they do best and try to build their strategy around their players.

➤ Mistakes (fumbles and interceptions) can be deadly and are a key indicator of what the score will be.

➤ Good teams can do everything, and do so because sometime in the season they will need everything.

➤ Teams need a huge arsenal of weapons no matter what kind of offense they run— West Coast, air-it-out, big play, smashmouth, or something else. They need guts and smarts in deciding when to take risks, and they need to be efficient when time is running out.

Chapter 12

Advanced Offensive Strategies: Like Rocket Science

In This Chapter

➤ How football teams communicate

➤ How audibles work

➤ The joy of creating mismatches

Sometimes, you'd swear that some Silicon Valley software firm is designing NFL offenses. But it really isn't being done by nerds (no offense intended) with pocket protectors. This stuff is being designed by *football guys* and these guys are smart. Let me tell you, if these football guys had gone into software instead of the NFL, they'd be kicking butt in Silicon Valley.

I admit it. This stuff *is* complex. But, as you will see, a lot of it is also common sense. Some things in football aren't logical, they just *are*. But most of football, even the complex stuff, makes sense. After all, folks have been winning football games for a long time—and every one of them understood it. So can you.

This chapter will deal with the stuff that NFL players deal with, including the communication system among the players and with the coach during the game, the rules and strategies regarding motion and shifting, the importance of mismatches, and why intelligence is so important for a football team. The best part is that I am going to simplify it. No downloading required.

The Communication System—Say What?

I speak two languages—English and *football*. The two languages are not similar. Whereas one language, English, has nouns, pronouns, verbs, adjectives, and the like, football has abbreviations.

The language of football is one of quick communication because on the field there just isn't time to say, "*All right, Jerry, I think you should run an out pattern, and Michael, you should run a post, and Ben, I'd like you to run a slant, and gosh Emmitt, maybe you could run a little swing pattern off to the right, and Daryl, if you could hang out near me and block any of those big defensive linemen, I would really appreciate it. Oh, and you offensive linemen, could you please do a slide block to the right because I think I might move a little to the right before I pass the ball.*"

Instead of all that, the quarterback might instead just say, "*Boomerang.*"

In the context of a football game, you have to be able to communicate very quickly, very succinctly. There just isn't time for a long monologue. Instead, teams use one word or one number or a combination of them to describe what the plan is for any particular play. Every team has a different communication system. It can be done in a number of ways.

Think back to the passing trees illustrated in Chapter 9 for wide receivers and Chapter 10 for running backs. Each tree has nine numbers or names of patterns. Running backs patterns usually will have names. Each number or name stands for specific pattern. For instance, a 9 route on wide receiver passing tree is a Go route. A 1 route is a Quick Out.

All teams run essentially the same routes. The key to understand is that every route has a number and that every receiver and quarterback knows those numbers.

Got that? Good. Okay, next step.

There are usually two wide receivers and a tight end. The play is called with a pattern for each player, starting on the single receiver (split end) side. Each one will run a pattern that is described by one of the patterns in the passing tree. So, let's say the split end runs a 9 route. And let's say that the tight end runs a 7 route, and the flanker on the tight end side runs a 6 route. Remember, you can flip back to Chapters 9 and 10 to refresh your memory of what each route looks like.

Then, let's say that the halfback runs an H-Post route, and the fullback runs a swing.

Let's review:

➤ Split end: 9 route

➤ Tight end: 7 route

➤ Flanker: 6 route

➤ Halfback: H-post

➤ Fullback: Swing

This is a play. And, if it were called by the numbering system, the quarterback would set the formation, by saying, *"Split right,"* and then he would say, *"9-7-6 H-Post Swing."* And everyone would know what to do. See, it's a foreign language.

Here is what that play looks like:

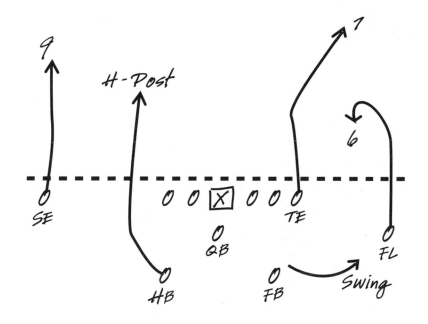

The play is 9-7-6 H-Post, Swing, in which five players are given specific pass routes to run.

Many teams run the same play. But the thing is, every team calls it something different. The numbers for the patterns could be different in some systems.

But in another system, the entire play could be called by two words, say, "Ohio pass." Yet another team could call the same play "Twenty-four," and still another team could call it something else.

It is the same play, called something different in different systems. Not only is football a different language, but clearly there are many dialects.

There is a difference in philosophy, though, between naming every pattern for every player and simply calling one name that stands for everything. For instance, the 9-7-6 H-Post, Swing, tells every player specifically what to do. Calling the same play *Ohio pass* requires more memorization on the part of each player. A lot more. Here's why. When the quarterback says, "9-7-6, H-Post, Swing," each player listens for his number—the one that tells him the pattern he should run. But, if the quarterback says, "Ohio pass," each player must automatically know their pattern. Sure, it sounds the same. But wait.

Joe's Tips

It would be good if every player on the field knew where every other player on the field is going on every play. It would be good, but it is not absolutely necessary. It is, however, essential for the quarterback to know what everyone is going to do. That's just another reason why quarterback is such a difficult job, and why quarterbacks get the big bucks.

Joe's Tips

When Joe Gibbs, my coach with the Washington Redskins, talked about putting a football team together, he had three criteria: character, intelligence, and ability. He ranked them in that order. Gibbs, a coach that took four teams to the Super Bowl, ranked intelligence above ability. That should tell you a lot. Remember, the game is 85 percent mental and 15 percent physical.

Let's say the quarterback calls *3-7-6, H-Post, Swing.* It is nearly an identical play except for the single-side receiver who runs a 3 pattern instead of a 9 pattern. Every other player runs the exact same pattern. This is easy to figure if the name of the play is 3-7-6, H-Post, Swing. However, another team could call that play *Utah pass.* The play is the same as Ohio pass except for one guy. It is a different name, but only one player does something different.

Now, you can take it a step further. You can even run a *9-7-6 H-Post, Swing* from a different formation. This is easy to do if the quarterback calls the formation in the huddle. But some teams actually use the formation as part of the play call. So, the same play, which is called an *Omaha pass* from one formation, is suddenly a *Boomerang pass* from another formation. Same play, same patterns—different formation and different name.

If a team uses numbers, 7 is a route. If the team puts three numbers together, it is a play. Those three numbers equal, in another system, a word. A communication system is either numbers or a word.

It is a foreign language. Really. The best analogy I can give for why some systems are easier to learn than others, is from when I was in high school. Back then, many of my friends and I took Spanish instead of Latin because we thought it was easier to learn.

Some offensive systems are easier to learn than others. This doesn't make any one system better than any other, but it does make some systems better suited to certain players than others. If you remember back to the early chapters of this book, I said that football is 85 percent mental and 15 percent physical. The truth is that a team with smart players can really win games with smarts and deception. And football is a game of smarts and deception.

Where Do the Runners Run?

You know about the numbering system for the passing tree. But the holes in the line where the running backs are supposed to run are numbered as well, and the quarterback will direct the running game as much as the passing game. See the following illustration.

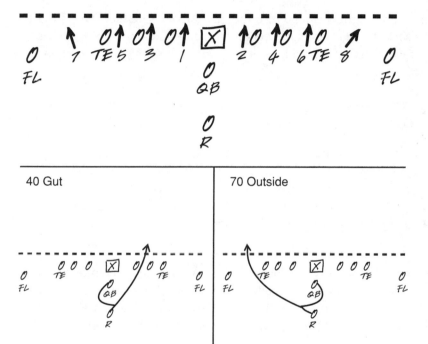

Running holes for a two-tight-end offense, and two examples of plays: The 40 Gut and the 70 Outside.

Teams usually use odd numbers for the holes left of the center and even numbers for the running patterns on the right. The coaching staff decides the numbering system.

For instance, if you wanted to run the play 40 Gut, you could do it from any number of formations. In the huddle, you would say "Trips Right, 40 Gut." This gives the formation and the play. The line has memorized the blocking scheme for a Gut run. The 40 tells them that the running back will run at the 4 hole. The way players know the difference between a running play and a passing play is through memorization of plays. When players hear a play called, they know what to do.

The Quarterback Isn't Listening to Elvis

In the old days—the early part of my career, for instance—quarterbacks used to call their own plays. When I played under George Allen, I called my own plays. But offenses continue to get more and more sophisticated, and quarterbacks are only allowed to call audibles (you'll learn about these next) when they spot either a weakness in their own plan or a weakness in the defense. Otherwise, coaches call plays. That is, the offensive coordinator sends a message to the quarterback in the huddle to tell the quarterback which play to run.

It is now done with a radio signal beamed into the quarterback's helmet. That's right, quarterbacks wear a sort of walkman—speakers inside his helmet. He's not listening to Elvis, The Beatles, or Celine Dion. Instead, he is listening to his offensive coordinator tell him which play to run.

Joe's Rules

The radio communication is shut off 10 seconds before a play is run. The coach cannot keep talking to the quarterback as he walks to the line of scrimmage. And believe me, from a quarterback's perspective, they don't shut them off soon enough. A quarterback has his own thoughts but the coach always seems to have something more to say.

On occasion, technology breaks down. In other words, every once in a while, the radio doesn't work. In those cases, plays are still called from the sidelines but with baseball-type signals that you would see a third base coach use. This was how it was done when I played and was one of the fun parts of the game for me. Players got a chance to make up their own signals.

If the person giving the signal touched the top of his head, that meant a certain number. If he grabbed his nose, that meant a certain number. If he put his hands in a "V," that meant a certain formation. Or, if he made a muscle like a muscle-man, showing me his bicep, that meant strength—where the tight end should go. So, if he showed me his right bicep, that meant the strength of the formation was to the right. Following is an example of how a team might use the numbering system with signals.

Usually, at least two and often three people were giving signals from the sidelines at once. The reason is that teams don't want the defense to be able to steal the signals. Only one person is giving the real signals. The quarterback knows which one.

Hands next to thighs = 1

Hands on front of thigh = 2

Hand on front of belt = 3

Hand on side of belt = 4

Hand on stomach = 5

Hand grabbing neck = 6

Grabbing the nose = 7

Hand on shoulders = 8

Hand on head = 9

Audibles, Changing the Play

Sometimes, the play that is called into the huddle by the coach is not a good idea. It could be because the defense has anticipated the play and is loaded up to stop it. Or, it could be because the defense has lined up in a vulnerable alignment and the offense could take advantage of it with a different play. In either case, the offense wants a chance to change.

But clearly, the offense does not want to tell the defense what they plan. So, they have to have a system of communicating at the line of scrimmage. It starts in the huddle, where the quarterback gives a formation. There, he calls a play, or he calls a *check-with-me*. A check-with-me tells the team the quarterback will call the play at the line of scrimmage (LOS). It works the same as an audible, except it is not changing the play, it is setting it at the LOS.

Audible plays are usually called with colors as the code. The offense has a *live color* that signals an

> **Joe's Gridiron Talk**
> A *check-with-me* is where the quarterback gets in the huddle and calls, "Check with me." What he is saying is, "I'm not going to call a play now. I'll call it at the line." He sets the formation, and then when he gets to the line of scrimmage, he looks at the defense and calls the play.

137

audible is coming. For instance, that live color could be *black*. This means that if the quarterback comes to the line of scrimmage and sees a reason to change the play, he could first yell the color of the live audible—"Black!"

By yelling "Black," he tells the offense that he wants to change the play. Whatever he yells after yelling black, he is telling the team the new play. If he yells, "Black Utah," he is switching to the Utah play. If he yells, "Black Boomerang," he is switching to the Boomerang play.

But…

There are other colors in the rainbow besides black (okay, black isn't in the rainbow, but bear with me). For instance, there is yellow, my personal favorite.

So, if black is the live color but the quarterback comes to the line and yells, "Yellow 31," the defense may think he is calling an audible to change to play 31. But in reality, yellow means nothing, nothing at all.

Joe's Gridiron Talk
Almost every team snaps the ball *on two*, meaning the snap will come when the quarterback says, "Hut one, hut two." When he says, "hut two," the ball is snapped. But sometimes, to fool the other team, the center will try snapping on "hut three." However, when an audible is called, the snap automatically reverts to snapping the ball at "hut two."

And, if you remember back to Chapter 7, there is a thing called a dummy audible. This works with the live color. If the live color is black, the quarterback will call a play in the huddle and then tell everyone that he is going to call a dummy audible. The reason for this is obvious. The quarterback does not want the defense to know the live color. He is, in effect, fooling the defense into thinking that the live color audible is actually a dummy color. So, the quarterback calls the play and then he says, "No matter what I say, we are running this play."

At the line, he yells, "Black." The defense, in the game, has already sort of noticed that black appears to be the live audible. But this time, there is now a dummy audible. Black is called but the play doesn't change. Remember, football's a head game. It is one of those, *I want you to think that I am going to do this, but I'll do something else instead.*

Audibles are called about 10 percent of the time. If they are used much more, that means the offensive team did not do a very good job of preparing a game plan.

Shifting

When the quarterback comes to the LOS, the first thing he yells is, "Set." That tells everyone to get in their set position. At that point, the offensive line cannot move. However, the other players on offense can *shift*, meaning they are allowed to release from their set position, move to another place on the field, and then get set again. This is called *shifting*.

An example of shifting would be if the tight end first lined up on the right side of the formation. Then, after the quarterback made the first sound, he would shift to the other side of the line and reestablish himself before the ball is snapped.

Defensive players can move all they want before the snap of the ball.

Motion

There is a difference between shifting and motion. When players shift, they have to come to a stop before the play begins. Five players can shift at one time as long as they all come to a stop.

Motion, on the other hand, is when a player is still moving when the ball is snapped. Motion cannot begin until all shifting has ended.

Joe's Rules

When the ball is snapped, a player in motion must be moving parallel to the line or away from the line. Players in motion can move in any direction before the ball is snapped, but cannot be moving toward the line of scrimmage when the ball is snapped. If the player is moving toward the line of scrimmage, that is *illegal motion*—a 5-yard penalty.

Motion is used for a number of reasons. For one thing, motion helps tell an offense what the defense is planning for that play. If the offense sends a man in motion (a running back, tight end, or a wide receiver), and a defensive player is mirroring him, it probably means the defense is in a man-to-man coverage rather than zone coverage. If the defense doesn't send one man with him, but instead just slides in the direction of the motion, it usually means there is zone coverage.

Motion can also give certain receivers an advantage in getting out into routes. For instance, Art Monk, early in his career, was not very good at getting away from the *press*. A press is when a defensive back lines up within one yard of the receiver and tries to stop him from getting off the line.

Now, Art, who I played with and was one of the greatest receivers of all time, had this difficulty. However, when he got past the press and into his route, he was incredible. So quite often, we would send him in motion. After all, it is harder to hit a moving target, and Art was very good at getting away from the press when he had a chance to be moving first. Also, he was smart enough to handle motion, and we clearly wanted to get him the ball. When you have a guy who is that good, you want the ball in his hands as much as possible.

Mismatches

Motion can also be used to create *mismatches*—when a defensive player doesn't have the necessary skills to cover an offensive player. For instance, motion can be used to get a running back covered by a linebacker instead of a safety. Defenses don't want a linebacker covering a running back because normally running backs are faster than linebackers. Teams can also get mismatches in the running game. That was part of philosophy of the two-tight-end offense.

Normally, a defense plays a safety in the middle of the football field. He is responsible for protecting the deep middle, and the strong side safety lines up on the side of the tight end. The problem for the defense is that when there are two tight ends, there are not enough safeties. The defense certainly doesn't want to take the free safety out of the middle of the field. So, instead, a run to the side without the safety can create a mismatch because there should be enough blockers to cover all the defensive people. This gives the running back room because the defense doesn't have any *support,* or defensive backs, to come up and help stop the run.

There is one more example of how a mismatch can occur in the running game. If the offense has a 300-pound guard and wants to run a sweep to the right, it would like to force a cornerback to come up and support that run. The cornerback may be about 185 pounds. If that 300-pound guard is going to block that 185-pound defensive back, the offense has created a mismatch. When there is a 300-pound mass of body that is agile and quick, and in all likelihood quite nasty, going up against a smaller individual who really doesn't look forward to contact anyway, *that* is a mismatch.

Picking Up Blitzes

Sometimes, the defense will try to bring more people at the quarterback than the offense has people to block. This is called a *blitz*. You will learn more about these in Chapter 17.

For now, though, you should know that normally, the defense will *rush* three or four linemen.

Joe's Gridiron Talk
When the defense *rushes* the quarterback, it means it is charging at him trying to tackle or disrupt him.

When the defense also rushes a linebacker, it is called a *dog,* not a blitz. When the defense brings more than one linebacker, or rushes more than five people, it is called a blitz. The idea is to attack *so fast* that the offense is hurried into making a mistake.

The offense knows that the defense might blitz. So, it tries to figure a way to beat it. So remember:

➤ Blitz = More than five rushing

➤ Dog = Five rushing

Normally, when a defense blitzes, it means the defensive backs are in man-to-man coverage. Recognizing the blitz is the job of everyone, but especially the quarterback and wide receivers. The quarterback and wide receivers need to make a very quick adjustment.

The wide receiver must run a shorter route, and the quarterback has to throw the ball quickly. If the quarterback and wide receiver know a blitz is coming, the blitzer doesn't even need to be blocked. The quarterback has about 1.5 seconds to throw the ball. In a blitz situation, the quarterback will take three steps back and then the ball will be gone to the receiver who should run a quick slant at a 45 degree angle up the field. Blitzes can really hurt the offense, but if the offense knows they are coming, they can backfire on the defense.

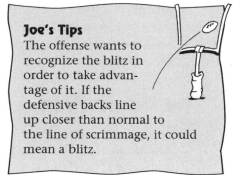

Joe's Tips
The offense wants to recognize the blitz in order to take advantage of it. If the defensive backs line up closer than normal to the line of scrimmage, it could mean a blitz.

Tackle Eligible to Catch a Pass

Remember that only the two outside men on the line of scrimmage are eligible to catch a pass, all others on the line of scrimmage cannot. Sometimes, especially in a short-yardage situation, the offense will put lots of big bodies right on the line of scrimmage. A short-yardage situation is one in which the offense needs two yards or less for a first down or for a touchdown. In these situations, the offense may try to simply use a power run to get the little bit of real estate it needs. Thus, it may line up an extra tackle—because he is big—on the outside of the formation.

The rule that the outside guys on the line of scrimmage are eligible to catch a pass does not automatically apply to the tackle. The reason is simple. He is wearing a number in the 70s. And the defense knows that a guy wearing a 70s number on his jersey is ineligible. So in order to be eligible to catch a pass, the tackle must report to the official as an eligible receiver. The official then informs the defense. The tackle must actually go to the official and say something like, *"Mr. Official, I am reporting as an eligible receiver."*

The official will then allow him to be eligible. And sometimes, the offense won't run the ball but instead will actually throw the ball to the tackle, who is eligible. Everybody on offense, especially the tackle, gets a kick out of that. The defense usually is not amused.

Trick Plays

Speaking of amusing the defense, there is nothing like a good trick play—one designed to trick the defense into thinking one thing is happening when in fact, something completely different is happening. When they work, trick plays are wonderful. When they don't, they can really backfire.

It's all a matter of timing. An example of trick play is a *flea flicker*, in which the quarterback takes the snap and hands the ball to the running back as if it is a running play. This play works if the defense has really been expecting a running play because the running back heads right for the line of scrimmage. But just before he gets to the LOS, he turns and pitches (throws the ball two-handed underhand) the ball back to the quarterback. If the fake run worked, the defense is all geared up to stop the runner. And the split end should be wide open downfield to catch a bomb from the quarterback, who should have time to throw.

The Game Plan

Every team has a game plan—simply a choice of plays that they want to use in specific situations. It is usually on one sheet of paper and it has different situations—such as *first down and 10 yards,* or *second down less than seven, two minute, goal line/short-yardage (GL/SY)*. Under each situation, there are a choice of plays that the team plans to use. See the example game plan that I've created below. This example won't show you every play a team might have and you might not understand what all the play abbreviations mean (after all, each team has its own play names), but it will give you an idea of the complexity of a game plan.

OFFENSE

1st & 10

RUN	FORMATIONS	PASS
1. 40/50 Gut	(Split, I, 2TE)	1. 585
2. 60/70 Outside	(R, I, Trips)	2. Scram 3/7
3. 60/70 Counter	(R, Trips)	3. Ch. 10
4. 20/30 AOI	(I, Stag, I)	4. Flash/Lightning

2nd & 7–

RUN	FORMATIONS	PASS
1. 20/30 Reach	(I, Trips)	1. Ch.20/30 18 Pass
2. 40/50 Sprint Draw	(Trips)	2. Scram 3/7
3. 60/70 Outside	(R, Br.)	3. Scat Dodge
4. 80/90 Toss	(Trips, Double)	4. 989 ycs

2nd & 7+

RUN	FORMATIONS	PASS
1. 40/50 Gut	(R, I, Open)	1. Hi/Lo 63
2. 60/70 Outside	(R, Trips)	2. 79 R Wide
3. 20/30 Lead Draw	(I, Sh.mo)	3. 33 Run it
4. 40/50 Dive	(Split, R)	4. 363 Pump (all)

3rd+7 (3-7)

RUN	FORMATIONS	PASS
1. 20/30 T-Trap	(Trips, F.mo)	1. Scram 3 (pump)
2. 40/50 Speed Draw	(R, Sh.mo)	2. Utah Pass
3. 40/50 Lead Nose	(I, Wham)	3. "O" 88 Roll Rt.
		4. Speed 3

3rd+7 (3-7)

RUN	FORMATIONS	PASS
1. 20/30 Trap	(Trips, Gun)	1. 989 ycs
2. 40/50 Stutter	(Trips, 4w, G)	2. Dash 39 CB
3. 80/90 Q Sweep	(Trips Gun)	3. 933 Under Sc.
		4. 428 Wide Swing

GAME PLAN

+20 RED ZONE

RUN	FORMATIONS	PASS
1. 20/30 AOI	(Split, Trips)	1. 976 HP Swing
2. 40/50 Gut	(Trips, Over, I)	2. Ch. 10 212
3. 60/70 Counter	(2TE, Pop I)	3. RunPass 40/50 Gun
4. 40 Gut/Around	(Spread, Trips)	4. 333 Pump
	(Gun, Trips)	5. QB Draw

2 MINUTE

RUN	FORMATIONS	PASS
1. 20/30 Draw	(Trips-Double)	1. Dash 875
2. 80/90 Quick Sweep	(Trips)	2. Dash Pump
3. 20/30 T. Trap	(Trips, Double)	3. 428 ycs
4. 60/70 Over Draw	(Trips Rk. Whiz)	4. Scram 3
	(Whiz, Trip W)	5. 44/76

GL/SY

RUN	FORMATIONS	PASS
1. 60/70 Chip	(IRTW, F mo.)	1. RollPass (Z)
2. 60/70 Blast	(IRTW, St. I)	2. Juke 97 "o"
3. 20/30 Pop Trap	(Brown, F mo.)	3. Spring Draw
	(IRTW-Y mo.)	4. Ch. 50 Yove

TRICK PLAYS

RUN	FORMATIONS
1. Flea Flicker	(Trips mo.)
2. Run-Pass 60/70 Outside	(2 TE)
3. Hook & Ladder	(Trips Fake mo.)

2 PT.

RUN	FORMATIONS	PASS
1. 70 Chip	(I Tight Wing)	1. Speed
2. 60/70 Blast	(I F mo., Trips)	2. Punt
	(I Tight Wing)	3. Run/Pass

The Least You Need to Know

➤ Football is a foreign language that relies on colors, numbers, and abbreviations.

➤ There is one live color that the quarterback yells to the offense to tell them an audible is coming.

➤ The offense wants to create mismatches to take advantage of the defense. Offenses want to get their best guy on the defense's worst guy.

➤ Football is a microcosm of society. Just as you a plan to be successful in anything in life, you need a game plan to be successful in a football game.

Chapter 13

The Guys Who Control the Chaos

> **In This Chapter**
>
> ➤ What each official does
>
> ➤ Learning the penalties you'll see during a game
>
> ➤ Those funky referee signals and what they mean

They call them *zebras*, because they wear black-and-white striped shirts, but their real title is *officials*, and they have very difficult jobs. They stand in the middle of these huge humans wearing armor, and they decide when someone has broken the rules, when someone has caught the ball, or when someone goes out of bounds.

Think about it. No two people ever see something exactly the same way, but officials are supposed to see things exactly as they *really* occurred. They have the unenviable task of trying to make a split-second decision in a game that is played in fractions of inches. They have to make a decision based on something that happens literally in the blink of an eye.

Referees are put under a microscope. The players are looking at them and their decisions. The coaches are looking too, so are the fans in the stadiums, and so is that big eye in the sky called television.

This chapter will cover the officials, who they are, what each one's responsibility is, and where they are on the field. It will list the various penalties, what the cost is of each one, and what the signal is that tells you which penalty occurred.

Joe's Gridiron Talk
An *inadvertent whistle* is when a whistle is blown by mistake. When this happens, the play stops. Whatever happens after the whistle is insignificant.

Who Are These Guys and Where Are They?

Officials are part-time employees of the National Football League. Some work full-time as teachers, some as insurance salesmen, some as principals. All are dedicated to football.

All have whistles. A whistle, when blown, signifies the end of a play either due to a tackle or a penalty.

But who are they when they are on the field? There are seven of them, and each has a distinct responsibility, as described next.

Referee

The *referee* is in charge of the game. He is the one you see on television making those funky signals, and he is also the one who makes the final decision for all rules interpretations. He is also the one who wears the white hat. (All other officials wear black hats with thin white stripes.) He stands in the backfield behind the quarterback, on the side of the quarterback's throwing arm. So if the quarterback is right-handed, the referee stands behind the quarterback's right side.

The referee is responsible for determining whether the snap is legal and whether the backs have been in legal motion. The referee is also the quarterback's best friend (maybe even more so than the offensive line) because he is responsible for looking for any fouls on the quarterback, such as roughing the passer. In fact, even on running plays, the referee stays near the quarterback before, during, and after the hand-off. After the action has cleared away from the quarterback, the referee follows him downfield looking at the contact that follows behind him.

He also makes decisions about possession of the ball, such as whether the ball is free on a fumble or dead on an incomplete pass.

Umpire

The *umpire* is concerned with actions near the LOS during the play. He stands about four or five yards on the defensive side of the ball, between where the guards line up. He is on the lookout for any false starts by the offense, and he is also checking on the legality of the contact between the linemen. The umpire checks to make sure offensive linemen do not move illegally downfield on pass plays, and he is also responsible for ruling on players' equipment.

Head Linesman

The *head linesman* is responsible for what happens at the LOS prior to or at the snap. He calls offside and encroachment. He straddles the LOS and focuses on the closest back to his side of the field. He also makes rulings concerning illegal action by defenders to prevent receivers from moving downfield, and he must make rulings concerning the sideline on his side of the field—in other words, whether a ball carrier or receiver is out of bounds. Also, with the referee, the head linesman keeps track of the number of downs. He helps determine forward progress by a runner on his side of the field. He also makes calls regarding the legality of action of receivers and defenders on his side of the field, including pass interference. The head linesman sometimes wraps a string around his finger to keep track of downs. For example, a string around his index finger means it is first down. A string around the middle finger equals second down, a string around ring finger equals third down, and a string around his pinky means it is fourth down.

Line Judge

The *line judge* keeps time as a backup in case the official clock operator's clock does not work. He straddles the LOS on the side of the field opposite the head linesman. Like the head linesman, he judges actions just prior to or at the snap, such as encroachment and offside. He focuses on the closest back to his side of the field and rules on any passes thrown to him—whether they are forward or backward passes. He also judges whether the quarterback is behind or beyond the LOS when a pass is thrown, and also assists in observing contact between lineman on his side of the field. The line judge tells the Referee when time has expired at the end of each quarter.

Back Judge

The *back judge* is in a deep position in the defense. He is on the same side of the field as the line judge, but is 20 yards deep on the defensive side. His focus is the wide receiver on his side. He observes the legality of actions surrounding that receiver and those defending that receiver. He makes decisions regarding his sideline—whether a ball carrier or receiver is out of bounds. He also makes decisions about catching, recovery, or illegal possession of a loose ball beyond the line of scrimmage and rules on interference calls.

Side Judge

The *side judge* is in a deep position in the defense. He is on the same side of the field as the head linesman, 20 yards deep on the defensive side. He focuses on the legality of action between the offensive end and back and those guarding the end and back. He also has responsibility for making decisions regarding the sideline—whether a ball carrier or receiver is out of bounds. And he makes decisions about catching, recovery, or illegal possession of a loose ball beyond the line of scrimmage. He rules on interference calls.

Field Judge

The *field judge* keeps the 40/25 second clock. He is located 25 yards down the field, generally on the tight end side of the ball. The Field Judge focuses on the tight end and observes the legality of the tight end's actions and the actions that defenders take against the tight end. He rules on holding or illegal use of the hands by the end or the back or on the defensive player guarding the end or the back. He makes decisions about catching, recovery, or illegal touching of a loose ball beyond the line of scrimmage. He makes calls on pass interference.

Where officials line up.

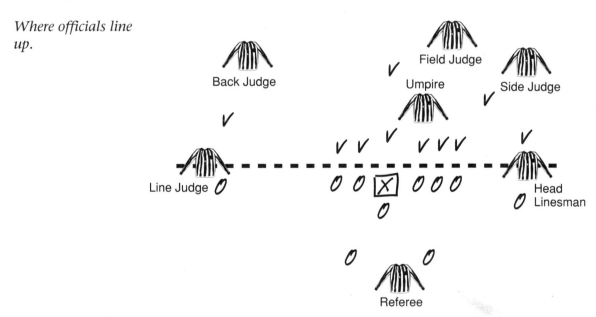

A Few Basic Referee Signals

When there is a score, a completion, or an incompletion, an official will also use hand and body signals to communicate. Table 13.1 shows some of the basic signals that you are likely to see.

Table 13.1 General Signals You Should Know

Signal	Description
	A scoring attempt isn't good until you see this get signal, which signifies a **TOUCHDOWN**, a **FIELD GOAL**, or a successful **EXTRA POINT** or **TWO POINT CONVERSION**.
	This signal means a team has earned a **FIRST DOWN**. The referee points his hand toward the defense.
	The signal here has many meanings. It is used if a **PENALTY IS REFUSED**. It also signifies a **PASS IS INCOMPLETE**, a **PLAY IS OVER**, or a **FIELD GOAL OR EXTRA POINT ATTEMPT HAS BEEN MISSED**.
	This signifies a **SAFETY** has been scored.

continues

149

Table 13.1 Continued

Signal	Description
	This signal means a **TIME OUT** has been called. If the referee uses the same signal and then follows it by putting one hand on top of the cap, it signifies a **REFEREE'S TIME OUT**. The same signal followed by an arm swung at the side means **TOUCHBACK**.
	This signal, in which the referee blows the whistle while spinning his arm in a circle to simulate a moving clock, means **TIME IN**.

Controlling the Chaos

There sometimes appears to be chaos on the field. There really isn't. There are a lot of rules that govern the game, and sometimes those rules are broken. When there is a penalty, the referee will use hand and body signals to tell the crowd and both teams what went wrong. Here are some of the basic penalty signals you are likely to run across:

Table 13.2 Penalty Signals You Should Know

Penalty Signal	Description
	This is the signal for the **CROWD NOISE** penalty—loss of team time out, or a five-yard penalty on the defense for excessive crowd noise. This signal also can mean **DEAD BALL**. Excessive crowd noise is when crowd noise makes it virtually impossible for the visiting offense to communicate. A dead ball is a ball that is on the field but is no longer live. It describes the football after a play has ended.

Penalty Signal	Description
	This signal means a **BALL HAS BEEN ILLEGALLY TOUCHED, KICKED, OR BATTED.** The penalty is a loss of down.
	This signal means **DELAY OF GAME OR EXCESSIVE TIME OUTS.** A team is only given three time outs in a half. If it tries to call more, or if it takes too long to get a play off, this is a penalty of five yards. Teams are given 45 seconds from the end of a play to start a new play. If an official becomes involved, teams are given 25 seconds to start a play once the administrative stoppage is finished.
	This signal, when the referee rotates his forearms over and over, means **FALSE START, ILLEGAL FORMATION,** or **KICKOFF** or **SAFETY KICK OUT OF BOUNDS.** These are 5-yard penalties.
	This signal means **PERSONAL FOUL.** It is often, though not always, followed by a signal that describes the type of personal foul. For instance, if it is followed by a swinging leg, it means **ROUGHING THE KICKER.** If it is followed by a raised arm swinging forward, it means **ROUGHING THE PASSER.** And the same signal followed by a simulated grasp of the face mask means it is a **MAJOR FACE MASK,** which is considered intentional. The penalty for a personal foul is 15 yards and sometimes an automatic first down.

continues

151

Table 13.2 Continued

Penalty Signal	Description
	This is the signal for **HOLDING**, which is a 10-yard penalty. For more information, see Chapter 8.
	This signal means **ILLEGAL USE OF THE HANDS**. This is a 10-yard penalty. It occurs when an offensive player uses his hands in the face of a defensive player or pushes him from behind. There are many other interpretations of this rule.
	This is a signal that is used as an explanation for the incomplete pass signal that will follow. This signal means a **PASS WAS JUGGLED IN BOUNDS AND CAUGHT OUT OF BOUNDS**. The referee moves his hands up and down in front of his chest.
	This is a signal for **INTENTIONAL GROUNDING**, which means that the quarterback threw a pass that he had no intention of trying to complete. This is a 10-yard penalty and loss of down.

Penalty Signal	Description
	This signal means **ILLEGAL FORWARD PASS**. One hand is waved behind the back, and then it is followed by the loss of down signal. An illegal forward pass is one that is thrown after the quarterback has gone past the LOS, or if it is the second forward pass thrown (since only one is allowed).
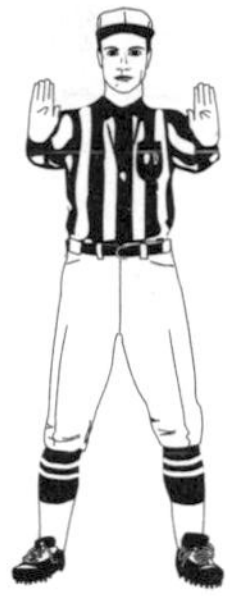	This signal means **INTERFERENCE**. Interference is when a player illegally disrupts an opposing player's ability to catch the ball. The ball is placed at the site of the infraction.
	This signal is used to signify an **INVALID FAIR-CATCH** signal. This is 5-yard penalty.
	This is a signal that means an **INELIGIBLE RECEIVER OR INELIGIBLE MEMBER OF THE KICKING TEAM** is downfield. This is a 5-yard penalty.

continues

153

Table 13.2   Continued

Penalty Signal	Description
	This is the signal for **OFFSIDE**. (See Chapter 8 for more information).
	This is the signal for **ILLEGAL MOTION AT THE SNAP**. The penalty is five yards.
	This signals **LOSS OF DOWN**, coming from any of a number of penalties.
	This is a signal for **UNSPORTSMANLIKE CONDUCT**, which is a 15-yard penalty. Roughing the kicker or roughing the passer are examples of unsportsmanlike conduct.

Penalty Signal	Description
	This is the signal for **CHOP BLOCK or CLIPPING**. (See Chapter 8 for a further description.) If the referee uses both hands to strike his thighs, followed by the personal-foul signal, it is a chop block signal. If he uses only one hand striking the back of his calf, followed by the personal-foul signal, it is a clipping signal. Both are 15-yard penalties.
	This is the signal for a **PLAYER BEING DISQUALIFIED**.
	The signal for **TRIPPING** is when the referee repeatedly bangs his right foot into the back of his left heel. This is a 10-yard penalty.
	This is the signal for an **ILLEGAL SUBSTITUTION** or for **TOO MANY MEN ON THE FIELD**. These are five-yard penalties.

continues

155

Table 13.2 Continued

Penalty Signal	Description
	This is the signal for illegally grasping **THE FACE MASK**, which is a five-yard penalty if it is not considered deliberate.
	When a referee moves his hands in horizontal arcs like the this illustration, it means **ILLEGAL SHIFT**. This is a five-yard penalty. An illegal shift occurs after an offensive lineman has assumed his stance and then lifts his hand up prior to the snap.

Instant Replay

The officials are amazing. They see things that normal folks really do miss. Part of it is training but part of it is just like the rest of the NFL—these guys are very good at what they do.

However, sometimes officials make mistakes. Unfortunately, those mistakes can change the outcome of games. And, the mistake are visible for all to see because every game is televised and every television broadcast will replay controversial plays. Announcers have been known to say something like, *"It looks like they blew that call."* (Of course, I've never said that.)

For a few years, the NFL tried to remedy this by allowing certain calls to be reviewed by video replay. If the call was clearly wrong, quite often it was reversed. However, the NFL stopped the policy of using replays. The League is still trying to decide how to use this powerful tool and even though you probably won't see it again until after the turn of the century, you should know that this is a great topic for debate.

The Least You Need to Know

➤ Different officials have different responsibilities and different parts of the field to cover.

➤ Different penalties cost different amounts—some costing yards, some costing downs, some costing both.

➤ The referee signals with his hands and body to indicate the type of penalty or other action that happened.

➤ The instant replay sometimes catches mistakes that officials make, but the truth is that the NFL officials are amazingly accurate.

Part 3
Learning the Defense and Special Teams

The most important part of a football team is its defense. Ask any quarterback. Despite everything I might have said in the previous part, the best friend of a quarterback is a good defense. It's not a good running back, or a good line, or even a good arm or brain. A quarterback loves it when his own defense is dominant. I once played for George Allen, a defensive guru. I swear, George's dream game would have been 2-0. His offense didn't score but didn't make any mistakes, and his defense was perfect while actually scoring points. George understood that if the other team scored zero points, it was easier to win.

This part will teach about the defense—the different positions and what they do and the strategies players at each position use to outsmart the offense. It will also discuss the overall defensive strategies that teams implement to try to stop the offense, and finally it will discuss the third unit in football—the special teams.

(<u>DEFENSE</u>! GET IT!)

Chapter 14

YOU OK, DUDE?

AAACK...

The Defensive Line: Get the Ball, Hit the Quarterback

In This Chapter

➤ How defenses can be successful even when they don't make tackles

➤ The different techniques defensive linemen use

➤ Stopping the runner and passer

➤ Why stunts aren't only in the movies

Line play on defense is not that different from the offensive side of the ball. On the line of scrimmage, big men hit big men. For instance, on running plays, the offensive line is trying to move the defensive people so that the running back can find holes and move through it. Defensive linemen are trying to move the offensive linemen so that the line-backers can get into the holes and hit the running back.

The chess game continues.

This chapter will deal with the defensive line—the different positions, their job in stopping the run and stopping the pass, and a few of the techniques linemen use in their attempt to control the line of scrimmage. It will also give my personal list of the five best of all time.

Who Are These Guys?

Defensive linemen play on the defensive side of the line of scrimmage. They are huge, agile, and powerful. They have to be because they are playing against offensive linemen who are, well, huge, agile, and powerful. It certainly makes for some interesting matchups.

Some teams use three defensive linemen, others use four. In either case, they line up in a lot of different places on the line. The following illustration shows a basic three-man line.

A three-man defensive line has a numbers disadvantage against the five-man offensive line.

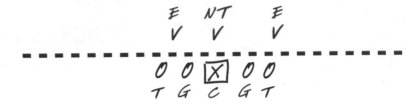

The most interesting of these positions—or maybe the most brutal—is that of the nose tackle. He is so named because he lines up right on the nose of the center, literally in his face. Talk about a rough day at the office. Sheesh. This is a man who could get hit on every play from the front, the left, and the right by 300-pound linemen. Three of them, all within hitting distance of one nose tackle. Imagine getting hit by 900 pounds of fury. Now imagine it again, and again, and again. Imagine a three-hour football game in which your job is to stand your ground no matter what hits you. If you can imagine it, you can imagine being a nose tackle.

A four-man line has two tackles instead of one nose tackle. It looks like the following illustration.

A four-man defensive line.

Generally, tackles are bigger than ends and serve a little different purpose. The prototype NFL tackle of the 1990s is Gilbert Brown, the 350-pound behemoth who plays for the Green Bay Packers. He kind of dares people to move him out of the way. They don't. Tackles are supposed to stand their ground, occupy blockers, and capture any ballcarrier that comes within reaching distance. A defensive tackle wants to be like a stubborn mule.

If you push, pull, tug, or do anything to him, he's not moving. That's his space and he's not moving. He may go forward, but as far as he's concerned no one is pushing him anywhere.

Ends, on the other hand are a little bit smaller and quicker. They aren't small—unless you consider 300 pounds to be small. But 300 pounds is less than 350, so it's relative. Because ends are quicker, they have a tendency to get into the *backfield* more often than tackles. Getting into the backfield is good. It means that the defensive player has pushed beyond where the offensive line started. The area behind the offensive line is called the backfield. That's where the quarterback and running backs start. When defensive players get into the backfield, they have a good chance to get a sack.

The primary objective of defensive linemen is to break through the offensive line and penetrate into the backfield. By doing that, they can create holes in the offensive line so that linebackers and other defensive players can have a free shot at the ball-carrier or quarterback. Also, if they have an opportunity to make a play on the quarterback or the ballcarrier, they certainly won't pass it up.

> **Joe's Record Book**
> Records for sacks have only been kept since 1982. Since then, the record for the most sacks in a season is 22 by Mark Gastineau of the New York Jets in 1984. The most sacks in one game is seven, by Derrick Thomas of the Kansas City Chiefs against the Seattle Seahawks on November 11, 1990.
>
> Reggie White of the Philadelphia Eagles and Green Bay Packers is the career leader for sacks with 165.5 sacks through the 1996 season.

Stopping the Run

Quite often, defensive linemen are like sacrificial lambs being offered forth in the *tackle box*. When there is a running play, they want to get to the runner, but their job is more than that. Frankly, they want to get hit by offensive linemen. If a defensive lineman can tie up two offensive linemen, that means there is one less offensive player to block the rest of the defensive players.

Defensive linemen don't go out of their way not to make tackles. Certainly they are there to stop the run, but they do more. Consider a guy like the aforementioned Gilbert Brown. He is 350 pounds. He will make an effort to try and tackle a runner, but on some plays his primary role is to occupy two linemen and allow the linebackers to pursue and make the play. If the

> **Joe's Gridiron Talk**
> The *tackle box* is the area along the line of scrimmage between where the two offensive tackles line up. It includes about three yards on either side of the line of scrimmage and features some interesting battles.

163

runner heads toward him, he will try to tackle him. But if he can get two linemen to block him, he has done his job.

Pass Rushing

Linemen start out closer to the quarterback than anybody on the defense. Sometimes, as a quarterback, defensive linemen can make you feel like an item on a menu. They just want to order you up.

They want to hit you, smack you, and knock you to the ground. You can tell they get an adrenaline rush from drilling you. Defensive guys get a thrill from making a tackle. It's like a first kiss—they get a tingle all through their body. It's a real sense of accomplishment. The idea is not just to bring the offensive player to the ground. They want to try and, not deflate, but actually destroy the confidence of the people with the ball. They want them to remember what it feels like to be hit.

Now, I don't think this is a good way for anyone to get their jollies, but that's just one man's opinion. Let me tell you how I got that opinion—from being tackled. Tackling hurts.

In my career, I had five concussions—I have post-concussion syndrome. I can remember things from 20 years ago, but sometimes I can't remember what I did yesterday. The concussions are just the start of my list. Here's the rest:

➤ broken collarbone (1)

➤ broken ribs (3)

➤ broken nose (7)

➤ broken thumb (1)

➤ broken leg (2—one really bad)

➤ torn up knee (left)

➤ dislocated elbow (left)

And my three front teeth—well, just don't look close. They really aren't mine, but I have a great dentist. In fact, I'll bet the NFL has brought business to more than a few dentists over the years. Interestingly enough, the most painful injury I ever had was called a hip pointer—when the muscles around the hip are literally torn away, and the last thing you want to do is sneeze. That's right, sneeze.

Before pass rushers can get to the quarterback, they have to get past the guys trying to block them. Defensive linemen rush the quarterback and linebackers blitz the quarterback but the only difference is where they come from—the hits all hurt. (See Chapter 17 for a further discussion of blitzing.)

When defensive linemen take on offensive linemen, it is an interesting confrontation. Since both men are approximately the same size—that is, the size of a small truck—there are not many times either one is going to overpower the other. That's not to say it's unheard of, but usually defensive linemen need to rely on using technique and smarts to get past their opponent. Many techniques are used and allowed but one, the *head slap*, has been outlawed.

Techniques are only good if they work. And they work if they accomplish the main agenda of the defensive line, which is to attack. The defensive line doesn't even need to get to the quarterback to disrupt him. Sometimes they can just *push the pocket* into his face. When a quarterback throws, he steps forward. It is very hard for a quarterback to even want to step forward when there is a mass of bodies coming at him. Instead, he may throw off his back foot, which gives him a lot less accuracy and arm strength. When the pocket is pushed back into his face, it messes up his rhythm and his ability to throw with confidence, and blocks his vision. When that happens, he may make a mistake. And when a quarterback makes a mistake, it usually costs the offense.

Pass rushers want to get the blocker they are facing off balance. If they can, they have a distinct advantage. They want to get them off balance physically and mentally. Football is *always* a chess game and defensive linemen are playing it just like everybody else. For instance, a defensive lineman might go outside on an offensive lineman for a pass rush and may do it again and again.

Everybody has an agenda in football and this defensive guy is trying to get the offensive guy to get comfortable with blocking him to the outside. The defensive player may go outside five or six or more times in a row. He's establishing a pattern, a tendency, but what he really is doing is setting up the offensive lineman. He's playing chess. In Super Bowl XXXI, that's exactly what Reggie White of the Green Bay Packers did to Max Lane of the New England Patriots. For a while, it appeared Lane was having a fairly good game against White. Then, in a critical situation, White came inside and Lane ended up

> **Joe's Gridiron Talk**
> A *head slap* is not allowed. Deacon Jones, who played for the Los Angeles Rams in the 1960s, used it a lot. Old offensive linemen still have headaches from Deacon. Imagine putting a helmet on and having somebody take a baseball bat and banging it upside your head about a dozen times—you just played against Deacon Jones. Ouch.

> **Joe's Tips**
> If a defensive lineman can get one sack a game, just one, he will get 16 in a season. If he can get 16 in a season, he will go to the Pro Bowl, which is the name of the NFL All-Star game. Heck, he may get a lifetime pass. That's right, get one sack a game and you are a superstar.

watching as White smashed Patriots quarterback Drew Bledsoe to the ground. When White got up and walked past Lane, he didn't say anything but he could have said, "checkmate."

Defensive linemen are trying to figure out what offensive linemen are planning. Film study is essential, and so is experience.

> **Joe's Gridiron Talk**
>
> When a defensive lineman *shades a guy's shoulder,* he moves slightly off the center of his opposing lineman. If he shades the right shoulder, he takes his helmet and puts it over the offensive lineman's right shoulder. It's only a move of about eight inches but it allows him to work on one side of the body.

For example, consider an offensive lineman is in a three-point stance with his hand on the ground in front of him. Clearly, he is either going to go forward to run block or backward to pass block. If he is going forward, he is probably leaning forward a little onto his hand, getting ready to push forward. If he is going backward, his weight distribution is slightly different. How does a defensive lineman know? He looks at the offensive lineman's finger-tips and knuckles. If the offensive lineman's fingertips and knuckles turn white, that means he is putting a lot of pressure on his hand and is probably leaning a bit forward.

Linemen also line up in various places along the LOS to gain an angle advantage on their offensive line opponents. Sometimes they will go straight at them, sometimes they will line up in the gap between them, or sometimes they will *shade their shoulder.*

Also, defensive linemen will look at the eyes of offensive linemen. Often, offensive linemen will look where they are going to go. If a guard is going to pull right, he might be looking in that direction. Everybody is trying to climb inside everybody else's head.

Stunts

There are other ways to get to the quarterback as well. Defensive linemen sometimes use *stunts* to rush the passer. This means that two men on the line will switch positions as the ball is snapped. There are lots of stunts. Here are two—a TT and an ET. A TT is simply when the two tackles switch positions. When a TT stunt occurs, one tackle will go first in front of the other and then the other tackle will come around and go into the line where the first tackle was lined up—just like a criss-cross. It looks like the following illustration.

An ET stunt works the same way, only the end and the tackle switch the position of their rush lanes. An ET stunt looks like the next illustration.

In a stunt, the second guy always hesitates for a half second. It's all just part of the head game—trying to make the offensive line worry about what the defensive line might do.

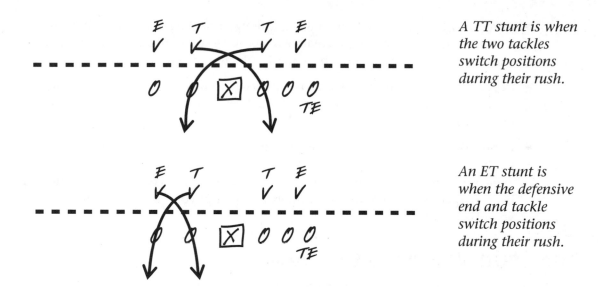

A TT stunt is when the two tackles switch positions during their rush.

An ET stunt is when the defensive end and tackle switch positions during their rush.

Bull Rushing

Sometimes, defensive linemen don't want to be cute or fancy. They just want to go straight forward. When they do, it is called a *bull rush*. The only thing missing from the bull rush is a pair of horns on the defensive lineman as he digs his feet into the ground. Other than that, it's just like a bull charging. When it works, the offensive lineman ends up flat on his back because the defensive lineman just ran him over. It looks like somebody breaking down a door and walking over it. The bull rush should only be used occasionally when the defensive lineman catches the offensive lineman off balance. Otherwise it's not going to work. After all, a 300-pound man is not going to overpower another 300-pound man very often. But it does happen.

Joe's Top Five Defensive Linemen

In the history of the NFL, there have been some great defensive linemen. I have picked five that I think are the best of all time and listed them here in no particular order.

➤ **Bob Lilly**, tackle for the Dallas Cowboys, was the cornerstone of the Dallas Doomsday Defense. He had the strength and quickness to control the line from tackle to tackle.

➤ **Deacon Jones**, end for the Los Angeles Rams, is considered the grandfather of the sack. He actually invented the name *sack*. If statistics were kept at the time he played, he would probably be the all-time sack leader.

167

➤ **Bruce Smith**, end for the Buffalo Bills. Although not a big defensive end, he plays with tremendous quickness, incredible upper body strength, and a tenacity that makes every offensive lineman have to play their best game against him.

➤ **Reggie White**, end for the Green Bay Packers, is an unstoppable force. No one in the game of football has ever possessed the sheer power and strength of this one man. He is affectionately called "The Reverend."

➤ **Randy White**, tackle for the Dallas Cowboys. His nickname was "Manster," meaning he was half man, half monster. This man could make you feel like a football game was a nightmare. It didn't matter whether you played offensive line, running back, or quarterback, he would definitely be a part of your dreams the night after you played him.

The Least You Need to Know

➤ Defensive linemen often want to occupy blockers to let others make tackles.

➤ A stunt is when defensive linemen switch positions as a play starts.

➤ A bull rush is when a defensß ive lineman overpowers an offensive lineman.

➤ When the defensive line tries to tackle the quarterback, it is called a rush.

➤ The stunt and bull rush are two main pass rushing techniques.

Chapter 15

Linebackers Do Everything

In This Chapter

➤ Lining up the linebackers

➤ The different roles of inside and outside linebackers

➤ How a linebacker reads and responds to the offense

There is something about the linebackers standing a few yards back from the ball, staring down a quarterback. You think of Ray Nitschke, the middle linebacker of the Green Bay Packers in the 1960s, with the missing teeth and the furious glare that told you how insulted he was that you would even dare try to move the ball against him. Or you think of Lawrence Taylor, who was like a hungry predator as he readied to roar off the line.

Defenses are set up for linebackers to be stars. Plus they just seem to glare better than anybody else. They usually line up a few steps away from the trenches, so that they have time to act and react. Essentially, linebackers make plays.

They can control a game—both stopping a run and thwarting a pass. Linebackers are the best athletes on the football field because they have to do everything, and by doing everything, they get to be stars. They have to be able to run with wide receivers and running backs, yet they have to be strong enough to take on 300-plus pound offensive linemen. Linebackers also have to be smart enough to recognize what's going on on the other side of the field.

Just as offenses are set up to make quarterbacks into stars, defenses are set up for the linebackers to become the stars. Linebackers should be the playmakers, and playmakers are always stars.

When you think of the greats in the game of football, the first thing you think of is the quarterback. Being one, I am partial. But certainly, the next group that comes to my mind even before the great running backs are the linebackers. Dick Butkus, Ray Nitschke, Sam Huff, Mike Singletary, and Lawrence Taylor.

Those are *names*.

This is a chapter about the stars of the defense, the linebackers. It will cover who they are, where they line up, what they do, and when they do it. It will discuss inside linebackers and outside linebackers, and the differences between run stopping, pass coverage, and pass rushing. Finally, this chapter will discuss those *names* and why they are my top five.

The Menu—Three Linebackers, or Four?

Every team has a linebacker on each side of the tackle box. Those are the *outside linebackers* because they, yes, line up on the outside. Inside the tackle box, teams usually use either one linebacker or two. If a team uses one linebacker in the middle, he is called a *middle linebacker*. Two linebackers who line up inside the tackle box are called *inside linebackers*.

So, to review:

There are either three or four linebackers, who are trying to make tackles. Their job is to be playmakers, not occupy offensive blockers. Remember, blocking is when offensive players try to push or knock defensive players in a certain direction.

Two of them are outside linebackers. If there are two in the middle, they are called inside linebackers. If there is only one in the middle, he is called a middle linebacker.

If there are only three linebackers, it looks like the following illustration.

The front seven of a 4-3 defense features four down linemen and three linebackers.

If there are four linebackers, it looks like the following illustration.

The front seven of a 3-4 defense features three down linemen and four linebackers.

When football people refer to a 3-4 defense or a 4-3, the first number always refers to the amount of defensive linemen and the second number refers to the amount of linebackers.

In the Middle

The role of linebackers in the middle of the alignment is the same whether there are two inside linebackers or one middle linebacker. When there are two inside linebackers, the role is shared. There is also more flexibility to rush the passer from inside.

In any linebacker configuration, the inside linebackers or the middle linebacker are not asked to go into pass coverage as much as the outside linebackers. The inside guys are usually bigger and more suited to stop the run. They may not be as fast as the outside guys, but they are ready to hit running backs and fight off guards and centers and tackles and tight ends and fullbacks and an occasional wide receiver. Their main job is to get to running backs, who run between the tackles.

They can also drop back into pass coverage—man-to-man on a tight end or running back, or zone coverage in which they have an area of the field to cover. When there are two inside linebackers, they can sometimes fool the offensive line into thinking that they are dropping into pass coverage. They can hesitate. They can make believe that they are going into a pass drop and then rush—sort of give the offensive line a false look and hope to get them off balance. By taking a lineman away and putting in an extra inside linebacker, a defense has less power but more versatility.

The inside linebackers are usually lined up at Level 2 of the defense, meaning they are a few yards off of the line of scrimmage.

Joe's Gridiron Talk
The defense is divided into three levels. Those players on the line of scrimmage (LOS), including the outside linebackers, are on *Level 1*. Those lined up about five yards off of the LOS, including the inside linebackers, are at *Level 2*. The defensive backs who line up behind the linebackers are at *Level 3*.

No matter the alignment, the man in the middle is usually calling the play for the defense. He is quarterbacking the whole defensive approach. He is communicating right up until the ball is snapped. He has the best perspective to do this—he is in the middle.

The middle linebacker is like the quarterback on defense. He doesn't throw passes, but he does call plays. When the offense huddles up, so does the defense, and it is the middle linebacker who calls the defense in the huddle. When the offensive huddle breaks, the middle linebacker will start yelling to his teammates the things that he sees. For instance, if the offense comes out in a one-back formation, he will start yelling, "Ace! Ace!" Or, in another situation, he could shout, "Naked! Naked!" No, that doesn't mean he has seen someone with no clothes on running through the stands. It means the offense came out with no backs in the backfield.

He could yell where the tight end is lined up—"Strength right!" or "Strength left!" Or, he could be alerting his teammates about the number of wide receivers. Perhaps he'll yell, "Four wides! Four wides!"

As quickly and succinctly as possible, he is trying to communicate with his teammates what he sees from the offense. When the play begins, he uses his smarts, instincts, will, and physical ability to try to react to the play.

The middle linebacker used to be the most glamorous position on the defense. Most of the linebackers I mentioned early in the chapter were middle linebackers. The reason was that the middle linebacker has the advantage of his position on the field and can literally make plays from sideline to sideline. He sees it all.

But in recent years, the outside linebackers have taken on much of the glamour.

The middle linebacker is not as important as in the Nitschke/Butkus days of the 1960s. There are more complex offenses and, therefore more complex defenses. Part of it just has to do with playing time. In the old days, all of the greats played on every down. Very few middle linebackers play on every down anymore.

Everything in football has become specialized. If you've got a linebacker who's good against the run, he's probably not going to be in the game on third down and long. Because of that, the aura of middle linebackers has lost a little of its shine. And, not only that but a lot of teams play a 3-4 alignment, meaning that there are two inside linebackers instead of just one big mean one.

> **Joe's Tips**
> If the linebackers are close to the LOS, they are usually anticipating a run. If they are backed away from the LOS, they are usually anticipating a pass.

The Outside—A Place to Raise Havoc

Linebackers are the most athletic players and outside linebackers are the most athletic of the linebackers. The best of the best is the outside linebacker who plays on the side away from the tight end (the open side)—usually the right linebacker. Remember, the defense's left is the offense's right.

The *outside linebackers* are the ones who are operating out in *space,* which is the area outside of the tackle box. There is room to move around out there, room to maneuver and a launching pad from which to attack. Outside linebackers are now so athletic that they can move from sideline to sideline just like middle linebackers. Outside linebackers can cover a lot of area, but mostly they cover their own area.

They have a very flexible role. They have to cover people on pass patterns who are fast and quick. They have to defend against the run just like the inside linebackers. And normally, they wind up getting people with a bigger head of steam heading their way. An outside linebacker has to face a 300-pound guard coming at him with a head of steam.

When that guard goes at an inside linebacker, he only has a step or two before they collide. But by the time he reaches the outside linebacker, the big guy is really moving. The outside linebacker has to have the agility to make the guard miss and then he has to make a play on the running back.

Normally, a linebacker doesn't want to be hit by a blocker. Linebackers exist to make plays, not to take on blockers. Linebackers are supposed to be stars. The blockers are supposed to be taken up by others so that linebackers can be stars. But inevitably, linebackers have to shed blocks.

The one thing that linebackers fear most is staying blocked. That means exactly what it says, that the blocker controlled the defensive player. It is a sin for a linebacker to get knocked to the ground, but it is a bigger sin for a linebacker to stay on the ground. He has to bounce back up like a rubber ball.

> **Joe's Tips**
> Left is right and right is left when you compare offenses and defenses. The right wide receiver is guarded by the left cornerback. The left tackle faces the right outside linebacker. Just remember, both sides are looking at it from their perspective going forward. And they are facing each other. Left is right and right is left.

> **Joe's Gridiron Talk**
> Despite not wanting to get hit, linebackers get hit. The idea for linebackers is to *play off (or shed) a block* and then make a play. Get one hand free, that's all that is needed to start to get free of a block. Some players use a forearm, others shoulders, while they try to focus on the ball.

There are different techniques that are used to avoid staying blocked. One is to be able to bounce up like a rubber ball. But others include not getting knocked to the ground in the first place. Linebackers have to be able to run, they have to be strong, and be able to use their hands.

They need to keep their heads up to see what's going on. They certainly can't be an ostrich at the linebacker position. There is action all around them. If somebody comes at them and they get locked up, everything is gone. They are dead meat. If a linebacker loses vision he loses everything. The linebacker position, especially the outside linebacker position, requires vision, hands, agility, speed, and strength.

> **Joe's Tips**
> If a linebacker is able to keep one arm free while he is fighting off of a block, he has a much better chance of making the play.

If an outside linebacker is facing a back coming outside, he has to match his quickness with somebody who could be quicker than him, he also has to match his strength against a running back who may be stronger than him, and he has to match his wits against an offensive lineman who is surely bigger than him. Linebackers do everything but they are smaller than defensive linemen and slower than defensive backs.

Splitting the Outside Guys

There is a *strong side* of an offensive formation and a *weak side*. The strong side is the side that has the tight end. There is strong-side-outside linebacker, and a weak-side-outside linebacker. The strong-side-outside linebacker lines up over the tight end.

The linebacker who plays over the tight end is equally involved in stopping the pass as stopping the run. After all, the tight end can be a receiver or a run blocker. The linebacker on the tight end side must be a little more physical than the linebacker away from the tight end.

> **Joe's Gridiron Talk**
> The *open side* and *closed side* of a formation are directly related to the placement of the tight end. The open side is the side without the tight end. The closed side has the tight end.

The weak-side linebacker is more concerned with passes—whether he is in coverage on a running back, in a zone, or rushing the passer.

If the tight end switches sides, usually the outside linebackers will switch places too, but not always. Sometimes they will just let the tight end switch, which is why the outside linebackers must be close in skill levels. It doesn't always work out that way. And the offense would love to get a big, physical tight end blocking a smaller, quicker, more athletic linebacker.

But the weak side outside linebacker now is in the position to be the star of the defense. He has the positioning to disrupt things in the most chaotic manner. This phenomenal athlete is standing a few steps away from the quarterback and there is no tight end in his way. Thus, offenses are forced to pay special attention to a weak side linebacker.

In the Mind of a Linebacker

Linebackers think that they know what the offense is thinking. As the play begins to set itself up, the linebacker is running a checklist through his mind at Pentium speed.

He is pre-reading the formation. He is thinking down and distance. If it is first down and 10, the offense will maybe run or maybe throw. But if it is third down and 15, there is a pretty good chance that the offense is going to pass. The linebacker has thought of that. He is a smart guy.

Next, he looks at the formation. If, for instance, the offense has three receivers on his side and only one to the other side, he knows that there is a strong likelihood that a pass is coming to his side of the field.

Then he thinks through what he remembers from film study of what the other team liked to run out of that particular formation. He remembers a specific pass route.

Then he thinks about the defense that has been called and where he is expected to be in that defense.

And then the play starts and he reacts—really fast.

First, he is keeping one eye on the quarterback and another on the receiver in front of him. If he is entering a zone coverage, he just wants to get to his area of responsibility. He is not necessarily covering any particular receiver.

Joe's Rules

Defensive holding is a penalty that linebackers have to be careful to avoid. It is illegal to hold a receiver who is trying to run a pattern, and the penalty is five yards. However, linebackers can run into a gray area of interpretation because the linebacker may just be trying to protect himself from being blocked.

The quarterback's actions tell the linebacker what to do next. The amount of steps a quarterback takes is usually related to the depth of the pass route. The linebacker knows this. Again, he is smart. If a quarterback drops and stops at three steps, the linebacker has to stop his drop at the same time and look around his area.

175

Also, linebackers are more than willing to use the *five-yard chuck rule*, which allows them to hit a receiver within five yards of the LOS. If a running back is starting five yards behind the LOS, that means he must travel 10 yards before the linebacker isn't allowed to hit him. In those 10 yards, maulings have been known to occur. And it doesn't have to even be a mauling to be effective. If the linebacker can disrupt the pass pattern of a running back or tight end by even one step, it could disrupt the timing of the entire play. And timing, as you know, is everything.

The linebacker also has an advantage in giving a chuck in the legal five-yard zone. He knows that there is someone behind him to help on the receiver. The linebacker just makes it harder for the receiver to get there, and then the linebacker moves on to his next assignment.

The Spy

Football is full of espionage. On the field, sometimes teams will ask a linebacker to keep an eye on a particularly mobile quarterback in obvious passing situations. There are certain quarterbacks—Steve Young, John Elway, and Mark Brunell come to mind—who have such great athletic ability that they are almost as much of a threat to run as they are to throw. Therefore, the number one consideration of the spy is the ability to run as fast or faster than the guy he is spying on—the quarterback.

The spy could be a linebacker or a defensive back. In either case, the spy pretends to go about his business, but really his actions are mirroring those of the quarterback.

If the quarterback slides to the right, the spy slides with him. If the quarterback slides to the left, same thing. Like a mirror. When a team uses a spy, it is showing great respect for the running ability of the quarterback.

Joe's Top Five Linebackers

In the history of the NFL, some of the greatest names in football played at linebacker. This is my personal list of the top five of all time in no particular order.

> ➤ **Ray Nitschke**, middle linebacker of the great Green Bay Packers teams of the 1960s. He brought new meaning to the phrase, *No pain, no gain.*

> ➤ **Dick Butkus**, middle linebacker of the Chicago Bears. Dick wasn't interested in making friends, just leaving a lasting impression on people's bodies.

> ➤ **Sam Huff**, middle linebacker of the New York Giants in the 1950s and 1960s. A film featuring Sam took people into the violent world of the Middle Linebacker.

➤ **Mike Singletary**, middle linebacker of the Chicago Bears in the 1980s and 1990s. Mike wasn't very big by football standards, but he was a great student of the game and often knew where you were going before you got there.

➤ **Lawrence Taylor**, right side linebacker for the New York Giants in the 1980s, is credited with revolutionizing the game and the position of outside linebacker. On one fateful day in November 1985, he ended my career. I figure, if you've got to go, it may as well be by a hit from the best.

The Least You Need to Know

➤ There are two outside linebackers and either one middle linebacker or two inside linebackers. The guys in the middle are more responsible for stopping the run than the pass. And one of the guys in the middle calls the plays for the defense.

➤ The outside linebacker away from the tight end is usually the most athletic and is often known to cause the most havoc.

➤ A spy is a defensive player, often a linebacker, who is responsible for mirroring a particularly athletic quarterback.

Chapter 16

The Secondary: The Last Best Hope

In This Chapter

➤ A look at the skills that secondary players need

➤ The difference between cornerbacks and safeties

➤ Understanding zone coverage

➤ When man-on-man coverage is used

Defensive backs, the guys who cover the receivers, have to have short memories and thick skins because, inevitably, they are going to give up a big play. It's the nature of the job. Someone will make a incredible catch or a perfect throw, or the defensive back will slip. It *will* happen, sometime. But then what? What happens next?

More than anything, the short memory is what I think of when I think of a defensive back. I admire the way they react, with the cockiness of a heavyweight boxer who has just taken a left hook to the head. It doesn't matter what just happened. The only thing that matters is what is going to happen next. They stare down the receiver. They stare down the quarterback. "So bring it on." There is no give at all.

This is a chapter about the last line of defense, the *secondary*—players who are also called *defensive backs*. The secondary usually consists of four guys—two cornerbacks and two safeties—who live away from the trenches. This chapter will deal with the skills that are needed, the duties of the cornerbacks and safeties, the difference between zone and man-to-man coverage, and my top five defensive backs in no particular order. All of them had short memories.

Small, Quick, and Fearless

It can seem to be an impossible job: stop wide receivers, who are usually the fastest players on the football field, from catching the ball. The receivers know where they are going. The defensive backs do not, but they have to stay with the receivers anyway.

It is not an impossible job. There are men who are capable of being an actual shadow on a wide receiver. Speed is important, but quickness is much more important. The ability to change direction and burst is what sets the good defensive backs apart. Defensive backs must have the ability to turn their hips because they have to make instantaneous adjustments that require contortionist-type turns in a fraction of a second. They must also have quick feet to be able to get into a proper defensive position—usually between the quarterback and the receiver or right next to the defender, but sometimes behind the receiver, or to one side or the other. The definition of "proper defensive position" could change from play to play. But defensive backs always need to be able to turn from backward to forward quickly because when the receiver gets next to them, they must turn. They must always be in proper defensive position. And they have to be fast enough to stay with speedy wide receivers. The best asset that a defensive back can have is quickness. Although a defensive back is most often playing against a wide receiver, each has different skills.

The most important skill of a wide receiver is his ability to catch the ball. If a defensive back has good hands and can catch the ball, it's a real plus. Nothing is sweeter than an interception. Turnovers help win games. But still, the ability to catch is not the most important thing. The defensive back needs to cover and tackle. Specifically, he needs to be able to cover, and that requires quickness.

> **Joe's Tips**
> Different skills are needed for a defensive back than for a wide receiver. If a defensive back has 10 balls thrown in his direction and he knocks all 10 down and but doesn't catch one, he's had a great day. But if a receiver has 10 balls thrown to him and he drops one, he's had a bad day.

One skill is needed in both positions—the ability to run without bobbing the head. If you remember from the section on speed guys as wide receivers in Chapter 9, if they are running and their head is bobbing, it's hard to focus on the ball. The same exact principle applies to defensive backs.

But the most important thing is quickness. A wide receiver can start, stop, come in, and go out. Or he could go left, right, or he could just head straight downfield. A good defensive back, in man-on-man coverage, has to stay with him no matter what he does.

Defensive backs are usually smaller by football standards. There are two sizes of defensive backs—cornerbacks and safeties. By weight, I would say they (and their fellow defensive players) average:

➤ Cornerback   185 pounds

➤ Safety   210 pounds

➤ Linebacker   250 pounds

➤ Lineman   300 pounds

Cornerbacks—Life on an Island

As you can see, *cornerbacks* are usually the smallest defensive players. These are the guys who make their living away from the trenches, out on islands. They hang out in the tropics, away from the cold fury of the tackle box. But their island sometimes gets invaded by wide receivers, and they find they must run the length of the island just to stop those receivers from catching the ball. Island life can be difficult.

Cornerbacks tend to be short as well as light. Some are as short as 5'9", and even though they could be covering a wide receiver who may be as tall as 6'5", their height doesn't really hurt them. Their vertical leap isn't that important. Instead, playing defense against receivers is all about body position and getting the *long arm* on the ball.

The only time that the defensive back's size is a factor is when the offense runs short, five-yard slant patterns. But the defense's thinking is that a cornerback's main job is to prevent bombs, not five-yard slants. After all, it takes a lot of five-yard slants to go 80 yards. In that time, the defense is thinking that the offense is bound to make a mistake. It is much more important to defend against the long bomb, and the best guys to do that tend to be short, quick, and fast.

> **Joe's Gridiron Talk**
> The *long arm* is the arm of the defensive player that is closest to the quarterback and furthest away from the receiver. In a jump, because of angles, that hand should be able to raise a little higher than the hand nearer the receiver, or *short arm*. The long arm is normally the one used to knock the ball away.

Cornerbacks have an ally on the island. That ally is the sideline—built-in help on one side of the field. A cornerback will try to favor the open side of the field, making the receiver run near the sideline.

> **Joe's Rules**
> If a receiver runs out of bounds, he is no longer eligible to catch a pass. However, if he was forced out of bounds because of a foul by a defender, he is legally eligible to catch a pass as soon he gets back in bounds.

The biggest concern of a cornerback is the big play. These players have quickness, as I said, and great reaction time to the ball. They also have an excellent ability to read wide receivers—to read routes. They can sense where receivers are going.

Joe's Tips

If a defensive back gives up a bomb and walks back to his team pointing at his chest mouthing some words, he is probably saying, "My bad. My bad." That is jock talk for "my mistake." And whenever I see that, I laugh. It's like, gee, no kidding. There's no one else within 30 yards. Yeah, your bad. We saw. We saw.

Although they are located way out on their island looking back at everything going on as if they were a spectator with a hot dog, they do participate in the game—but not always. Quite often, they are spectators. But when they participate, they are always big participants. Even for little guys.

Stopping a bomb, which is a primary concern of corner-backs, is an interesting job. In some ways, the job is much the same as a centerfielder in baseball. The ball may not be hit to the centerfielder for seven innings. But then in the eighth inning, the bases are loaded and there is a line shot into the gap and the centerfielder is expected to go get it. It's the same in football. Sometime, usually at a key time, the offense is going to test the cornerback, and the whole team is expecting him to make the play.

Safeties Are Enforcers

Safeties are smallish-type linebackers who can run. A lot of college linebackers become pro safeties. Safeties need to have good cover skills but they are also depended on to stop the run—especially big runs. They are the last line of defense. They are the safety—the name fits.

There are two safeties—the *strong safety* and the *free safety*. The skill levels required for the two positions are close to the same because formations switch so much that their roles could switch from play to play.

Basically, the strong safety plays behind the linebackers but in a little closer to the LOS than the free safety. The strong safety plays on the same side of the field as the tight end. He could cover the tight end or he could be asked to play in a zone, but he usually begins a play on the tight end side. His basic role is to be there to provide pass coverage against the tight end or running back and also to support in stopping the run game. He assists the linebackers.

The free safety is lined up right down the middle of the field. A line could be drawn from the halfback through the quarterback through the center through the middle linebacker to the free safety—right down the middle. See the following illustration for a look at the heart of the offense and defense.

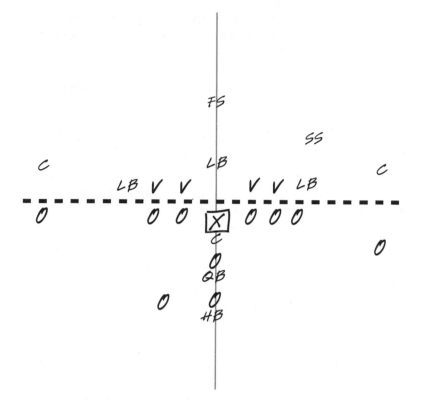

The heart of the offense and defense includes all the players in the middle of the offensive formation and defensive alignment.

The free safety is the furthest player back on defense and his primary responsibility is to stop the big play, pass, or run. His job is to roam, to be free to go from sideline to sideline to do what he thinks is right. He should always be as deep or deeper than the deepest receiver. He has to keep everything in front of him.

And, like everyone else, he plays head games. In fact, a free safety knows that most quarterbacks are looking at him (see Chapters 7, 11, and 12) as they try to read the defense. So free safeties play games. It is not unusual for a free safety who is supposed to be in the middle of the field for a particular defense to line up ten yards away from the middle. And then, just before the snap, he runs to the middle to play his role in the called defense. And the quarterback is supposed to figure that out. Everybody is playing head games. The whole game is a head game, and those free safeties can be quite a nuisance.

Joe's Tips
If both safeties are within eight yards of the LOS, it probably means there is some kind of blitz coming and the safeties will end up having to cover a tight end or a running back.

Free safeties know they can be a nuisance. I think they love it. And they are smart, too. They communicate, just like everyone on a football field communicates. Because of crowd noise, a safety will use a hand signal to call a defense, and get people into position. He could use a clenched fist to mean a zone, or an open palm could mean man-to-man coverage. Signals need to be easily seen, easily understood, but not easily stolen.

Zone or Man-to-Man Coverage

A *zone* is a defensive coverage scheme in which certain players cover certain parts of the field. Each covers an area, or a zone. It is not illegal to leave your zone, it just won't help your team. Essentially, linebackers, cornerbacks, and safeties are all assigned to a specific area of the field. Draw a circle, about eight yards in diameter, around each of these players, and you will see the zone that he is assigned.

If you are a defensive back and someone comes into your zone, you are supposed to prevent them from catching the ball. If no one is in your area, you can shade toward one side of your zone where you see receivers. You can slide to help out your buddies, but your team will be in big trouble if you leave your area. If you do, there is a wide open hole for the offense to attack. That spot? Your area. So, if the receiver leaves your area, just let him pass on to your buddy.

On the other hand, *man-to-man* coverage requires a defensive back stay with a wide receiver no matter where that receiver goes. If he starts on one side of the field and then goes in motion all the way to the other side, the defensive back must stay with him.

The position of a cornerback will often tell an offense whether the team is playing zone or man-to-man coverage. See the following illustration.

Although the theory of defenses is for players to provide help to each other, the idea of man-to-man coverage is to rely on the cover people to do the job. They are not given a lot of help.

One other thing to know about zone and man-to-man coverage is that the two can be combined on one play. Say, for instance, a team plays a zone on one side of the field and a man-to-man coverage on the other side. That is a combination coverage. See Chapter 18 for more information.

> **Joe's Gridiron Talk**
> When a team *rotates the zone,* it moves players toward one side of the field to be near a group of receivers who have gone into that area.

> **Joe's Tips**
> If a cornerback is shaded to the inside of the wide receiver, the coverage is probably man-to-man. If the cornerback is lined up outside the wide receiver, the coverage is probably some kind of zone.

Man-to-Man

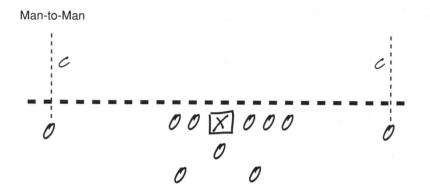

Cornerback positions in zone and man-to-man coverage.

Zone

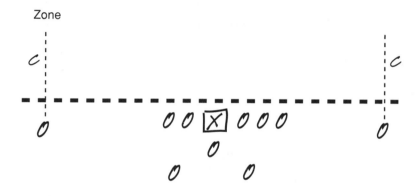

Bump and Run

In the first five yards off the LOS, defensive players can legally hit receivers. This is the *five-yard chuck rule*. In those first five yards, defensive players can chuck (hit) receivers. The bump and run strategy takes advantage of the five-yard chuck rule. Essentially, cornerbacks get up in the face of wide receivers and bump them as they come off the line. The idea is to disrupt the timing of the pass play.

Cornerbacks like to get a hand on the receiver's chest and get it away quick. He only needs to mess up one step. One step in a five-step route is quite a bit.

Joe's Top Five Defensive Backs

In the history of the NFL, there have been some amazing performers in the defensive backfield—players who can dominate half the field, or the middle of the field, or all of the field all by themselves. These are the top five defensive backs in NFL history (in no particular order), in my opinion.

➤ **Larry Wilson**, a safety for the St. Louis Cardinals. He was involved in so many hits that he was missing many teeth. It was quite a sight to see the toothless wonder staring at you.

➤ **Ken Houston**, a safety for the Houston Oilers. He was big for his time and had the strongest grip I have ever seen. When Ken grabbed you, you were stopped.

➤ **Mike Haynes**, cornerback for the New England Patriots and Oakland Raiders. His long arms made it hard to get away, and he was a master of the bump and run.

➤ **Ronnie Lott**, safety for the San Francisco 49ers, was known as a ferocious hitter.

➤ **Darrel Green**, cornerback for the Washington Redskins. He was a little guy with all the tools. He was quick, fast, and had a very short memory.

The Least You Need to Know

➤ The most important trait of a defensive back is a short memory. They will give up big plays from time to time but they cannot let it bother them.

➤ Defensive backs cover receivers by trying to be like a shadow, staying with them step for step and getting in the way of passes before receivers have a chance to catch them.

➤ Cornerbacks cover wide receivers and are the smallest players on the defense.

➤ The strong safety lines up on the side of the tight end and is very involved in stopping the run. The free safety is always supposed to be deeper or as deep as the deepest receiver, and stops the big play, pass or run.

➤ Players cover an area of the field in zone coverage. In man-to-man coverage, players stay with a specific receiver.

Chapter 17

Strategies: Attack or React

In This Chapter

➤ The difference between an attacking or reacting defense

➤ The advantages of zone and man-to-man coverage

➤ Why football is in the age of specialization, and when teams use situation substitutions

➤ Blitzing: a really aggressive defense

➤ Defending when an offense only needs short yardage

Defenses win championships. In the game of football, offenses get the glory, but that only means that the offense causes the most excitement. The defense will more than likely get you the wins. It's simple. If you can stop the other team from scoring, it is easy to win. Nothing else is more important. Stop the other team. After all, it is easier to outscore zero than any other number. Any idiot knows that.

Defense is a simple proposition. It really is, as I said in the beginning of this book, merely a matter of *"I don't want to let you to go across the street."* It is macho-physical, yet it is very logical and intellectual. At its core, the defense is always at a disadvantage because it is essentially trying to stop someone from doing something.

Defenses know what offenses are trying to do—put the ball in the end zone. They don't know how the offense is going to do it, but they do know that the offense wants to get to paydirt. And it really ticks the defense off. Heck, everything the offense does ticks them off. How could the offense even show up? How dare they?

There are two basic philosophies of playing defense. You can go after the ball, or you can wait and make sure the ball doesn't get past you. There are risks and rewards to both approaches.

There are also a couple of basic alignments, and a couple of different pass coverage styles. In this chapter, I will discuss all of that, plus the purpose of situational substitutions. So don't go across the street. Stay here and read this chapter.

Attacking Versus Reacting

If a defense attacks the offense, it does that to dictate the tempo of the game. It wants to make the offense react to what the defense is doing. The defense essentially makes the statement, *I'm not worried about what you're going to do, I am going to make you worry about what I am going to do.* The idea is to stop the other team from even being able to attempt what they want.

Joe's Gridiron Talk
A *rubber-band defense* is a bend-don't-break defense that allows short plays down the field. If the offense has to run a lot of short plays they are sooner or later going to make a mistake, or the rubber-band defense hopes so.

If a defense instead reacts to an offense, it waits and lets the offense dictate the tempo. The idea is to make no mistakes. Force the offense to be perfect. The reacting style defense lets the offense run a play and then gets people to where the ball goes. It is a bend-don't-break defense, just like a rubber band—the *rubber-band* defense.

I have never been a big fan of a reacting-type defense. I think you have to set the tempo on the offensive and defensive side of the ball. If you have a bend-don't-break defense, you are counting on the offense to screw up. Although a reactive defense will work against many offensive teams, an efficient offense can pick it apart.

I believe in an attacking defense because it sets the tempo. But there are risks. If the offense guesses right and finds all the people to block, the offense will have time to get the ball off. If they do, they can usually exploit the back of the defense. By attacking, the defense is asking a defensive back to basically cover half the football field. The reason why a defensive back will have to cover half the field is because against an attacking defense, the offense can usually only get two receivers out into their patterns. Therefore, the other two defensive backs are usually attacking. So, two defensive backs *are* asked to cover half the field and that is more than most defensive backs can handle. An attacking defense is clearly a bit of a gamble if you do it too much. But then, you can't do anything too much.

Basic Alignments—the 4-3 and the 3-4 Defenses

There are two basic defensive alignments—4 lineman and 3 linebackers (a 4-3 defense) *or* 3 linemen and 4 linebackers (a 3-4 defense). The usual secondary would include two cornerbacks and two safeties.

In both defenses, a lineman's job is to penetrate past the LOS and occupy some offensive linemen. The most important thing for defensive linemen is to not allow themselves to be moved.

In a basic defense, linebackers have a certain area in which to cover the run or the pass. The secondary can play either zone coverage or man-to-man coverage.

The key is that it is all coordinated together. The guys up front are involved in putting pressure on the quarterback, stopping the running game, and occupying blockers.

The guys behind the defensive line, the linebackers and defensive backs, usually work in coordination and rotation opposite one another. In a 4-3 alignment, because there are only seven men in the defensive backfield, there will always be an odd number. There will always be a hole in the defense somewhere. For instance, if the linebackers drop toward the right, the defensive backs will be asked to rotate toward the left. The void is there because you cannot have two defensive levels with four players each. One level only has three men. Therefore, a team cannot have even distribution of coverage on a football field. You just can't give the offense time to find that void.

The idea of bringing four people on the rush (using a 4-3 alignment) is to put as much pressure on the offense as possible while still giving yourself opportunities to protect the areas of the defensive backfield. Like everything in life, there is always a tradeoff. If you bring more people at the quarterback, there is less protection in the defensive backfield. If you add protection, the quarterback could have all day to throw.

When a team plays a 3-4 defense, the philosophy is nearly the same. It actually still brings four men on the rush. It just so happens that one of the men lines up a few yards back and usually wears a 50 number on his jersey. You are still committing seven men close to the line of scrimmage with a 3-4 defense, it's just that you have replaced a bigger defensive lineman with a linebacker who can give you more versatility and speed. In either formation, the idea is to contain the offense. The defense lines up in a certain way and tries to force the offense to do certain things. The defense wants to dictate to the offense what it can and cannot do.

Stopping the Run

Football is a macho game (I know, I said that already) and there is nothing more satisfying than stopping the run. Stopping the run means keeping running plays to three yards or less—on average. Three three-yard gains in a row would make it fourth down and one—resulting in a punt situation for most teams. So, the team that played defense on that drive stopped the run, because the other team could not run for a first down in three plays.

Stopping the run is the way a defense stands up to an offense and says, *"I don't think so."* The offense would like nothing more than to stuff the ball down the defense's throat. The defense, knowing this, would equally like nothing more than stopping the offense cold in its tracks.

One of the most important and telling statistics from a football game is the number of yards per run (or yards per carry). If a team can stop the opponent from running the ball and keep the offense's yards per run low (3.0 yards or less per carry) they can stop the offense from controlling the game. It still all comes down to who controls the tempo of the game.

By stopping the run, the defense forces the offense to throw the ball. That takes away half of the options of an offense, making it one dimensional. After all, the only two options for an offense are to throw or run. If they can't run, there is only one option. Clearly, a lot worse things can happen when the ball goes in the air. Two of three things are bad—an incomplete pass or an interception. By stopping the run, the chance that the defense will succeed has gone up tremendously. And not only that, but the other team's offense will leave the field sooner because pass plays often stop the clock.

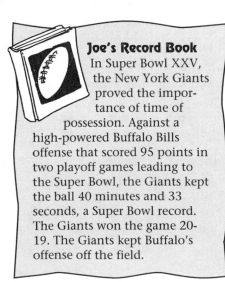

Joe's Record Book
In Super Bowl XXV, the New York Giants proved the importance of time of possession. Against a high-powered Buffalo Bills offense that scored 95 points in two playoff games leading to the Super Bowl, the Giants kept the ball 40 minutes and 33 seconds, a Super Bowl record. The Giants won the game 20-19. The Giants kept Buffalo's offense off the field.

Stopping the run always starts with the defensive linemen, who must get the offensive linemen tied up. And then the linebackers are supposed to make plays.

Remember, there is an average of about 65 offensive plays a game. If the defense forces the offense to throw 45 of those times, it means a few things. It means that the offense only ran the ball 20 times and probably 12 of those were unsuccessful. It also means that the team that is throwing the ball all those times probably will not have the ball as much time as a team with a balanced attack. Time of possession is another very telling statistic of which team is most likely winning (if your team has the ball longer, it has more opportunities to score).

Stopping the run is strategic for many reasons. Clearly, time of possession is a big factor, as is the safety of running the ball and not risking interceptions. It also is extremely important as a game nears the end. If the team with the ball is trying to protect a lead, it wants to run the ball because running the ball can eat up the clock. The game really does end when 60 minutes are gone. But if the defense can stop the running game, it forces the offense to either turn over the ball with a punt after three runs, or to take the riskier course of putting the ball in the air.

Stopping the Pass—Zone or Man-to-Man Coverage

The way the defense tries to stop the pass reveals something about the personality of the team. If it uses man-to-man coverage, it has an aggressive personality. A zone coverage is more reactive.

A *zone* defense, in which the linebackers and defensive backs each cover a specific area on the field, is a statement that the defense doesn't want to get beat deep by a long pass. (See the following illustration of a basic zone defense.) The zone coverage approach allows the offense a chance to get short gains, and counts on the fact that somewhere in a drive the offense is going to make a mistake. A defensive team using zone coverage believes the offense cannot go 80 yards without making one.

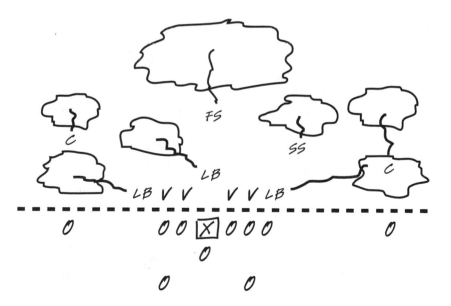

A basic zone coverage has each player behind the defensive line responsible for covering an area (zone) on the field.

A zone defense is patient. It is also careful. Zone defense is often played when a team does not have enough talented defensive backs to run an efficient man-to-man defense. It takes less chances and forces the offense to be perfect. A team playing zone defense believes the offense can't just march down the field mistake free. In all likelihood, they are right. The offense probably will make a mistake. A zone defense will wait for the offense to make that mistake and plans to capitalize on it.

But if an offense is efficient and doesn't make a mistake, it can take advantage of a zone defense by throwing to *soft spots* where the offense can make play after play.

When the defensive line rushes the quarterback and the linebackers drop back into coverage, there is a soft spot in between them of about 10 yards. If the linebackers keep dropping back and the quarterback keeps dumping the ball over the top of the line to a running back, the offense can get eight or 10 yards on every play. If the linebackers come up a little closer, a soft spot opens up between the linebackers and the free safety, who, as you remember, is the last line of defense.

On the other hand, *man-to-man* defense, in which the linebackers and defensive backs each cover a particular offensive player, is pure guts and confidence. The defense puts its faith in its defensive backs and uses the extra players who would normally be in coverage on a zone defense to attack the quarterback. The idea of playing man-to-man coverage is that the defense doesn't want to wait for the offense to make a mistake. It wants to force mistakes.

Man-to-man coverage is simply man-to-man coverage— one defensive guy follows another offensive one all over the football field. Think of your shadow on a sunny day and you will have a good understanding of the complexity of man-to-man coverage. It's not complex. Your shadow simply follows you everywhere. It is really an amazing skill—one of the most amazing in all of athletics. Think about it. You have a guy who is a great athlete following another great athlete. Only the receiver knows

> **Joe's Tips**
> A goal of any football team is that in every game it wants two drives of 60 yards or more for a touchdown. That says a lot about how hard it is to go down the field. If a head coach wants only two drives of 60 yards for a score, what are the chances of a team going 80 yards even once? A zone philsophy works by the math.

> **Joe's Gridiron Talk**
> A *soft spot* is an area in a zone defense between defensive players.

> **Joe's Gridiron Talk**
> A *pick* occurs when receivers criss-cross and two defensive players run into each other. If an offensive player runs into a defensive player who is covering someone else, it is an illegal pick (if he is caught). If two defensive players run into each other, they're just not very smart.

where he wants to go. The defensive back will try to stay with him. This really is amazing. And even more amazing is a defensive back's attitude when he does happen to give up a big play. A cornerback will never say he was beaten by a receiver. Instead, according to a cornerback, he made a mistake. Nobody ever beats them.

Following is an illustration of man-to-man coverage.

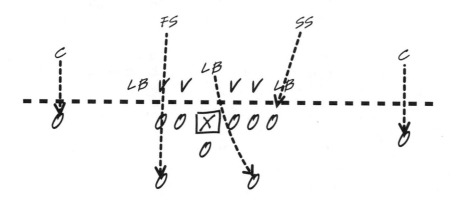

Basic man-to-man coverage involves one defensive player covering one offensive player all over the field.

One thing that defensive coaches worry about is having their players get *picked.*

Coaches worry about offensive players making defensive players change direction or hesitate as they try to cover a different offensive player. Offensive players try to not look like they are getting in someone's way when they really are because if they can make a defensive back to fall one or two steps behind his receiver, there is big play potential.

Situation Subsitutions—Welcome to the Age of Specialization

Every player who lines up on a football field has a very specific set of skills suited to his position. Some guys have even more specific skills—suited to their position for specific situations. Thus, football is a game of many situation substitutions—bringing in players with specific skills for specific situations.

For instance, if a team has two big defensive linemen who are very good against run, but it is an obvious passing situation, say third down and 12 yards to go, the defense may very well replace those run stoppers with a couple of men who are a little bit lighter and quicker because they probably have slightly better pass rush skills.

Late in a game, when the offense may line up in a four-receiver set, the defense may take out a safety and substitute a cornerback who has slightly better pass-coverage skills. The defense will not take out both safeties. It will usually leave its best pass coverage safety in because the defense will still want a good tackler deep in its secondary in case there is a big run.

Linebackers are also subject to situation substitutions—especially the middle linebacker. The defense still wants a guy who is a good run stopper, but in certain situations it may not necessarily need their best run stopper hammering up the middle. The guy who comes in to replace the middle linebacker will still be a good run stopper, but he is more needed for pass coverage so he is probably a little bit faster and more agile. On third down and long, if he stops the run six or seven yards down the field instead of at the LOS, it is okay. It is more important to have someone in who can cover a running back or a tight end. To learn more about this, see Chapter 18.

The key for substitutions is to get a better matchup on the field for what the offense is expected to do. This is the age of specialization. Some guys are making football teams these days because they have an ability to do just one thing. It is a given that on every football team there are two or three guys who are there for their ability to do one thing. On the other hand, there are guys who make the team because they have an ability to do many things. The guys who are multi-dimensional give a team the flexibility to carry the specialists.

For instance, maybe a team has an older defensive lineman who cannot play 65 plays a game anymore. Maybe he can only give a team 20 plays a game. But in those 20 plays, he may be able to get pressure on the quarterback a couple times, and maybe get one sack. Every team wants a guy like that. He could determine the outcome of the game. It only takes one play to determine the outcome, and this guy could be the guy.

But in order to carry him, a defense will need other guys with versatility. For instance, a team would love to have a defensive end at 300 pounds who can also play defensive tackle. This allows the team to carry the older guy who is the pass rush specialist. That way, the versatile guy can play end when the older guy isn't in, and is also available to substitute in at tackle and give the starting tackles a breather. Versatility is on the roster to save a spot for specialization.

Another example of a situation substition is the man who is known as the long snapper, who has the skill to snap the ball between his legs 15 yards back on punts.

Despite the continual evolution of the game, I believe it has reached the level of saturation for specialization. After all, the size of the rosters is still the same.

As much as the game has evolved, it still involves blocking, tackling, throwing, catching, and running. Those five elements have not changed one bit. It may be a different game because of the size and speed of the players, but if you've got two big guys going up against two other big guys, it's still the same game. It's just bigger.

Blitzing

The idea of *blitzing* (bringing more than five defensive players on a rush at the quarterback and forcing a bad throw or getting a sack) is to dictate the tempo of the play. Blitzing is aggressive. It is, quite simply, an attack mode.

It is one of the few times the defense actually can dictate to the offense where they want the offense to throw the ball. It works because defenses know how offenses think.

Defenses know that how they rush on a blitz will determine who the *hot* receiver is and where that receiver will be as the play develops.

Defenses are always trying to get the numbers game on their side when they blitz. They understand the blocking scheme of the offensive line and then overload one side in order to have more people coming than the offense has people to block. It serves two purposes. First of all, obviously, it puts an extreme amount of pressure on the quarterback. Secondly, and just as importantly, it forces the quarterback to make a decision that the defense presumes is beneficial to its cause—go to the hot receiver.

Defenses know that when they blitz, the quarterback doesn't have a lot of time to throw the football. They know he has to hurry, and he probably won't be very accurate. Now, of course, most offenses have blitz adjustments, but defenses know those as well. (How? You might ask. From film study.) And, frankly, the purpose of a blitz is to force those adjustments.

For instance, if the defense blitzes from the side of the tight end on a specific team, it may know that the blitz adjustment is to throw a five-yard quick post to that tight end. If it is third down and 12 yards to go, a five-yard post is not much of a worry. The defense still has a seven-yard cushion to bring that tight end down. By blitzing from that side, the defense knows the quarterback has to throw that specific pass. He'll throw it, unless he is an idiot. And if he is an NFL quarterback, he's not an idiot.

> **Joe's Gridiron Talk**
>
> A *blitz adjustment* is an automatic decision a quarterback must make when he sees a blitz coming from a certain area. The blitz adjustment requires the quarterback to go to the hot receiver.

> **Joe's Gridiron Talk**
>
> A *hot* receiver is one who is supposed to get the ball when the defense is blitzing. As soon as the receiver realizes he is hot, he must turn and look for the ball, because the quarterback will have limited time to get it to him. There are different hot receivers for different blitzes.

Blitzing is a great defensive tool, but offenses can beat the blitz. If an offense gets a hot pass off and the defense doesn't make a tackle, the hot receiver can go for a lot of yards. Nevertheless, I think the blitz is just not used enough. Being the aggressive individual that I am, and being a believer that football is a game that rewards aggressive individuals and teams, I think the blitz can cause all sorts of havoc for the offense.

That said, I also know that there are ways to beat the blitz. Remember, offensive lines can slide. They can pick up the blitz. Quarterbacks can call audibles. When I played, I was burned by the blitz on more than one occasion. I also burned the blitz more than once. I know I've said this a million times in this book already, but a million and one times is not enough, so I'll say it again—football is a head game. The concept of blitzing fits perfectly into that head game.

Short Yardage/Goal Line

Sometimes, the offense only needs to get a tiny chunk of real estate to get a first down or a touchdown. If the offense needs a small amount in order to get a first down, it brings in a *short-yardage* offense on third down. If it is before third down, it doesn't need a full-power offense (which is what a short-yardage offense is) because it has more than one play before fourth down.

However, when an offense needs two yards or less and only has one play to get it, it very often will line up in a close formation and try to simply bully its way past the defense. Power versus power.

The same situation exists when the offense is close to the goal line. The difference between a goal-line situation and a short-yardage one is that the offense may run a power offense on four consecutive plays near the goal line. If they get those two yards or less, they get six points. A lot is on the line.

Defenses know what offenses want to do. They want to advance the ball a short distance. In these situations, defenses can be quite stubborn—or at least they'd like to be. There is some attitude going on when the ball only needs to go a couple of yards or less. Often, it is less. It could be a matter of inches. Heck, it could be a fraction of an inch. And sometimes, if the defense is good, that fraction of an inch can be equal to a mile or more.

So what happens? There are eight basic gaps along the LOS. The area between two offensive players is considered a gap. There is one on either side of the center, one to the outside of each guard, one to the outside of each tackle, and one on the outside of the tight end (depending on which side the tight end is lined up on). The defense wants to plug those gaps. The offense wants to push the ball through one of them. It is power versus power. Big guys against big guys.

In these situations, everybody on defense is within three or four yards of the LOS. The defense does *not* want to get pushed back. These are usually critical situations and the defense has every intention of being as stubborn as a mule. Of course, the offense feels the exact same way and is not in a cooperative mood. Thus, there are some fabulous collisions.

These are almost always running plays, and often the running back will leap in the air to try to get the little bit of yardage needed to get the first down or the touchdown. The defense knows this, so they have their middle linebacker ready as a *jumper*.

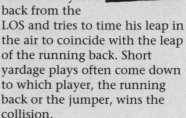

Joe's Gridiron Talk

A *jumper* is a linebacker who starts a few yards back from the LOS and tries to time his leap in the air to coincide with the leap of the running back. Short yardage plays often come down to which player, the running back or the jumper, wins the collision.

The Prevent Defense

At the end of a game or the end of a half, when the defense is worried about a big play, it will often employ what is called a *prevent defense*. The idea is to prevent a big pass play, but in reality it often gives up many small pass plays that are just as damaging.

This is not one of my favorite strategies. First of all, if your team is winning, and it got to that point in the game by using one defensive strategy, it makes very little sense to change it at the very end of the game. Why change what has worked all game?

But coaches do. Because they fear the big play so much, coaches employ the prevent defense. Essentially, the prevent defense uses only three men to rush the quarterback and puts eight men in coverage. The eight men are set up like a big umbrella, designed to make sure the offense cannot complete a long pass and also designed to make sure the offense cannot get a pass near the sideline so it can stop the clock. Remember, a ticking clock is the ally of a winning team. So, it sort of makes sense.

But it only makes sense if the team on defense is winning by more than one score and the other team is out of time-outs.

A prevent defense is a zone defense that tries to force every pass into the middle of the field. Sure, the soft spots in the zone are small because there are so many men in the defensive backfield. But on the other hand, the defense is giving the quarterback lots of time to throw the ball. And any NFL quarterback, if given time, can complete most of his passes. If he couldn't, he wouldn't be in the NFL.

The Least You Need to Know

➤ An attacking defense wants to set the tempo of a game and force the offense to make a mistake, while a reacting defense waits for the offense to make a mistake.

➤ Some players are on teams because they have specific skills that are useful in certain situations. When they are brought in, it is a situation substitution.

➤ Teams blitz in order to put pressure on the quarterback and to force the offense to throw to a specific receiver.

➤ The prevent defense is willing to give the offense short passes in order to prevent one long pass, but those short passes can be just as damaging.

Chapter 18

Advanced Defensive Strategies

In This Chapter

➤ The evolution of defensive philosophies

➤ A few coverage packages to defend against the pass

➤ The latest wrinkle, the zone blitz

The game of football has evolved. Great strategists have encountered other great strategists, and although at its core football will always be a confrontation between athletes, it has become much more than that.

The chess match aspect of the game that I have referred to so often in this book really has developed into a battle of masters. Offensive innovations are followed by defensive innovations. Sometimes, defensive innovations come first. There is no rule. The chicken? The egg? Hey, who knows. All I know is that this game has spawned strategies that have spawned strategies, and every time something new comes along, I can only shake my head in amazement.

This chapter will cover some of the advanced defensive strategies that teams have used and still use to contain the offense. Defenses want nothing more than to confuse the offense. That is the purpose of advanced strategies. Although football really is about athletes, strategy has become increasingly more important over the years.

This chapter will cover the evolution of some more advanced defensive philosophies, the different coverage packages that are commonly used, and the newest wrinkle in the evolution of the game, the zone blitz.

Who knows what is coming next?

How Defensive Philosophies Became Important

Once upon a time, say a few decades ago, defenses wanted to tackle the guy with the ball. They didn't want passes to be caught by receivers. Defenses used to be just a bunch of tough guys with no teeth, trying to stop the run and pressure the quarterback.

The tough guys with no teeth are still around, but the philosophy of how to tackle the guy with the ball and how to stop passes from being caught by receivers has evolved into a science. The game has become, in many ways, a battle of wits between coaches. But still, if a team doesn't have capable athletes, it cannot run the defensive schemes.

Schemes are very important now. Imagine taking four defensive linemen and three linebackers and lining them up in every conceivable way opposite an offensive line. As far as your imagination can go, it exists in football today.

Offenses have evolved as well as the defenses. Offenses have evolved for the same reason that defenses evolve: Film study. The number of things each side can do with 11 people is, by my best guess, almost infinite. One thing leads to another. It is fascinating.

Coaches study what other coaches have already figured out and then they build on it.

The Flex Defense

One of the first stages of defensive evolution came in the late 1960s and early 1970s with Coach Tom Landry's Dallas Cowboys. Landry and his staff developed what was called a *flex defense*, in which the defensive linemen did not all line up right on the line of scrimmage, but rather two of them were actually lined up a couple feet away. Because two men were off the ball, it became harder for the offensive line to block them. Remember, the offensive line must work in perfect coordination, almost like a chorus line. But when two of the defensive linemen are lined up off the ball, the offensive line had difficulties moving in synch and therefore spacing was created. When the gaps opened, people could fire through them and attack the ball or the quarterback. It was the beginning of the evolutionary process.

See the below illustration to learn how the flex defense lined up.

The flex defense is not used anymore, but for a while it totally confused offenses, especially offensive lines.

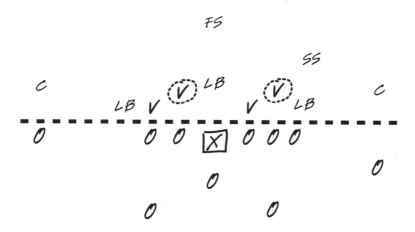

The flex defense was made popular by Tom Landry, coach of the Dallas Cowboys. The idea was to disrupt the blocking schemes of the offensive line.

The Over Defense and the Under Defense

The great Pittsburgh Steelers "Steel Curtain" defense of the 1970s used the *over defense* and the *under defense*. The over defense meant that the defensive line shifted over toward the tight end, and the middle linebacker also shifted from the middle of the defense to one player over. The under defense meant that the shift was made to the weak side. The strength of these two defenses was that they always had someone over the center, which made it difficult for the center to help block any other player.

The following is an illustration of the over defense and the under defense.

The over defense and the under defense was popularized by the great Pittsburgh Steelers teams of the 1970s as a way to put pressure on certain areas of the offense—such as the center.

THE OVER DEFENSE:

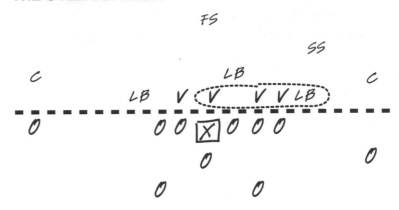

THE UNDER DEFENSE:

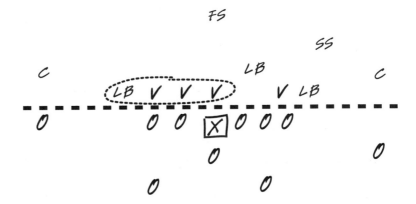

The 3-4 Defense

The next step in the evolution came when teams decided to use four linebackers instead of three—the *3-4 defense*. You have seen this illustrated in Chapter 15. This defensive scheme was created so teams could have linebackers run in pursuit of the ballcarrier. However, offenses thought it gave them a chance to run at the "bubble" because the linebackers were actually backed off the ball. There was, in fact, a natural bubble. The 3-4 defense did give offenses a slight advantage in trying to stuff the ball up the middle. But, it also gave defenses an advantage in pursuit across the entire field, and made it difficult for offensive lines to both run-block and pass-block.

Another advantage the defense has gained was that the 3-4 defense created a lot of possible ways to blitz. The defense could bring both inside linebackers on a blitz. It could bring two from one side. It could bring all four. It made an offensive lines coach's life miserable.

An offensive line will usually rely on one of the three inside guys—the center or two guards—to be a helper on a pass rush. But the 3-4 defense makes, for instance, a left guard have a *double response* when considering who he is supposed to block.

The 46 Defense

In the mid-1980s, Buddy Ryan was the defensive coordinator of the Chicago Bears, and he developed what was for one season one of the most dominating defenses in the history of the NFL—the *46 defense*. Having played against it and having been beaten up by it, I know the 46 defense was an attacking, man-to-man style. That defense wanted offenses to do everything in a hurry. First of all, the defense lined up with linemen over all three middle offensive linemen, who, as I said, are usually the helping linemen. Thus, these middle offensive linemen couldn't help anyone. They were busy fighting off 300 pounds coming at their face.

The 46 defense also relied upon having two great outside pass-rushing linebackers. And, those linebackers were both put on the same side, right over the tight end. This created a dilemma for the tight end. Who should he block? Both might come at the quarterback. Or maybe only one will. Or, maybe neither one will come at him. Should he just go out for a pass?

The key to that defense was to have these great outside pass rushers. If they weren't top-notch, the 46 defense was not as effective. The Chicago Bears of the mid-1980s happened to have some of the best linebackers in football—Mike Singletary in the middle and Wilbur Marshall and Otis Wilson on the outside.

> **Joe's Gridiron Talk**
> When an offensive lineman has a *double response*, he is responsible for a linebacker in front of him and off the ball, and also for an outside linebacker to that side. Normally, only one will rush. The question for the offensive lineman is, which one? He first checks the man in front of him, then checks the outside rusher, and he had better do it fast.

> **Joe's Gridiron Talk**
> A *hurry* is when a quarterback is forced to throw the ball quicker than he would like. It is not a sack, but it can be just as valuable. It hurries the quarterback up. It may just be pushing the pocket back in his face or it could be a rush that disrupts his timing.

Here is an illustration of the 46 defense.

The 46 defense was played by the 1985 Chicago Bears. The distinguishing feature of this defense was that it covered the three interior linemen (center and both guards) with defensive linemen.

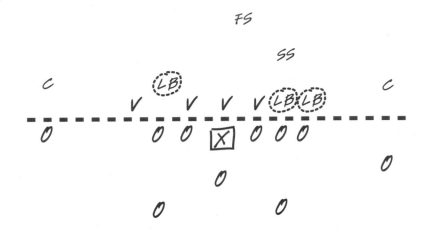

The 46 defense put tremendous pressure on the quarterback. If you were the quarterback, it seemed you had to hurry every play.

Joe's Record Book
The Chicago Bears defense was so dominating in the 1985 season that it actually held both of its opponents in the playoffs to 0 points. The team beat the New York Giants 21-0 in the divisional playoffs and it beat the Los Angeles Rams 24-0 in the NFC Championship Game. The Bears beat the New England Patriots 46-10 in Super Bowl XX.

And then, just when you thought you knew how to quickly get rid of the ball, the Bears would only rush three linemen. You would be standing in the pocket expecting extreme pressure and wanting to get rid of the ball quickly, but they would have eight players in coverage. So, you now had all this time with nowhere to throw the ball. This was the original head-game defense.

The Eagle Defense

An *eagle defense* is one where the outside linebacker who is normally on the left outside LOS is moved inside and a couple feet off the ball. The defensive end on that side is then moved slightly to the outside. The idea is to give that linebacker some room to pursue plays on the side of the field furthest from him. It moves him one player closer to the middle of the field.

Here is an illustration of the eagle defense.

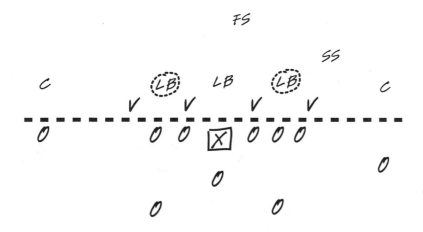

The eagle defense uses a linebacker on the inside of the tackle box and puts a lineman on the outside.

The idea of the eagle defense is to funnel the play to the linebacker by putting the big lineman on the outside.

The Double Eagle Defense

The *double eagle* is a 4-3 defense in which both outside linebackers are moved inside the perimeter of the defensive line. Again, the idea is to use the big people on the line to funnel the ball to the linebackers. This defense does give the offense a chance to attack the bubbles, and the defense has to be strong at the point of attack in order to stop runs. However, it gives the linebackers more latitude to pursue plays across the entire field.

Here is an illustration of the double eagle defense.

The double eagle defense uses two linebackers on the inside of the tackle box and moves two linemen outside.

Pass Coverage Packages

You have learned about zones and man-on-man coverages in the previous chapter. That was basic stuff. It is now time to graduate to some more advanced pass coverage packages. A pass coverage package is the way a defensive team positions its players on the field to defend against the pass. These are called by various names. So reach in your pocket and grab a nickel, a dime, and a quarter. These are your reference materials. Well, not really, but remember those names.

The Nickel Package

The idea of the *nickel package* is to bring in an extra defensive back. Normally, there are four defensive backs. In a nickel package, there are five defensive backs. Five cents in a nickel coin, five defensive backs in a nickel defense. Easy. (This simple memorization trick won't work for the dime or the quarter, but it works for the nickel, so remember it.)

A nickel back is brought in as a situation substitution on passing plays. He is usually brought in in place of the middle linebacker.

Defenses normally bring in the nickel back when the offense is using three wide receivers, four wide receivers, or in an obvious passing situation such as second down and 15 yards to go or third down and 12 yards plus to go. He is there to help in pass coverage.

By going to the nickel, the defense is sacrificing a bit of its run defense by playing percentages and playing more toward pass defense. It expects a pass, and it wants to give itself the best chance to stop it.

The extra defensive back, the nickel back, is usually there to cover the extra wide receiver although he could also be in to play a zone. All basic coverages are used with a nickel package.

Here is an example of a nickel package.

The nickel package is usually used in passing situations. One linebacker is removed and a defensive back (nickel back) is added.

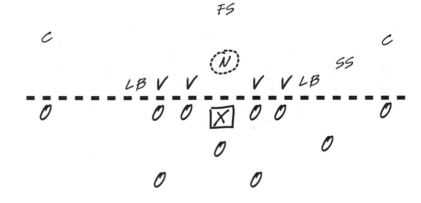

The Dime Package

A *dime package* involves bringing in yet another defensive back in place of a linebacker. By using a Dime, the defense is only leaving in one linebacker, usually the team's best coverage linebacker.

The dime package is mostly used when the offense brings in four wide receivers. It is used to match up coverage men against receivers. Again, just as with a nickel package, the dime can be played man-to-man or zone.

Why is it called a dime? It's bigger than a nickel, I suppose. Here is my honest answer: I really don't know.

Here is an illustration of a dime package.

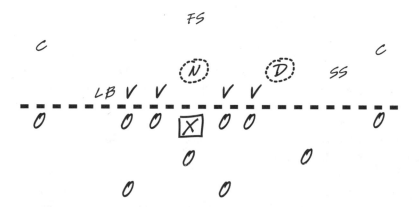

The dime package is usually used in obvious passing situations. Two defensive players (linebackers or defensive linemen) are removed and replaced with two defensive backs.

Combination Coverages

Sometimes, a team has a tremendous cornerback that they believe can cover any wide receiver in the world. But the offense may have two great receivers. The defense will want to use two people to cover the other receiver. To use a simple basketball term, they are double-covering (putting two people on one) that other receiver. In this situation, the defensive coach may choose to use a *combination coverage*, in which the one tremendous cornerback covers a receiver man-to-man, and the other receiver is double teamed.

Here is an illustration of a combination coverage.

Combination coverage uses some man-on-man coverage along with some zone coverage.

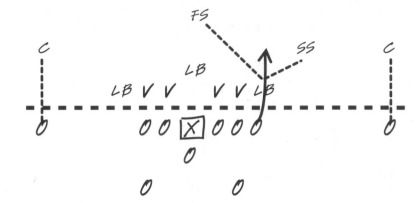

Quarter Coverage

Yet another coin word, it's a new kind of meaning. *Quarter coverage* means the secondary divides the field into four long strips from the LOS to the end zone, with each defensive back covering a quarter of the field. In quarter coverage, the cornerbacks and safeties line up in essentially a row—a flat line across the field. The cornerbacks are off the wide receivers and the safeties are in at the same depth as the cornerbacks. The advantage of this type of coverage is that, to a quarterback, it looks like man-to-man coverage. But it, in essence, is not. If the quarterback reads man-to-man coverage and thinks that the receiver will run away from one of the defensive backs into an open area, he's in for a big surprise and so is the receiver. This is one of the more deceptive coverage pacakages.

Here is an illustration of quarter coverage.

Quarter coverage divides the field into four quadrants and assigns one player to cover each quadrant.

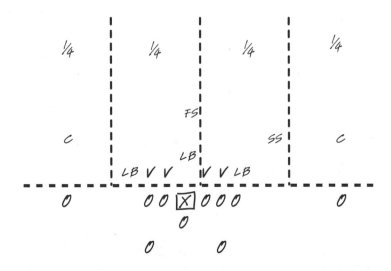

Each of the cornerbacks and safeties is responsible for his quadrant of the field. In his quadrant, he is in man-to-man coverage. But when a receiver leaves his quadrant, the defensive back passes him along to the next defensive back. For instance, a cornerback will chase a receiver through his quadrant and then the safety will pick him up in the next quadrant. The cornerback will then lay back in the zone to wait to see if someone else is coming into his quadrant. And, the nickel back is in the game to help in any of the quadrants. Receivers are passed along by *cut calls*.

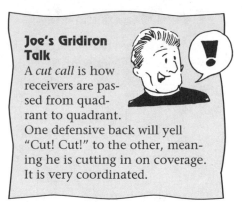

Joe's Gridiron Talk
A *cut call* is how receivers are passed from quadrant to quadrant. One defensive back will yell "Cut! Cut!" to the other, meaning he is cutting in on coverage. It is very coordinated.

Nickel Combination Coverage

When there are three wide receivers and the defense has its nickel package in, it can double cover two of the three wide receivers. In double coverage, one defensive back is usually to the inside of the receiver and the other defensive back is to the outside.

Two-Deep Zone

In a *two-deep zone*, the safeties each cover a zone deep and the cornerbacks and linebackers cover zones closer to the left outside. This defense tries to prevent passes that are thrown to the outside receivers in the 10-12–yard area. Because the defensive back (cornerback) knows he has backup help in the deep zone behind him, he can cover his receiver more closely. See the next illustration, which shows the two-deep zone.

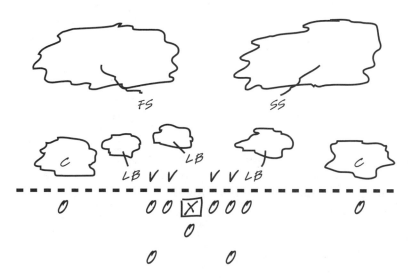

In a two-deep zone coverage, the two safeties back up the cornerbacks, who are playing aggressive defense.

Two-Deep Man-Under

A *two-deep man-under* has the safeties playing the same role as in the two-deep zone—each covers a deep zone that encompasses half of the field. But the cornerbacks play man-to-man coverage—in which they are more than a wide receivers' shadow, they are stuck to him like Velcro—all over the field. This type of defense allows the man-to-man cover people the opportuntiy to take risks because they have friends in deep places. But the vulnerable part of the field is the center of the field.

This is an illustration of a two-deep man-under.

The two-deep man-under is a combination of zone and man-to-man coverage in which the safeties play zone and the underneath cover men play man-to-man.

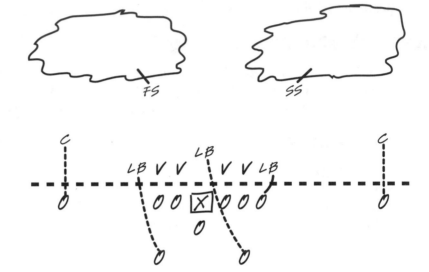

Zone Blitz

Defensive and coverage schemes can only work if teams have the athletes to execute them. When teams have the athletes, coaching imaginations seem to be never-ending. It is from that endless wealth of imagination that arose the newest NFL defensive craze—the *zone blitz*.

The concept of the zone blitz starts with film study, as all do. Teams need to understand the offensive blitz adjustment for a specific kind of blitz—bringing a middle linebacker, another linebacker, and a safety. In that situation the offense will probably run something like a five-yard quick post.

Hypothetically, the defense knows from film study that the quarterback coach has probably been telling the quarterback all year that if he gets a safety and a linebacker blitzing from the same side, he has to throw to the receiver on that side for a five-yard quick post. From film study, it is clear that that is the rule.

The zone blitz anticipates the blitz adjustment perfectly. It brings the linebacker and safety, but it drops a defensive lineman (yes, a 300-pound defensive lineman) into zone coverage. It's not a far back zone—only protecting against a five-yard pattern. And the defensive lineman doesn't have to cover anyone. He just has to be in between the quarterback and the spot film study has said that the five-yard quick post goes. The zone blitz. What will they think of next?

The Least You Need to Know

➤ Defensive strategies have evolved and continue to evolve as teams take things that have already been done and innovate further.

➤ A nickel package has five defensive backs. A dime package has six defensive backs. A quarter package divides the field into four quadrants, each covered by one defensive back. The quarter package has five defensive backs. The fifth back, the nickel back, can roam through all the quadrants.

➤ A combination coverage is a combination of zone coverage with man-on-man on a particular receiver.

➤ The zone blitz brings linebackers on the rush and drops a defensive lineman into zone coverage.

Chapter 19

Special Teams Really Are Special

In This Chapter

➤ Why special teams are so important

➤ Strategies for kickoff and kickoff returns

➤ Punt and punt return practices

There have always been different parts of the military, but the Special Forces have been the ones that come across as a little crazier than all the rest. Their training is a lot more rigorous. Their missions are a lot more dangerous. It is no different in football.

The *special teams* in football are the Special Forces. These are the madmen. When a team kicks off, for instance, it sends men running 40 yards at full speed into a wall of 300-pound men. These are human bowling balls aimed at some very big pins. But yet, on another part of the special teams, there are technical experts. On a field goal, a team of three will work out a precision drill of a snap, a hold, and a kick in less than two seconds. Yet other times, some of the biggest hits and most memorable plays occur when the game involves special teams.

I believe Desmond Howard and his 10 kick-return teammates won Super Bowl XXXI for the Green Bay Packers when Howard returned a kickoff 99 yards for a touchdown. It swung the momentum in a spectacular fashion. In some games, one special teams' play can be worth dozens of regular offensive and defensive plays. In Super Bowl XXXI, special teams brought the world championship to the Green Bay Packers.

This chapter will cover the importance of special teams, the mentality of the players who play on special teams, and the various skills and strategies of units that are involved in kickoffs, punts, field goals, and extra points. This is a special chapter.

Games Can Turn on Special Teams Play

It can be easy to overlook the importance of special teams to a football team. After all, special teams only handle about 17 percent of all plays in a game. Offense and defense play the rest. But any coach will tell you that special teams are as important as offense or defense—the full 33-⅓ percent.

I use the word "special" a lot. It's true. These guys are special. Special teams plays involve either a direct attempt to get points, or a large chunk of yards. In either case, they take on more significance than a normal play from scrimmage.

You can almost always count on special teams to provide a big play—whether it is a blocked punt, a great punt return, or a last-second field goal. There is a high probability that a special teams play will be exciting.

First of all, games always begin with special teams—a kickoff. Therefore, special teams are the guys who are on the field first. Because of this, coaches are constantly preaching that these are the guys that set the tempo of the game. It's true. A big hit to open the game sets a completely different tone than a big runback. Just as offenses and defenses from the same team can feed off of each other, both units are also directly affected by the performance of special teams.

Joe's Record Book

George Allen, coach of the Los Angeles Rams and then the Washington Redskins, was the first coach in the NFL to recognize how important special teams are by hiring a coach just for them. Now, all teams understand. Many print up T-shirts just for the special teams.

If a team goes down the field and knocks someone into snot-bubble land, everybody gets fired up. Guys jump around like maniacs when somebody knocks the snot out of someone. It sends a message to the other team: *"All afternoon you are going to be in for a real battle."*

Now, if I am the quarterback and my guy just got the heck kicked out of him, I am thinking that these guys came to play today. The first words I would say in huddle would be, "Listen, these guys have come to play, we better strap it up and get our butts in gear."

But if my guy just had a good runback, I'd say, "We've got them going, we've got them on the ropes. Let's not waste this opportunity."

Two Ways to Be Special

Special teams can be divided into essentially two categories—*change of possession plays* (punts and kickoffs) and *plays for points* (field goals and extra points).

The plays for points often involve a good portion of the players from the regular starting offense and the regular starting defense. The biggest wildcard in those plays is the *place-kicker*, a solitary man who must have the make-up of an individual-sport athlete, such as a golfer.

On the other hand, the change-of-possession plays involve maniacs. They involve players who may not be regulars on offense or defense. Some of the players on special teams (although certainly not all) are those who are on the fringes of the roster. Coaches like to put players on special teams to evaluate them. They can check the size of a guy's heart, his toughness, and his level of intelligence. Yet other guys are on special teams because they are experts at the art of flying down the field. Many of the guys on a special teams unit are specialists. This includes almost all *kick returners*.

Although change-of-possession plays are high-velocity collision type plays, they are also very organized. It may not look that way on television or from the stands, but there is great coordination on both sides. Coaches quickly learn about the intelligence level of a player by putting him on special teams. As for his toughness and his heart—just watch a kickoff sometime. Maniacs, I'm telling you, maniacs.

Kickoffs—Rolling Thunder

Games begin with kickoffs. Halves begin with kickoffs. There is a kickoff after every score. These are very important plays that go a long way in determining field position and momentum. They can set the energy level.

I believe the opening kickoff is the most important kickoff in a game because it does set the tone for how the game begins.

Joe's Rules

If the ball is kicked out of bounds on a kickoff, the return team gets the ball on its own 35-yard line, with first down and 10 yards to go.

You should first know a few words.

➤ The kicking team is the team that kicks the ball.

➤ The receiving team is the team that receives the kick.

➤ The kick returner is the player who catches the ball and runs it back. His runback is called, yes, a *runback*. Cool, huh?

Coaches always talk about wanting to hold the opponent inside their own 20-yard line on a kickoff. If a team tackles a kickoff returner on the 10- or 15-yard line, the defense is given a huge advantage. First of all, it puts the offense 85 or 90 yards away from a score. That gives it bad field position. Also, it sends a message to the offense that the team that just kicked off has come to play hard that day. As you have learned, football is a very mental and emotional game. The emotion of early success or failure can go a long way in determining what happens next.

On the other hand, if a runback gets to the 35-yard line, it's a positive for the receiving team. Even if that team only gains five yards in the next three plays and then punts on fourth down, it is punting from good field position and a good punt will pin the other team deep in its own end. There is always psychology at work in a football game, but maybe never more so than in special teams play.

The ball is always kicked off from the 30-yard line. The ball is placed in the center of the field. On the kicking team, usually five players line up on each side of the kicker. Each player is given a number and an assignment. On the left side of the kicker, players are numbered L1, L2, L3, L4, and L5. On the right side of the kicker, players are numbered R1, R2, R3, R4, and R5.

> **Joe's Gridiron Talk**
>
> A *wedge* is a wall of big players who are supposed to form a blocking wall in front of the kick returner. The players get into a formation that resembles a "V," or a wedge. The idea is to throw blocks on the kickoff coverage team in order to spring the kick returner loose for a big return.

The two guys closest to the kicker are L1 and R1. Their job is to be the craziest on the field. They are usually extremely fast and without a care at all for their own bodies. They take off straight down the field toward the *wedge*.

These guys, L1 and R1, are aiming for the wedge. They literally want to blow it up and are more than willing to sacrifice their bodies in order to accomplish their task. These are the guys that want to get down the field the fastest. The rule is that no one can run past the 30-yard line until the ball is kicked. Some guys will line up on the 15-yard line, just to get a head of steam. They don't need all 15 yards. They start that far back because…well, because they are wackos. They want to be roaring down the field and the 15-yard head start gives them a boost of adrenaline that makes them actually gain momentum. They start running before the kicker starts. They are about two or three steps behind the kicker when the kicker begins to move forward. They have it timed perfectly, just like a dragster coming out with lights. The ball is kicked and they are roaring and rolling toward that wedge and soon there is the sound of thunder.

The next guys, L2 and R2, are trying to keep the kick returner near the middle of the field. Then L3 and R3 come in from a little bit further outside. This continues all the way out to L5 and R5, who are supposed to make absolutely sure that the kick returner does not get outside.

Often, though, a kicking team will designate one of the outside men, L5 or R5, to stay back with the kicker. Usually, when the team does this, the man who stays back with the kicker is one of the fastest players on the team. His role is to be a safety—to make sure that even if the kick returner does break out for a big return, he does not score a touchdown. The kicking team wants someone as a safety who is fast enough to catch the kick returner. The thinking is that even if the kick returner is tackled on the kicking team's 15-yard line, at least he has not scored a touchdown. At least you give your defense a chance.

Here is an illustration of a snapshot in time of a kicking team covering a kickoff.

Joe's Tips
Often, the kicking team will want the kick returner to have his ball-carrying arm to the side facing them. They know his ball-carrying arm from film study. So, a kicking team would kick the ball to a right-handed return man's right side. He would return to the left, and his right arm would be exposed to their hits.

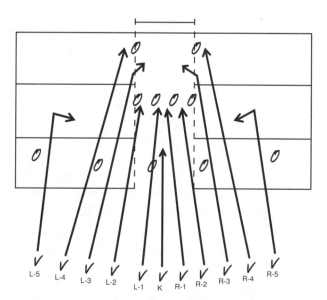

This is a snapshot in time of a kicking team covering a kickoff.

The Five Parts of This Kicking Team Coverage

1. Go down as fast as possible, maintaining proper lateral spacing. Be ready to react to the ball.

2. R1, R2, L1, L2: Landmark inside shoulders of Wedge men.

3. R3, L3: Spring around the Wedge, force the play. Make the tackle.

4. R4, L4: Contain the play. Be alert for the ball carrier "bouncing" outside, and be alert for reverse.

5. R5, L5, K: Act as safeties. Keep everything in front and inside of you.

There is a whole philosophy and strategy to a kickoff. Despite the look of chaos, every player really does have a different assignment and it is very specific. Each covers a very specific lane. Lanes are like passing lanes—about a six-foot strip all the way down the field. Players are supposed to stay in their lanes. If one gets knocked to one side of a two-yard area and the player next to him gets knocked to the other side of his two-yard area, there is a four-yard hole for a return man to pass through—and he can get through it in the blink of an eye. Go ahead, blink. That's all it takes. Two players get out of lanes and the score changes.

There are different approaches to a kickoff as well. One strategy is to kick the ball to the returner's right. In this strategy, the coverage men on that side of the field (their left) move down the field a little faster than the guys on the right side—creating a cup-like effect as they attempt to surround and swarm the returner and pin him to that side.

Another strategy is to kick the ball high down the middle to land at about the 10-yard line. The idea is that by the time the ball is caught, the coverage team has already run into the wedge, been blocked, and shed the blocks. They know they are going to be blocked. The key is to get up and get away.

Kickoff Returns—A Flash of Lightning

If the ball is kicked 70 yards down the field, it will probably land in the kick returner's arms at the goal line. The kick returner is a man with a flair for the dramatic. He has great opportunity, a wide open field, and ten blockers in front of him. He has the ball and maybe a 15-yard head start before he starts to run into other colored jerseys. He needs vision, he needs speed, and he needs quickness. He needs one more thing too—a little luck. If the right guy gets blocked at just the right time, he could go all the way.

The return team sets up two waves of blockers. The first group begins ten yards from the kicking team. These are smaller, faster players with good hands who are near the kick in case the kicking team tries an *onside kick* (keep reading for information on onside kicks). Usually, though, these guys will begin running backwards as soon as the ball is kicked. Their job is to time their blocks to coincide with the immediate needs of the return man. So they get back to help him.

Further back are the men who form the wedge. These are big guys who choreograph their blocks so they hit simultaneously. Again, they want to be hitting the other team at just the right time. If they get on their blocks too soon, the other team can get up and still make a play. In a wedge, everybody has a guy to hit. The worst thing that can happen is for somebody to hit your guy. If a man in a wedge is supposed to hit L3, and somebody else hits him, the timing of the blocking is thrown off.

And then behind the wedge is the man who catches the ball.

These are the guys who can make you miss. They have great quickness, great speed, and move like ballet performers in gladiator gear. Their strategy is simple. They have time for one move. Otherwise, their entire job is to get the ball forward, fast. The longer they wait, the more men wearing the wrong color will show up. They eye the field, look for lanes, watch how blocks are being set up, and then, boom, they're gone.

Some teams will have one return man back. Some will have two. When there are two, the one who doesn't catch the ball automatically assumes the role of *personal protector* for the return man.

As for strategies, teams can call:

> ➤ Left return

> ➤ Right return

> ➤ Middle return

> **Joe's Gridiron Talk**
>
> A *personal protector* runs right in front of the return man and throws what is hoped to be a key block to bust the return man loose for a long run. The return man follows the personal protector and reads his block as he plans his cuts.

These strategies determine which direction the return man will run. This is called by the special teams' coach. The wedge slides in the direction called, just like an offensive line.

In addition, teams can run trick plays on a kickoff return in which they execute a reverse with a wing man coming around behind a return man. Or they could have the return man start up field and then stop and throw it backwards to another player. A forward pass on a kickoff is illegal. But a backward pass is just a long hand-off (it is also called a *lateral)*, and it is legal. It is dangerous. It has a big risk/reward factor.

The Onside Kick

This is an attempt by the kicking team to gain posssession of the ball with a short kick that has a predictable bounce. An *onside kick* is a strategy that a kicking team uses when it is behind in the game and it needs to get the ball back. It is an all-or-nothing play.

When the ball is kicked, it must go 10 yards before it can be recovered by the kicking team. The receiving team can recover the ball before that. In an onside kick, the kicking team wants the ball to start out low bouncing end over end and then hopes that it takes a high bounce just before it reaches 10 yards. Then the kicking team tries to recover it.

Usually, the kicking team lines up nine of its men on one side of the field and then kicks the ball to that side. Both sides use what they call their *hands team*.

> **Joe's Gridiron Talk**
> The *hands team* are guys who normally handle the ball—wide receivers, running backs, and defensive backs. The most important skill for both teams in an onside kick is the ability to grab and hold onto the ball.

Punts—Your Turn

When an offense is unable to advance the ball 10 yards in three plays, it will often elect to punt on fourth down. A *punt* is a kick from the offensive team to the other team to change ball possession between. The team that receives the kick becomes the offensive team.

Remember, there is a difference between a kick and a punt. A kick is kicked from a tee, while the punter drops the ball to kick it. The kicker and punter are usually two different players because the types of kicks are very different, requiring different skills.

The *punter* (the guy kicking the ball) lines up 15 yards behind the center. Halfway between him and the offensive line is a *personal protector* for the punter, who is there to block anyone who might get past someone else.

A punt is measured from the LOS, not from where it is kicked. Therefore a punt of 40 yards actually traveled almost 55 yards. There are two ways punts are measured—gross yards (how far it travels from the LOS), and net yards (gross yards minus the number of return yards).

On the outside of the line are the only two people who can leave the LOS at the snap. These two, who are legally receivers (remember, it is usually fourth down and the offense has the ball), are known as *headhunters*. Their job is to get down the field at the same time as the ball in order to tackle the punt returner.

The punting team has two concerns. The first is protecting the punter, and second is to get the return man. The line blocks for the punter. And the punter can help his line, depending on how many steps he takes. Some punters only take one step and then kick the ball. Those guys don't have many of their punts blocked. (A blocked punt occurs when a defensive player hits the ball with his hands or some part of his body just as it is punted—thus stopping it from flying in the air.) But some guys take two, or even three steps. For one thing, extra steps take the punter closer to the LOS. For another, extra steps take time. Both can make punts easier to block.

Ideally, the punter wants to kick the ball far and high. A far kick pins the other team back. A high kick gives his men time to get down to cover the return. A punter almost always wants good *hang time.*

In certain situations, a punter may try to aim his kicks. For instance, if his team is too far away to kick a field goal, but too close to really boom a long punt, he may try a *pooch punt.*

The punting team could also try a *coffin corner kick* in which the ball is kicked out of bounds near the end zone. If it goes out right near the the end zone, it is called a *coffin corner kick.* The receiving team gets the ball at the yard line that the ball went out of bounds.

Another strategy for long punts is a *directional punt,* in which the ball is kicked to one side of the field to try to pin a returner in and make it harder for him to return the ball.

Finally, you should be aware that a punt is really an offensive play. The team could fake a punt and throw a pass or run the ball in a last ditch effort for a first down.

> **Joe's Gridiron Talk**
>
> *Hang time* is the amount of time a ball is in the air after it is punted. It is the time from when the ball leaves punter's foot until it lands on the ground or in the returner's arms. If you have great hang time (4.0 seconds or longer), the chances of someone returning a punt very far aren't very good.

> **Joe's Gridiron Talk**
>
> A *pooch punt* is a short, high kick designed to land around the 10-yard line in order to give the punting team a chance to down the ball. As long as the receiving team doesn't touch the ball, the punting team can touch it and down it—making it first down and 10 yards to go for the receiving team at the spot the ball was downed.

Punt Returns—Life on the Edge

There was nothing I enjoyed more in football than returning punts. It was the most macho, adrenaline-filled challenge that the game offered. First of all, you have to catch the ball. If you drop one, you probably won't return many more punts. If you don't drop it, you provide tremendous highlights—and most are at your expense.

But it's fun, the ultimate rush. It takes nerve, guts, and a logical approach to insanity. This is *not* craziness. There is a method to the madness. The punt returner (the guy who must catch the punt and run it back) stands under the ball, eyes the defense, and then makes a split-second decision whether to *fair catch*.

His decision is based on a quick glance at the approaching headhunters. If they have made it past the first wave of blockers, who stand across the LOS from the headhunters and try to hit them as soon as the ball is snapped, the returner knows he will have to fair catch. If not, he begins eyeing lanes to run up. And then he starts running. He doesn't have time to build a head of steam. He is working in a more compact area than a kickoff returner, the hang time of a punt ensures that. Thus, he actually needs to be a guy with a few more moves than a kick returner. He may need to juke and dart to get past the headhunters.

The headhunters are on overdrive by the time they get to him. One little elusive move sends them flying past.

But before the punt returner ever touches the ball, the punt return team may want to try to block the punt. They figure how to do this, once again, from film study. They learn how the punter punts, which way he steps, and how many steps. They go into each punt knowing exactly where to dive.

> **Joe's Gridiron Talk**
>
> When a punt returner signals for a *fair catch*, he waves an arm over his head. When he does this it means he plans to catch the ball and promises not to advance it. When he does this, the punting team is not allowed to hit him or interfere with his ability to catch the ball.

> **Joe's Rules**
>
> *Running into the kicker* is a five-yard penalty and not an automatic first down. But *roughing the kicker* (tackling or knocking down the kicker) is a 15-yard penalty and is an automatic first down. The difference, in theory, is about the intention of the man running into the kicker. The reality is that it is about the acting ability of the kicker. They all want to win an Oscar.

For instance, if a punter steps to the right, the defense may want to overload that side with more players. The defense may want to bring two people from the corner. The idea may not even be to block the punt. It may just be to disrupt the timing of the punter. He could just push the personal protector near the punter, and that would certainly disrupt his timing.

Here is an example of how a team may want to plan to rush a punter in order to try to block his punt. It is called a 10-man rush left.

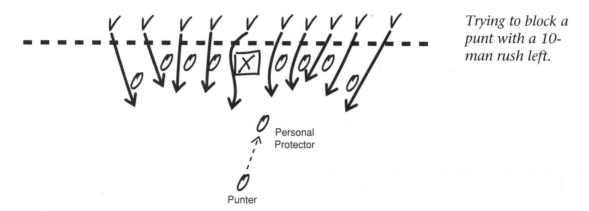

Trying to block a punt with a 10-man rush left.

Personal Protector

Punter

When players dive to block a punt, they should not try to swat at the ball. Instead, players have a better chance if they just lay their hands out. In the time it takes them to swat at the ball, it could be kicked away.

To set up for the return, the receiving team is most concerned about the headhunters. First of all, the receiving team recognizes that a punt is really an offensive play so it is on the lookout for a fake punt. And, it has at least one man on each headhunter. Sometimes, teams put two men on the headhunters, trying to stop them from getting down the field.

Field Goals and Extra Points

Field goals and extra points work on the same principle—kick the ball through the goal posts. In each case, the ball is snapped seven yards back from the LOS to a kneeling holder, who places the ball on the ground. A kicker then kicks the ball.

A field goal, as you know, is worth 3 points. An extra point is worth 1 point.

Kickers are a strange breed. They each have their own idiosyncrasies. Some want the ball tilted toward them. Some want it away. Most, but not all, want the laces pointed away from them. There is a chemistry that must develop between a snapper, holder, and kicker or else the kicker will not be confident. And kicking is all about confidence.

It is also about distance. As you can see from Table 19.1, kickers are more accurate when they are close to the goal posts.

Table 19.1 Field Goal Percentages From Various Distances, 1996

Distance (yards)	Made	Attempted	Percentage
1-19	20	20	100%
20-29	266	281	94.7%
30-39	244	288	84.7%
40-49	172	268	64.2%
50 or longer	30	58	51.7%

The Least You Need to Know

➤ Special teams play about 17 percent of all plays but coaches look upon them as being equal in value to offense and defense. Part of the reason is because special teams plays either involve potential points or a large exchange of yardage.

➤ Kickoff teams try to keep the runner contained in the middle of the field. Kick return teams want to spring the return man loose with well-timed blocks.

➤ Punters try for lots of hang time to give the coverage team time to get to the returner. Punt returners are slightly crazy.

➤ A field goal requires great coordination between a snapper, holder, and kicker.

Part 4
College and Pro

Football comes in levels. Young men play Pop Warner (little league football) to learn to compete. Some of those young men and little boys move on to play high school football, and then the lucky ones get to the higher levels.

College football is the beginning of the spotlight, when the big eye called television begins to take account of the skills of young men. But professional football is "The Show."

This part will examine college and pro ball. It will discuss the relationship of the college game to the professional game and then it will cover the NFL—why the league is the best in the world, how teams advance to the Super Bowl, and how money continues to take on greater importance for everyone involved.

Chapter 20

College Football: More Than Marching Bands and Cheerleaders

> ## In This Chapter
>
> ➤ How college football is different
>
> ➤ Why there is such pageantry
>
> ➤ The divisions and the conferences
>
> ➤ The relationship between the colleges and the pros

College football is full of pageantry, pom-poms, cheerleaders, and big brass marching bands that play tuba-waving fight songs. College football is also where the NFL gets its players.

Unlike pro baseball, pro football doesn't have a minor league. So the feeder for the NFL is college football. Thus, if you want to be a professional football fan, you cannot ignore the college game.

The relationship between college and the pros is very close, although at times the colleges would not like it to be quite so close. One problem of recent vintage is the tendency of underclassmen to leave school early for the lucrative paychecks of the National Football League. Many colleges, who count on the senior season for a player to be his most productive, are not happy when players skip their senior season for the pros.

College players go to the pros. Some college coaches go to the pros. And some pro coaches leave the pros and end up coaching in college.

But for all the similarities and closeness, college football is different. This chapter will examine the college game, its relationship to the pros, and the similarities and differences between the two games. There are even a couple of rule differences that will be discussed. This chapter will briefly discuss the various divisions, the importance of competition in college, and why all those New Year's Day bowl games are important to fans of the pro game.

The Pageantry

College football sounds different. It is younger—a vibrant atmosphere of exuberance and joyous noise. There are horns, honest-to-goodness brass, and big pounding drums mixed in with chants that always seem to echo like an instant memory. You've got to go.

There are acrobatic cheerleaders and squads of young men who live for Saturday afternoons in the fall. These young men dream of being able to play on Sunday afternoons. They all want to be drafted. And they step toward those dreams in the world of holy-mackerel euphoria that is college football.

What Is the NCAA?

The NCAA is the National Collegiate Athletic Association, which is the governing body of college athletics that was formed in 1906. As a fan, you don't need to know a lot about the NCAA, but you should be aware that it exists, and that it can make rulings on whether players are eligible to play, and whether teams have violated any recruiting rules.

Joe's Rules

There a few rules differences on the field between college football and pro football.

> ➤ In college ball, a receiver is ruled in-bounds if he catches the ball and lands with one foot in-bounds before going out-of-bounds. In the pros, a receiver must land both feet in-bounds.

➤ In college ball, if a ballcarrier falls to the ground, he is automatically down. In the pros, if a ballcarrier falls to the ground and a defensive player does not touch him, he may get up and continue to advance the ball. In the pros, he is only down if a defensive player touches him while he is on the ground.

➤ In college ball the hashmarks are closer to the sidelines.

The NCAA has very specific rules regarding college players getting any money besides scholarship money. Essentially, college players are not allowed to receive any money. And that's about all you need to know. College players are supposed to be amateurs.

This can create a dilemma for a college player, especially one from a poor family. That player may find the lure of big money too hard to pass up even if an extra year of college would help him grow as both a player and a person.

Divisions I-A, I-AA, II, III

There are big schools and there are small schools, and the NCAA divides them into divisions to ensure a level playing field. That is, the NCAA assumes that schools with more resources should play each other, while schools with less to invest in football should play each other. Big schools have big football programs and are on television a lot. These are the schools whose teams you see on Saturday afternoons. The big schools are in Division I-A—which simply means that the school is at the top levels of collegiate athletics. Smaller schools, which normally would not have much of a chance competing against the really big schools, compete against each other. The next level is Division I-AA. The one after that is Division II, and finally there is Division III.

Table 20.1 gives a list of how many schools and players are in each division.

Table 20.1   Schools and Players in Each Division, 1995 Season

Division	# of Schools	# of Players
I-A	108	12,344
I-AA	120	11,315
II	156	12,967
III	216	17,274
Total	**600**	**53,900**

This is important to pro football fans because, as I said, almost all professional football players come from college programs. If a player comes from a Division I-A school, the competition he faced will be of a higher caliber than those players who came from Division I-AA, II, or III schools. This does not mean that players coming from smaller schools can't make it in the NFL. In fact, some of the greatest players ever came from small schools. However, the majority of players come from bigger schools, where the competition more closely resembles that of the NFL.

Table 20.2 gives a list of the seven schools that had the most former players on NFL rosters at the beginning of the 1996 season.

Table 20.2   Schools with the Most Players on NFL Rosters in 1996

School	Number Of Players
Notre Dame	43
Ohio State	35
University of Miami (Florida)	34
University of Tennessee	33
Florida State	32
Penn State	32
University of Southern California	32

The schools listed in Table 20.2 are all big schools. The level of competition between these schools is very high. In other words, if a kid is a 6'4", 300-pound lineman playing at a Division II school, he is not facing many guys his size. Therefore, his chances of success against NFL-level competition is completely unknown. Sure, a player's success can't really be evaluated until he reaches the league and competes. But success in big conference greatly increases the probability of success in the NFL. Success in a small conference does not.

Joe's Record Book

At least two of the greatest players in the history of the game, wide receiver Jerry Rice of Mississipi Valley State and then the San Francisco 49ers, and running back Walter Payton of Jackson State and then the Chicago Bears, both attended Division I-AA schools.

There are other advantages to coming from a big school. Big schools are now huge entertainment corporations, and the players on these teams are unpaid *stars*. They know how to deal with media. They have walked into a stadium of 80,000 or 100,000 (as in the case of the Michigan Wolverines in Ann Arbor, Michigan) hostile fans. They have, in essence, played on a *stage*.

Nevertheless, a player from a big school will still make a *huge* step to reach the NFL. Some make it. Most though…most can only dream it.

The question is always there, no matter where a player went to school. In the NFL, they become freshmen again. There is that question. Every step of the way, they ask again, "Do I belong here?"

The Conferences

Although college football is separated into divisions based on the size of the school, it is further divided by geography. There are conferences.

For instance, there is the Pacific 10 (PAC 10)—which includes 10 teams from the far Western states. Then there is the Big 10, which has (really) 11 teams from the Midwest. There is the Atlantic Coast Conference, the Western Athletic Conference, the Mid-American Conference, the Southeastern Conference, the Big East, the Big West, and Conference USA. There are also conferences from the smaller divisions. College football has a rich potpourri of talent levels at all different schools. Usually, but not always, the top talent goes to the top schools. But there are so many schools and there are so many players.

And then, there is one major school that is not in a conference. It's Notre Dame, and it exists on its own plane.

> **Joe's Gridiron Talk**
> The *subway alumni* are folks who, though they did not attend the University of Notre Dame, for one reason or another have grown to identify with the school. I'm sure there are other subway alumni out there, but none have gotten the national attention like the ones of Notre Dame.

Notre Dame and Everybody Else

Almost every college in the country has a football team, but in the annals of history, there is really only one football team. Granted, I am an alumnus of that school, and I played quarterback when I was there, but even without my bias, it must be clear to anyone who follows football that there is Notre Dame University and then, well…. Now, I'm not saying everybody likes Notre Dame. Far from it. But, if you are going to follow college football even a little, you must either love or hate Notre Dame. You can't be ambivalent.

Notre Dame itself is small, with only about 7,000 full-time students. But the following of the university is tremendous, no matter which side of the fence you are on.

Although I am not Catholic, I know that a big part of the appeal is that Notre Dame is a Catholic school. But I think it goes back to the legendary Notre Dame teams that Knute Rockne coached earlier this century. There is tradition, a storied past full of heroes and gold helmets.

> **Joe's Gridiron Talk**
> *Touchdown Jesus* is the painting of Jesus that overlooks the stadium in South Bend, Indiana, home of Notre Dame. In the painting, Jesus has his arms upraised to the heavens (as if, some football fanatics have said, signaling a touchdown).

For myself, I looked upon a Notre Dame football career as a stepping stone to the NFL. Remember, earlier I referred to the different divisions in football and how the level of competition varied so much. Well, at Notre Dame, the competition is always intense. There aren't many walk-over games. I used to use the annual game against the University of Southern California (USC) as a measuring stick for whether I was ready for the NFL. I knew that USC had produced a number of players who went on to not only play in, but star, in the NFL. I figured that if I could do well against USC, I could compete at the pro level.

So I found plenty of reason to love the school. And, as I stated previously, so have many others. But, just the same, many have found lots of reasons not to like the school. For one thing, if you went to a school that is not called Notre Dame, I suppose you could be jealous of the success and exposure of the school. Notre Dame is the only school in the country with its own television contract—all its games are aired on NBC. Even decades ago, Notre Dame games used to be aired in condensed form on Sunday mornings. I can still recall the announcer's calm voice saying, "And now, we move to further action in the third quarter."

The Bowl Games

At the end of the regular season, various conference champions (and some second or third place finishers from the powerhouse conferences like the Big 10 or PAC 10) are given a chance to compete in bowl games. All told, there are 18 bowl games.

Bowls are great events, big games between teams that have been good that year. The NCAA tries to get the number one ranked team to play the number two ranked team in one of the bowls. But it gets tricky in college. There are just too many teams. They can't all play each other. There are no playoffs in college. Instead, there are big games called bowls.

The championship of college football is never decided on the field. Instead, it is decided by voters in two different polls. One poll, the *USA Today*/CNN poll is voted on by coaches. The other poll, the Associated Press poll, is voted on by the media.

The significance of the bowl games to the professional fan should be obvious. You see, pro football players come from college. The college bowl games usually feature the best college teams. It would stand to figure that some of the best college players would be on the best college teams. If you want to see who will be the next star of your pro team, watch a bowl game.

The All-Star Games

After the bowl games, the best seniors in the country are invited to play in all-star games. These are almost a direct showcase for the NFL. In fact, the Senior Bowl is actually coached by NFL coaches.

The four all-star games are the Hula Bowl, the Senior Bowl, The Blue-Gray Game, and the East-West Shrine Game.

These games are where players first start to get a feel for what it is like to be an NFL player. It is also where players, especially those from smaller schools, can show that they can play against top-level talent. It is an all-star game, and that means something.

The all-star games can give players a chance to showcase their talents outside their own college systems. For instance, a quarterback from a school that didn't throw the ball a lot may be a bit of an unknown to NFL scouts. But at an all-star game, he will be allowed to do pro football-type things. A good day could really help his chances of getting picked higher in the draft. It could be his one chance, and that's all he needs.

A bad day could hurt him some. I had a bad day at the Hula Bowl. Earlier in the week in practice I hit my funny bone and I lost the feeling in my ring finger and my pinkie that week. I couldn't throw. I couldn't feel the ball. The ball flew end over end all week. I threw *ducks*. It was my audition for professional football, and all I could do was throw ducks—no spirals. Luckily, I had a pretty good college career behind me, so my poor performance in the all-star game was somewhat overlooked by scouts.

The Heisman Trophy

The Heisman Trophy is the most prestigious award in college football, given annually to the best college player in the country. It was named after legendary coach John Heisman, and is given out by the Downtown Athletic Club of New York City. It is not necessarily given to someone who is expected to be the best pro. The two games are different. Some Heisman winners have succeeded magnificently in college but were unable to achieve the same success in pro football. Some were just as good in the NFL.

The Heisman is a very political award that has a lot to do with the previous reputation of the player and his school, the publicity department of his school, his position on the field, and also his year on the field. Sometimes, however, it has a lot to do with his name. When I went to Notre Dame, my last name was pronounced "Thees"-man. Our public relations director changed the pronunciation of my name to rhyme with Heisman my senior year because he believed it would give me a better chance to win the trophy. Just so you know, I finished second to Jim Plunkett that year (1970). Regardless of the massive amounts of public relations that occur, you still have to deliver on the field. It isn't always a name that counts. Even though I didn't win the Heisman Trophy, my name still rhymes with Heisman.

So What's All This Got to Do with the Pros?

Other than a few players, most notably Eric Swann, defensive lineman for the Arizona Cardinals, the NFL is loaded with ex-college players. Not all of them are graduates. But almost all played some college ball.

The two games are related. The interests of the two games are related, although not always parallel.

> **Joe's Gridiron Talk**
> The *draft* is the way college players are picked for the pros. Every year in the spring, all 30 teams take turns picking players at the annual draft. The worst team from the previous year picks first. The best team picks last.

Colleges want their players to stay in school for four years and get a diploma. The pros say the same thing, yet when a great junior running back declares he wants to be eligible for the draft, every team in the league would love to have him.

One problem is that colleges now allow freshmen to play varsity ball. This increases their worth to the pros early and also increases the chance that an underclassman will leave school early. And even though many underclassmen have gone on to great success in the NFL, there are even more who missed their last two years of college and didn't make the NFL. For the schools, usually a player's senior year is when they are going to be able to reap the benefits of this young man being a mature football player—athletically, academically, emotionally, and socially. And the NFL would get a more fully developed player if the player goes through that senior experience.

> **Joe's Gridiron Talk**
> *Redshirt* means a player doesn't play a certain year when he is in school and he is granted another year of eligibility to play later. This can happen, for instance, if a player gets hurt. He still attends classes and practices, but doesn't play and thus is still eligible to play four years.

It would be better for all involved if the students stayed in school an extra year. Notice, I said *students*. That's their job in college. They are students. Like many of today's juniors who leave school early, I only played three years of college ball. But they happened to be my last three years of school. When I played, freshmen were ineligible to play. I think that was a good rule.

Professional football is very different than college ball. The game is a lot simpler in college, where teams are only allowed to practice 20 hours a week—and that includes meeting time.

234

By contrast, in the pros, typically a player will arrive at the practice facility at 8 a.m. Normally, he won't leave until 6 p.m. And then some players, especially quarterbacks, would still do a few hours of film study a couple of nights each week at home. There is a short practice on Saturday and a game on Sunday. Professionals put in about 60 hours a week. It is their job.

The Draft

College players get to the pros by the *draft*. Each team picks players, one at a time. They each pick once, and then they each pick again, and again—seven times. There are seven rounds.

Players are then paid based upon where they were picked. The higher they are picked (with earlier rounds considered "higher"), the more they will be paid—usually. Occasionally, a player drafted a slot or two below another player will end up with more money. After all, all contracts are negotiated. But still, each position in the draft is generally slotted a certain amount to be paid. Thus, from a college player's perspective, the draft rules.

The Least You Need to Know

➤ College football sounds different, looks different and is different. There are even a couple of different rules. It is the same game as professional football, but there is more pageantry.

➤ Division I-A schools are the biggest, then Division I-AA, then Division II, then Division III.

➤ Divisions are divided into conferences like the PAC 10 and Big 10.

➤ Notre Dame is a successful independent team—like 'em or hate 'em.

➤ The bowls try to be championship games (but aren't quite) and the Heisman Trophy winner is the best college player in the country, but that does not mean he will be a good pro.

➤ Pro teams follow college teams because pro players are drafted (picked) from the college ranks.

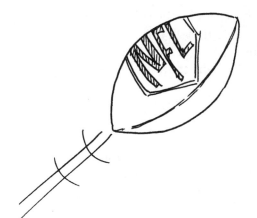

Chapter 21

The NFL: The Best in the World

> ### In This Chapter
>
> ➤ Thoughts on the show, the business, and the culture of the NFL
>
> ➤ Why the NFL is a superstar league
>
> ➤ Strategies for building champions

In playgrounds across America, there are dreamers—little boys who imagine themselves to be Dan Marino or Emmitt Smith or Jerry Rice. Once upon a time, Marino, Smith, and Rice maybe imagined themselves to be Joe Namath, Jimmy Brown, or Paul Warfield. It is a wonderful cycle that is fueled because boys have heroes and the heroes of football play in only one place—the NFL.

The National Football League is a professional league comprised of 30 teams that have the best football players in the world. It is the pinnacle of the game. A player can go no higher than the NFL. When a player is a boy, he plays Pop Warner (little league football) and hopes to play high school ball. When a young man is in high school, he hopes to play college ball. After college, the player hopes to play in the NFL. Once a player is in the NFL, there are no other worlds to conquer. Of course, conquering the NFL is no small feat.

This is a chapter about the greatest professional sports league in the world. It will touch on how the league is the pinnacle of the sport, and that although it is a sport it is also a business. The NFL is full of grown men playing a boy's game for a tycoon's fortune. This chapter will also discuss the culture of the league, and the different philosophies that teams use to build a winner.

The NFL Is "The Show"

The pinnacle of the stage is Broadway. The pinnacle for a screen actor is Hollywood. In football, there is only one place for a player to see if his talent is among the best in the world—the National Football League. It can be overwhelming for a player first walking into the league. Wow. The NFL. Imagine that. Players can all remember watching the games on television. Suddenly, the camera angle is reversed and the watchers become the watched.

Even if a player is the worst in the NFL, he is still among the best players in the world. There really is no higher mountain.

The NFL Is a Business

The NFL is a *professional* football league, meaning that players get paid to play. This means that although football is a game, in the NFL, football is a business. And it is big business.

Big business, of course, means big money for the players and the owners. It means that the boy's game that is played on the field often takes second place to the high-finance game that is played off the field. The game that once saw players begin and end their careers in the same uniform has given way to a new world order in which players bounce from team to team in search of the highest offer. Players have become, in effect, hired guns.

Teams used to have older players grooming younger players. It was like a passing of a baton. A player would play in a particular city for 10 years and, as his career was winding down, he would help his successor get ready to take over the job. And then, a decade later, the cycle would continue. No more. Now, there is basically an all-for-one and one-for-me type of attitude. It's like a free-for-all, and despite the fact that players do jump from team to team, I don't believe that there is anything more than human nature involved. Think of your job. If someone besides your employer offers you the same job at a huge pay hike, are you sticking around because of loyalty? Not likely. In the NFL, some players do still stick with a team out of loyalty. Sure, it's rare. But it happens.

Sure, sports are different. But you know what? It's really not that different. Football is a business.

There is another aspect to take into consideration. Players' careers do not last a long time. If a player is in the league for 10 years, he has had a very long career.

Therefore, even though players do make exorbitant amounts of money, the window of time in which to make this money is small. I actually believe players are loyal to their teams. But frankly, I think they are more loyal to their families. Who wouldn't be?

Joe's Record Book
The average career in the NFL 3.3 years.

There is one final point I'd like to make on the player loyalty subject. I have heard fans say that a player should stay with their team even if their team offers less money. The argument typically goes, "What is the difference between $3 million and $3.5 million?" Well, let me answer that. The difference is $500,000.

So, as you can see by all those zeros in the above number, the NFL is a big business. And really, that is a small number by NFL standards. The NFL is not about hundreds of thousands of dollars. It's about billions—that's with a *"B" and nine zeros.*

It's not just the players who are making money. Football is a cash cow for the folks who pay the players, too. After all, they wouldn't be paying the players millions if they weren't making more millions. The numbers are almost bizarre. A new franchise will cost about $140 million. Then, a stadium will cost at least $250 million. Owners spend all that money, so they can have the right to pay players $40 million a year—even though they know those players are only going to be around for three or four years before they sell their services to the highest bidder. It's a big Monopoly game, and everybody owns Boardwalk.

Oh, by the way, owners make money too. You know those tickets you buy? The money goes to the owners. You know all the beer, chips, and the cars—the products that are advertised on NFL broadcasts? Well, those companies all pay big money to sell their products on TV during NFL games. The broadcast networks sell the time, but only after paying the NFL exorbitant amounts of money. And guess who gets that money? Yes, the owners. Also, almost every stadium has *luxury boxes.*

Joe's Gridiron Talk
A *luxury box* is an enclosed room with a glass front that is inside of many stadiums. These are usually rented to corporations, and are located in some of the prime areas of stadiums. They are rented for tens of thousands of dollars or more per year. Television revenue is shared among all teams, but a portion of luxury box revenue is kept by the home team.

There was a time when some owners were just in it to make money. They are still in it for the money, but the initial investment is so huge now that all owners are more committed to winning. Not only is it more fun to win, but the owners finally figured out that there is money to be made from being successful. It's now about selling hats. It's about selling shirts and image and logos and dreams and jerseys and shoes. Money. Business is about money. Professional football is about money. Football is a business. (See Chapter 23 for more details).

The Superstar League

The pinnacle itself has a pinnacle. Yes, in a league that is filled with the best football players in the world, there are, indeed, the *very best* players. Superstars. It is an overused word in the age of hype but a true superstar has way more value to a team than any team ever pays him. Superstars sell tickets and T-shirts because there is one thing that superstars can be counted on for—winning. Superstars win.

It is impossible to win in the NFL without at least some of the best players in the league. Hard work and character and even smarts can go a long way, but it has to accompanied by talent because football is a physical game.

And superstars demand top dollar. The economics of football are governed by the simple rule of supply and demand. If there is a short supply of superstars at a particular position, and you are a superstar at that position, you will be one of the highest paid players in the game.

Some guys even have written into their contract a clause that says they must be, say, one of the top three paid players at their position. In other words, if player A has that clause but later four players come along and sign contracts bigger than his, player A will get his salary accelerated so that it equals the average of the top 3 players. Hey, it's good work if you can get it.

By the same token, if you have been a superstar for a team for 10 years and then you get hurt, the team may want to keep you, but it has to use your roster position for someone who can be productive *now*. Emotions and feelings have to be removed from the picture.

The superstar system has, in effect, created a sort of caste system in football. The superstars make exorbitant multi-million dollar salaries and the average players make a few hundred thousand a year.

Sure, a few hundred thousand may sound like a lot to most people. And it is. But remember, these are mostly short careers. And, the difference in salaries is huge. The middle class football player (go with me on this, it's a relative term) does not exist. There is the top of the mountain, and then there is everybody else. And that's just the way it is—it's not bad. Money has not ruined the game. The game is as popular as ever. Money has changed the game, but football on the field is still football.

But money creates a bit of pressure in locker rooms. Players know what other players make. If a player is making a ton of money and isn't getting the job done, his teammates will make sure he hears about it. Football is a microcosm of society. Families fight over money. So do football teams. Guys say things. There are spats. Superstars get pressure from everywhere. They better produce because fans know what players make. Owners obviously know. *Put up or shut up*. Superstars must put up.

Football honors the best who ever played in the Pro Football Hall of Fame in Canton, Ohio. The Hall of Fame is where the best of the best go. There is nothing more that can be accomplished than being elected to the Hall of Fame. And there is no greater honor than that.

Joe's Record Book

Players cannot be elected to the Hall of Fame until five years after they have retired. Coaches can go in immediately.

Although the world of professional football is obviously very competitive, superstars like it when other superstars receive an enormous contract. The bar goes up. The next contract negotiation will be even more mind-boggling. The National Football League has found the end of the rainbow and sure enough—there is a pot of gold. Just ask a superstar.

The Culture of the Game

I started playing football at 12 years old. When I left the game at 35, I was doing the exact same thing I did at 12.

And, as a father, when I was 34, for instance, I could come home from work and talk to my 13-year-old son about his day on the practice field and I compared it to mine. My son, Joey, would say, "Dad, I threw a couple of interceptions in practice today."

And I'd say, "So did I, Son. So did I. But I'll do better tomorrow."

"Me too, Dad," he'd answer.

The culture of the NFL is many things, but in many ways it is encompassed in that conversation I had with my son. Grown men playing a boys' game. There's your culture.

Of course, it is a culture of violence, of rare opportunity, and of money and fame. Every player is different. Although the culture is all male, it is also full of many races, religions, and nationalities. Just people. Happy-go-lucky guys have lockers next to whiners, who are next to practical jokers, who are next to born-again Christians, who are next to aspiring rap artists. It's just people who are judged on their athletic ability and on their ability to fit into a group. Character is important. By character, I mean, *"Can I count on you?"* Character is about work ethic, reliability, and accountability. Football players are highly talented and motivated individuals who have a healthy amount of ego and confidence. The culture of the NFL, especially on a winning team, is one of excellence. There is nothing more invigorating.

The culture also includes some of that history and lore that I spoke of earlier in the book (Chapter 6). Some players know more than others. The players who understand the traditions of the game have more of tendency to go into coaching.

The culture of the NFL does pass from one generation to the next. When I went up to Joe Namath and offered to carry his helmet to his locker room (see Chapter 1), it was ridiculous. I know that. But I wasn't embarrassed. Heck no. He was my hero. And then I think about our careers. He won a world championship. I won a world championship. Holy mackerel.

Professional football is like a fraternity. We, as football players, are criticized by people who have never done what we've done. We are under a microscope because of how much money we make. Our families are looked upon in a certain way because of what happened on a Sunday afternoon. We rely on each other for our own existence, our own success, and, to some degree, our own failures.

How Teams Are Built

Like Rome, championship teams are not built in a day. The strategies and philosophies of successful football teams (as you learned in the chapters on offensive and defensive strategies) are not clearly defined in black-and-white terms. There are different ways to do it.

But it all starts with organization. There must be a coherent philosophy, the contents of which are less important than the cohesiveness of the plan. It all has to fit together—people, philosophy, and talent.

There are really five aspects to a football team's organization, in addition to the players—the owner, the general manager, the coach, the assistant coaches, and the medical and equipment staff.

The owner pays the bills, makes the money, and hires the general manager.

The general manager picks the players. He is in charge of drafting players in the draft, acquiring free agents by outbidding other teams, and making player trades with other teams. Sometimes the head coach is also the general manager. It is the rare individual such as Jimmy Johnson, the coach of the Miami Dolphins who built the Dallas Cowboys and then coached them to two Super Bowl championships, who can handle both jobs. More typically, there is a matching of general manager and coach, such as Ron Wolf and Mike Holmgren, who together built the Green Bay Packers into the champions of Super Bowl XXXI.

The coach is the field general, planning overall strategy for the game and the season on the field. He devises strategies, motivates players, and makes decisions on playing time. He also decides who makes the roster.

Assistant coaches, I believe, have the greatest impact on a team. They work directly with the players. They teach specific on-the-field skills. They motivate. They are wired into a core group of players.

The medical staff makes sure the players stay healthy. The equipment staff makes sure the players have the proper equipment so that they can perform their jobs. It's just like any other business. The team is looking for good productivity from its people, who, after all, are a major investment.

It all has to fit together. Coaches and assistant coaches spend a lot of time together. Much of the time, they are tired. This can be a difficult situation. Think about it. If you are around friends or family and you are tired and they are tired, at times it is not a really happy place to be. If you are a coach, you need people around you who know you and know your moods and can put up with you, and who you can put up with. You want very smart people; people who think like you.

Finally, there are the players. You know about them. Or do you?

Rosters are set at 47 men—that's the most players that can be signed to any team. I have my own theory on the quality of players you need to compete for the championship. I call it the 8-14-25 Rule.

> **Joe's Tips**
>
> Occasionally, owners get involved in the football operations of their team. Sometimes, it's good, sometimes it's not, and sometimes it is inevitable. If two football men, say a coach and a general manager, are feuding about a personnel decision, the owner may need to step between them. Read your local newspapers to follow this kind of action in your home team.

> **Joe's Tips**
>
> Some coaches are teachers. Some are yellers. Some give pats on the back. Some give kicks in the butt. No one style works all the time, but usually all the coaches on one team are on the same page. They don't have to use the same style, but the styles of coaches must work together.

Joe's Gridiron Talk
The *Pro Bowl* is the All-Star Game of the National Football League. It is played every year in Honolulu, Hawaii.

Joe's Gridiron Talk
A *blue chip player* is considered by scouts to be one who cannot miss becoming a starter in the league, if not a superstar.

A *sleeper* is a player drafted in the later rounds of the draft who turns out to be something special.

Joe's Gridiron Talk
The *salary cap* is the amount of money the NFL designates each team may spend for players. The salary cap For 1997 is $41.45 million per team.

First, you need eight Pro Bowl players. Joe Gibbs, former coach of the Washington Redskins, used to say this. Get eight Pro Bowl players and you can compete for a title.

You then need 14 top-flight players who are borderline Pro Bowl players in any given year.

And then you need 25 quality NFL players.

The 8-14-25 Rule. That's a starting philosophy. The next question is where do you find the players?

Finding the Players

Every year, as you have learned, there is an annual draft in which the top college players who are eligible are picked. There are seven rounds, and each of the 30 teams picks in each round—unless there are trades. Sometimes teams trade draft picks for players or for other draft picks, or for a combination of both. Teams hope to get *blue chip players* in the early rounds, and *sleepers* in the later rounds.

Unlike other sports, trades are rarely made during the season. Football is too much of a team game. A player needs time to learn to work with his teammates and vice versa.

Even without team concerns, the league has a specific calendar for when certain personnel moves can be made, and when roster sizes must be set.

Nowadays, teams build through free agency as well. (See Chapter 23 for more details.) This is the area that may have the most impact on a team, because it almost always involves the most dollars. When a free agent superstar lands in a new city, he will most likely be making one of the highest salaries on his new team. Because of something called the *salary cap*, teams are only allowed to spend a certain amount each year.

Young Guys or Grizzled Veterans

A grand experiment was conducted in the NFL in 1995. Two new teams joined the league—the Carolina Panthers and the Jacksonville Jaguars. And the interesting thing was that they decided to build their teams completely differently. One team, the Jacksonville Jaguars, put together a team of mostly young players surrounded by a few key free agent players. The Carolina Panthers, on the other hand, pursued a number of free agents from other teams and put them together into a team with a few key young players. These were two completely different philosophies and they both were successful.

In their second season, the Jaguars were amazingly successful. They made it to AFC Championship game. If they had won that game, they would have gone to the Super Bowl.

In their second season, the Panthers were just as successful. They made it to the NFC Championship game. If they had won that game, they would have made it to the Super Bowl as well.

It would've been a heck of a Super Bowl.

Start with a Quarterback

Sure, I'm biased about the importance of quarterbacks. That doesn't mean I'm wrong. As a former quarterback, I know what is involved in the job.

Just look at how much quarterbacks get paid and you will see that I am right. An average NFL starting quarterback makes about $3 million per year. The better they are, the more they make. At any given time, there are about eight quarterbacks in the league who are superstars in the true sense of the word. Yet a quarterback who does not have superstar ability can do very well on a good team. Neal O'Donnel went with the Pittsburgh Steelers to Super Bowl XXX, a game they probably should have won but didn't. After that Super Bowl season, O'Donnell was rewarded with a $25 million, five-year contract to play for the New York Jets. Every team must have at least a decent quarterback. Most teams will have to settle for just that. About eight teams, as I said, are lucky enough to have a superstar at the most key position.

After quarterback, there are a few other key positions, starting with the offensive line, most specifically the left tackle, who protects a right-handed quarterback from hits from his blind side—the side behind him. Teams must also have a defensive lineman, a half-back, a cornerback, a pass rushing linebacker, and a quality wide receiver. If you make all those Pro Bowl players, throw in one more Pro Bowl player and you have eight Pro Bowl players. You can now compete for a championship. And that's when the NFL really becomes a show.

The Least You Need to Know

➤ The best players in the world play in the NFL, and the best of those are superstars.

➤ The NFL is a professional football league and money is the driving force.

➤ Owners pay for players and pick the general manager. The general manager picks the players. But sometimes, the owner wants to be both the owner and the general manager.

➤ Teams are put together in a number of ways. There is a college draft in which each team takes turns picking players, there are trades, and there is free agency, in which teams bid for a player's services.

➤ A team must have a good quarterback and follow the 8-14-25 Rule to contend for championships.

The Road to the Super Bowl

There is only one true prize in professional football, and that is the Vince Lombardi Trophy—given to the team that wins the Super Bowl. Nothing else matters.

If your team goes 15-1 in the regular season but loses in the first round of the playoffs, you've accomplished nothing. You are nobody. I know that winning the Super Bowl validated my career and that it validated the careers of all the players who ever played on winning teams. There are players who don't win the Super Bowl who say it isn't the end of the world. If they had won it, they'd feel differently. They'd feel like, if they hadn't won it, it would have been the end of the world.

It is not easy to get there. This chapter is about what it takes for a team to reach the Super Bowl, and how a team's performance in the regular season affects it chances in the playoffs. It describes the conferences and divisions that make up the National Football League, homefield advantage, scheduling, a round-by-round look at how the playoffs develop, and a description of what is so super about the Super Bowl.

Slice Up the League

The NFL is divided into two conferences, the American Football Conference (AFC), and the National Football Conference (NFC). Each of these conferences is further divided into three divisions, an East, a Central, and a West Division.

Table 22.1 covers how the league is divided.

Table 22.1 The National Football League

American Football Conference	National Football Conference
(AFC)	(NFC)
East	*East*
Buffalo Bills	Arizona Cardinals
Indianapolis Colts	Dallas Cowboys
Miami Dolphins	New York Giants
New England Patriots	Philadephia Eagles
New York Jets	Washington Redskins
Central	*Central*
Baltimore Ravens	Chicago Bears
Cincinnati Bengals	Detroit Lions
Houston Oilers	Green Bay Packers
Jacksonville Jaguars	Minnesota Vikings
Pittsburgh Steelers	Tampa Bay Buccaneers
West	*West*
Denver Broncos	Atlanta Falcons
Kansas City Chiefs	Carolina Panthers
Oakland Raiders	New Orleans Saints
San Diego Chargers	St. Louis Rams
Seattle Seahawks	San Francisco 49ers

You may think, by the titles of the divisions, that they are divided by regions of the country. You may think that, but you would be wrong. Just look again. For instance,

Atlanta is in the NFC West, and Arizona is in the NFC East. The NFL is the only place I know of that thinks Atlanta is west of Arizona.

The Regular Season Is Too Exciting to Be Just Regular

The NFL season is 16 games long. Each team plays the teams in its own division twice—once at home and once at the other team's stadium.

Teams want to win enough games in the regular season to qualify for the playoffs. Most teams just concentrate on making the playoffs and then figure that anything can happen once they get there. There is some truth to this, although it is also true that most champions would have considered the season a complete failure if they didn't win the Super Bowl. Champions have strong minds.

The regular season is important because, obviously, a team must first qualify for the playoffs in order to advance in the playoffs. But there is one other aspect too—homefield advantage. Teams that have the best regular season record get to play their playoff games at home. They also get to take the first week of the playoffs off.

Cheer Loud, Your Team Needs You

What's so good about playing at home? Oh gosh. Everything. Football fields are different. The wind, shadows, and weather all make a difference, and it's always nice to play on a field where those things are familiar. It's good not to travel and wake up in a hotel. But mostly, the reason why home field is such an advantage is the fans.

Remember, football is an emotional game. There is nothing that can toy with your emotions more than the difference between 70,000 fans cheering your every move versus 70,000 fans jeering your every move. Sure, it's a challenge to go into a foreign stadium and turn screaming maniacs into sullen spectators. But frankly, it's a lot easier to play in front of folks who are cheering for you. So go wild for your team. It really does help—more than you can imagine.

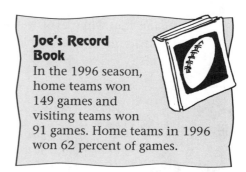

Joe's Record Book
In the 1996 season, home teams won 149 games and visiting teams won 91 games. Home teams in 1996 won 62 percent of games.

Scheduling

Football is full of pageantry and spectacle. Sunday afternoons in the fall are sun-drenched affairs of competitive fire. Games start at 1 p.m. or 4 p.m. Eastern Time. Professional football and Sunday afternoons are a perfect fit.

But one game a week is played on Sunday night at 8, and one game a week is played on Monday night at 9. On rare occasions, the NFL will give you a Thursday or Saturday game as a bonus.

When the game is played in prime time, the television audience is bigger. The game is bigger. The Monday night game is special—usually with the atmosphere of a playoff game. Players know that the biggest audience of the week is watching, as well as their peers. Although professional football is show business anyway, the Monday night game has taken on a special glitz.

Joe's Record Book
In the first Monday night game in 1970, the Cleveland Browns beat the New York Jets 31-21.

The game was originally known for its three announcers—Don Meredith, Frank Gifford, and Howard Cosell—as it was for the game. Now, the ABC broadcast opens with a rockin' Hank Williams, Jr. song, and the nation sets aside Monday nights to focus in on two football teams. They are always good teams because the NFL only schedules teams that did well the previous year for Monday night games. If you are scheduled for Monday night, you have already been rewarded for being a good team. If you win on Monday night, America sees. Players are very aware of that.

Sixteen Games, Then What?

When the season is over, there is a playoff tournament in which the teams that qualify for the tournament are matched up against other teams that qualify. Games are played. Whichever team wins gets to play again. When a team loses in the playoffs, its season is over.

Teams that win playoff games play against each other. This continues until there are only two teams left—a champion of the NFC and one of the AFC—and they meet in the Super Bowl.

Joe's Grid Iron Talk
A *wild-card team* is one that qualifies for the playoffs without winning its division. The three best non-division winners in each conference qualify as wild-card teams.

Six teams in each conference (AFC and NFC) make the playoffs. The winner of each division (East, Central, and West) makes the playoffs, and then three *wild-card teams* also play. Teams with the best win-loss record in their division win their division.

The two division winners with the best records in each conference get a week off before they must play a game. The first week of the playoffs is called the wild-card round, and it includes all three wild-card teams plus the division winner that had the worst record of the three division winners. The two division winners that had the best records in each conference get a *bye,* meaning they do not have to play that first week of the playoffs. They are rewarded for a suberb regular season by not having to risk elimination in the first round of the playoffs. And they are further rewarded by getting to play their first game at home—each against the winner of one of the games from the wild card round.

Each conference sends one team to the Super Bowl. There are two weeks between the conference championship game and the Super Bowl. Follow this chart to see how teams get to the Super Bowl.

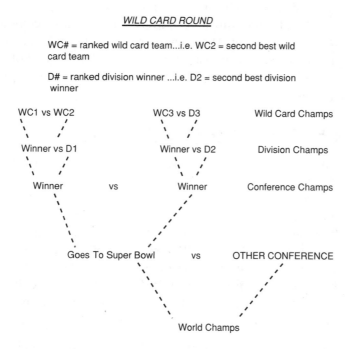

WILD CARD ROUND

WC# = ranked wild card team...i.e. WC2 = second best wild card team

D# = ranked division winner ...i.e. D2 = second best division winner

Getting to the Super Bowl—both conferences send one team. This is how each conference does it.

If there are ties at the end of the regular season, and this is very possible because it is only a 16-week season, there is an elaborate system of tie-breaking rules. For instance, if two teams tied for the championship of a division, nine steps would be taken until a champion is determined. Those nine steps are:

1. Head-to-head (best win-loss percentage in games between the clubs).

2. Best win-loss-tie percentage within games played in the division.

3. Best win-loss-tie percentage in games played within the conference.

4. Best win-loss-tie percentage in common games, if applicable.

Joe's Gridiron Talk
Strength of schedule refers to the record from the previous year of the current year's opponents. For instance, a team with six opponents that made the playoffs the previous year probably has a tougher schedule than a team facing only two teams that were in the playoffs the previous year. It is based on the win-loss record of all opponents.

5. Best net points in division games.

6. Best net points in all games.

7. Strength of schedule.

8. Best net touchdowns in all games.

9. Coin toss.

There are similar rules for breaking a three-way tie within a division, to break a tie for a wild card spot, and a procedure for breaking a tie between three or more clubs for a wild card spot. The rules are not exactly the same, but they are close. If your team finds itself tied at the end of the season, any local sports page will detail the entire procedure.

Jack Up the Intensity Level for the Playoffs

Now you know the math of how a team gets to the playoffs and the Super Bowl. But football ain't math. Football is passion and that becomes increasingly clear as each week of the playoffs goes on. Players and coaches like to talk about *intensity level* and how it goes up in the playoffs. Intensity level? Well, it's sort of *"How hard do you try?"* but it's more surreal. Every player (well, almost every player) already tries as hard as they can on every play of every game. So intensity level isn't really how hard you try. The best way to describe intensity level is not the level of effort, but rather the level of desire—*"How bad do you want it?"* No matter how bad you think you want it ("it" being the Super Bowl championship—there is no other "it") in week one of the season, you want it more when you get close. The closer you get, the more you can taste it. The intensity level goes up.

On the field, this means the holes a quarterback is throwing into are a little smaller. The holes a running back is trying to run through close a little quicker, and the tackling is a little harder. Everything is a bit more ferocious. *"How bad do I want it? Watch this."*

Of course, in the playoffs, there is such a finality to every game. Losers go home. I think the best week of the season is the week of the AFC Championship Game and the NFC Championship Game. I think those games are even better than the Super Bowl. All year, every team aims to get to the Super Bowl. Rare teams aim from the beginning to win it, but all teams aim to get there. That's why the week of the conference championships are so intense. Taste it? Good grief, one more game. One more win. So close, yet your opponent is guaranteed to be a strong team on a good run. It's almost silly—crazy, absolutely overwhelmingly insane that you could get this far and end up with nothing. But it happens—happens to half the teams that get there. Want it? Gimme a ring, a ring that goes to champions.

You want the world to know that, this year, there was no one better than our team. Want it? By the time you get to the conference championship games, you ache for it. Winners of conference championships go the Super Bowl. The winners of the Super Bowl have nothing more to do except sit at the summit in perfect bliss.

Joe's Record Book
The NFL gives Super Bowl Champion teams an allotment of $4,000 for each Super Bowl ring produced.

The Super Bowl

At the end of it all, it comes down to one game. It is not like other sports that play a best-of-seven championship series. In football's championship, there are no second chances. There is one game, one super game.

The AFC champs play the NFC champs at a neutral site—usually in a warm-weather city, but occasionally in a dome in cold weather. The Super Bowl is supposed to be played in perfect conditions.

It is a surreal event—bigger than the imagination. To give you an idea of how big it is, there is nothing to compare it to—it is the standard for events. The Super Bowl is a moniker that is used for other events. It is, in fact, the Super Bowl of football games. Get it? It's *that* big.

Joe's Record Book
The name *Super Bowl* was invented by Kansas City Chief's owner Lamar Hunt, who saw his daughter bouncing a hard rubber ball called a "Super Ball," and he thought the name was fascinating and could be changed slightly to represent the greatest game in football. He was right.

Each player on the winning team receives a ring. And the team gets the best trophy in the world, the Vince Lombardi Trophy—a regulation silver football mounted in a kicking position on a pyramid-like stand of three concave sides. It weighs 6.7 pounds and stands 20 ¾ inches tall. When it's yours, its even more beautiful. A Super Bowl ring and the Vince Lombardi Trophy look like the following illustration.

For the past 13 years, the NFC has won the Super Bowl. NFC teams seem to usually come in with a more physical team that is better at running the football and stopping the run. AFC teams usually seem to arrive at the Super Bowl with a marquee quarterback but not as much balance as NFC teams.

*A Super Bowl ring
and the Vince
Lombardi Trophy.*

The game is bizarre to both teams. Professional football has a show business aspect to it anyway, but the Super Bowl is off the charts. Players who normally talk to a dozen or so members of the media from their hometown are suddenly besieged by 1,500 or so reporters. Every one of them wants to ask the same questions and it can wear on them. But it is also exciting, tremendously exciting.

Joe's Record Book
The last NFC quarterback to lose a Super Bowl was some guy named Joe Theismann in January 1984.

In the middle of the two weeks leading to the Super Bowl, it can be hard to remember that you are there to play a football game. Coaches basically say to players, "Enjoy it, it's a special time in your life, but don't lose focus on why you're here." They know the tempations are great. All the world is watching, and everybody is in love with you. It can be hard to keep a clear head. But at the end of those two weeks, there *is* a game, the biggest game. The results of it can change your life. That's not a small thing.

The Least You Need to Know

➤ The NFL is divided into two conferences and three divisions in each conference. One team from each conference meets in the Super Bowl.

➤ Each team plays 16 games per season, two against each team in its division. Most games are played on Sundays, but there is one game a week on Monday night, which has a playoff-type atmosphere because the television audience is so big.

➤ The intensity level of playoff games goes up because the closer a team gets to the Super Bowl, the more they want to get there.

➤ The Super Bowl is so big that lives can change based on what happens for three hours in January.

The Business
of the Game

There is more than sports in the sports pages these days. There is money—a king's ransom that can warp perspective and has turned the boys' game known as football into a high-finance venture for everyone involved. Money hasn't ruined football. It has only changed it, and the changes have been, and continue to be, significant.

Professional football is a business. Although the fans don't see their money after they spend it on football, they hear about where the money goes. It is almost impossible not to know how much money players are making, and how much owners are making. This chapter will talk about the business of the game, describing a bit about the collective bargaining agreement between players and owners, the salary cap and how it works, free agency and its effect on teams, and the biggest source of revenue—television. In addition, it will touch on the recent trend of team free agency, in which teams actually move from one city to another in search of more dollars. You won't get paid to read this chapter, but you shouldn't skip it because it contains critical perspective to the modern game.

The Collective Bargaining Agreement— to Know It Is to Love It

There is a big pie of football money out there. Tickets, luxury boxes, television, souvenirs— big pie. When there is a big pie, everybody wants a piece, and there can and will be arguments about money. Thus, there must be a way to split the money that will satisfy everyone. Okay, I'm not an idiot. I know that no agreement can satisfy everyone, but the idea is to at least come as close as possible to satisfying everyone in order to play the games to grow the pie.

The way the NFL splits the pie is with a *collective bargaining agreement* (CBA), which is essentially a union contract between the NFL and the players that gives the players a certain amount of the revenue from the game. It is distributed via a salary cap—keep reading. The length of every CBA is different. The length of the contract is just one of many things that is negotiated. The CBA sets minimum salary levels for players. There are so many different elements that are covered in the CBA, we would need at least two or three more books to give you a complete picture. And just so you know, each year an agent or a team comes up with a new way to try to beat the cap. This stuff is as boring to players as it is to fans, except that it involves their financial futures. Are you bored by matters concerning your financial future?

How Many Superstars Fit in the Salary Cap? It's a Riddle

Every team is given a certain amount of money to spend every year on player salaries. The amount for 1997 is $41.45 million. Nowadays, the salary cap rules the NFL. If a team is good and is full of good players, it will not be able to keep all of them because they will simply demand salaries that are too high.

The idea of the salary cap is to prevent teams with greater financial resources (such as numerous luxury boxes) from spending exorbitant amounts of money and getting all the best players. The salary cap, in theory, evens the playing field.

Teams must be selective. They cannot spend as much as they want, even if they have it and are willing to spend it, because the NFL legislates how much teams may spend for players. The reason is that the league wants to keep teams on a equal plane. If one team spends $70 million, goes the thinking, and another only spends $20 million for player salaries, chances are that the team with the high payroll will have much higher quality players.

Thus, the salary cap. If a team wants to be stupid with its money (and many are), it cannot spend more than a team that wants to be smart. The key nowadays is to spend smart: Deciding which superstar can you afford, and which can be shown the door. Every team faces the same questions. Smart ones win, and those that aren't as smart find themselves with a few overpriced players that they thought were superstars but really weren't. The key for any team in managing the salary cap is the *capologist*.

The salary cap is a complicated matter that could be the subject of an entire book. I believe there are about four people in the world who completely understand it. I am not one of them and, trust me, you don't want to be one of them either. The salary cap is not really about sports. This is accounting stuff that, unfortunately, matters.

> **Joe's Gridiron Talk**
>
> The *capologist* is the person on an NFL team who is in charge of managing the salary cap. This person is a math whiz who helps the team figure what it can spend on players. Every team knows that one player could make a difference. In the 1990s, the capologist is as important as the general manager or coach.

But you should realize that there are loopholes that the good teams have figured out how to exploit. Consider a team that signs a star player to a contract for five years at $25 million. As part of the contract, the team could give that player a $10 million signing bonus. That player receives the bonus money on the day he signs the contract. Now, you would think that a $10 million chunk would put quite a dent in the $41.45 million cap. One player simply cannot take up 25 percent of a team's total salary. But the rules allow teams to spread the bonus over the length of the contract. So, a player who is given a $10 million bonus in a five-year contract would only count $2 million per year against the salary cap. That's a simple loophole, and there are more that I'm not going into here. If you want to know more about the loopholes in the cap, you should talk to one of those four people who know it. Then again, it may be more fun to watch grass grow.

The capologist today is more important than the coach or the general manager. He tells the team which players it can and cannot afford. The capologist is a magician, able to do infinite things with a finite number.

Loopholes? Yes, dealing with the cap is like dealing with the Internal Revenue Service. The IRS gives you ways to keep your money if you research it. The capologist, like a good accountant, studies his documentation and looks for loopholes. The accountant studies the tax code. The capologist studies the CBA. Teams find ways. They seem to always find ways.

Look. The cap doesn't work. Like everything else in football, there are creative people who have figured out a way to get around it. Someone is always going to find a way to circumvent it because there are people who are paid good money to figure exactly that.

Free Agency Isn't Free

If someone offers you more money to stay in the same job but switch companies, you would probably do it. If you did, you would be a free agent.

Joe's Rules

A *transition player* is a designation given to a player who is one of the best at his position. He must receive at least a salary equal to or greater than the average salary of the top 10 players at his position from the past season. When he becomes a free agent, his old club may match any offer given by another club. Every season, his salary must equal or exceed the average salary of the top ten players at his position. If the club doesn't offer that money, he loses his transition status and automatically becomes a free agent.

A *franchise player* is one who the team designates as its most important player. There are actually two types of franchise players. Teams only get one slot for a franchise player but can choose to use either designation. An *exclusive* franchise player cannot sign with another club. An exclusive franchise player must be offered a minimum of the average of the top five salaries at his position as of April 14, or 120 percent of his previous salary—whichever is greater. If, however, a player is only offered at least the average of the top five salaries *from last season*, he is a mere franchise player and can negotiate with other clubs. If he receives a higher offer, the old club can match the offer or it can receive two first-round Draft choices as compensation if it decides not to match the offer.

Clubs may elect to forgo using the franchise player. In that case, they are awarded one extra transition player slot.

The slots can only be used during the term of the CBA. In other words, if a team decides to release a transition player, it is not given another one. It can only name three during the term of the current CBA.

Free agency simply means that a player can offer his services to any team in the league. Usually, but not always, a player will sell his services to the highest bidder. Under the current CBA, there are two different types of free agents—restricted and unrestricted.

A restricted free agent is a player who has completed three seasons as a player in the NFL, and his contract has expired. He may offer his services to any team, but his team has a right to match any offer. In other words, if a player has finished playing three years and his contract expires, he can sell his services on the market. If he signs an offer sheet with a new club, his former club can match the offer and he will remain with his former club. If the old club does not match the offer, he becomes a member of the new club, but the old club may receive draft choice compensation.

An unrestricted free agent is a player who has played four or more seasons in the NFL, and his contract has expired. He is free to sign with any club, and his former club does not have the right to match the offer. The former club bids for him just like every other team.

Clubs can protect themselves from losing their superstars by designating three *transition players* and one *franchise player* over the course of the current CBA.

Different Kinds of Money— Defined Gross Revenues

Players receive, through the salary cap system, 62 percent of the NFL's *defined gross revenue* (DGR) which includes a number of items, as well as percentages of items. For instance, DGR includes all gate receipts from the games, the money from the television contract, 75 percent of luxury box money, and 75 percent of money from NFL Properties. That money equals the salary cap of $41.45 million that each of the 30 teams spend. Television is the largest chunk of money going into defined gross revenue.

Some money, such as 25 percent of luxury box money, is not counted towards the cap.

Joe's Record Book
The most recent set of television contracts with all the networks broadcasting games (ESPN, TNT, NBC, and Fox) is more than $1 billion per year. When Fox purchased the NFC package of games in 1993, it ended 38 consecutive years that CBS had carried NFC or NFL games.

Television—Football's Meal Ticket

I dare you to name anything that was more made for television than football. It is perfect. Full-contact gladiators. Two teams wearing uniforms and armor. Imagine. Uniforms. Right on your TV, face-to-face. Bang! They even put numbers on them.

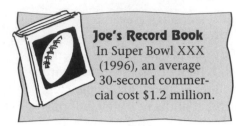

Joe's Record Book
In Super Bowl XXX (1996), an average 30-second commercial cost $1.2 million.

Football is the perfect television sport and absolutely everyone associated with the game understands this. That's right, everyone *gets it* when it comes to television because television is a large fountain of money for the NFL. You know why? Because you and I and everyone we know loves football. We all watch and the folks who want to sell us stuff understand this.

How Money Has Changed the Game

Athletes are commodities. They are not human beings any more, and there is no way to treat a $4 million player the same as a $400,000 player. The investment is different. Despite every intention to treat everyone on a team the same, it is inevitable that a team will have a star system. Stars win. Wins bring in money. Stars are treated differently.

For instance, if a $4-million-a-year player bangs up his knee a little, the team will take precautionary measures to make sure that he is okay. The investment will be protected. He may rest. But if a $400,000-a-year player bangs up his knee, the team will tape it, shoot it up with some cortisone and send him back on the field. *"Go earn your money, kid."* Teams want to know they can get their pound of flesh for the money that has been paid.

Joe's Rules

Superstars make millions of dollars per year, equaling hundreds of thousands per week. But their pay actually goes down come playoff time. In 1997, the division winner in the wild-card round received $15,000 per player. Players from the three wild-card teams received $10,000. Players on teams that played in the next round (the divisional round) each received $15,000, and for the conference championship, they received $30,000. The champions of the Super Bowl each receive $48,000, and the Super Bowl losers receive $30,000.

The championships are not for money (although a championship is worth money in endorsements and future contracts). A superstar could be making $350,000 per week during the season, but only earns $48,000 if he wins the week of the Super Bowl. Playoffs are about pride, desire. After all the money, it still comes down to, *"How good are you and how bad do you want it?"*

Stars are treated differently, and that is not unfair. Sure, coaches want to have rules for everyone, but stars know that if they produce on the field they can break a rule and there isn't anything anyone can do about it. That's the way of football. Usually, stars don't cause problems. They understand what it takes to produce at the highest possible levels. It is the marginal players who have caused teams trouble. They struggle sometimes with discipline because they just don't understand the price that must be paid in order to be great.

A classic example of money making a difference occurred during the off-season between 1996 and 1997 when the Houston Oilers traded Chris Chandler to the Atlanta Falcons for a couple of 1997 draft picks. In 1996, Chandler had his best year as a pro, throwing for 16 touchdown passes and 11 interceptions, but he was let go because the Oilers wanted to have a hotshot young quarterback, Steve McNair, who was drafted very high. Even though McNair could probably benefit from watching Chandler play one more year, he will be forced into service in 1997 because the Oilers simply can't justify paying him hotshot money (a lot) and having him sit on the bench. He is making too much money. They have to get him in the game.

Joe's Record Book
One player can make a difference. Cornerback Deion Sanders signed a free agent contract with the San Francisco 49ers for the 1994-95 season, and that year the 49ers won Super Bowl XXIX. The next year, Sanders signed a free agent contract with the Dallas Cowboys and that year the Cowboys won Super Bowl XXX.

Another example of how money has changed the game happened in New England in the 1996 draft. At the time, Patriots owner, Robert Kraft, had just signed young hotshot quarterback Drew Bledsoe to a seven-year, $42-million contract. At the time of the draft, the Patriots held the seventh pick. There was a disagreement as to who to pick. Patriots coach Bill Parcells wanted to draft a defensive lineman. Patriots general manager Bobby Grier wanted to draft a wide receiver, specifically the speedy Terry Glenn of Ohio State. The owner stepped in. Kraft sided with his general manager, because, among other reasons, his $42-million quarterback needed a superstar receiver to catch his passes. It proved to be a brilliant move. The Patriots, who were 6-10 in 1995 without Glenn, went to the Super Bowl in 1996 with him. Nevertheless, money played a part in the move.

There Used to Be a Team Called the Cleveland Browns

These days, you need a program to keep track of the teams from year to year, not just to keep track of the players and coaches. Money, of course is the culprit. The astronomical sums of money that the players and, now, the owners can get by moving to a different city has made professional football a different kind of game. It's still exciting, but a bit of the long-term sentiment has disappeared. It is sad, because the fans are still loyal.

Here are the list of teams that have moved since 1983. One team, the Raiders, moved twice.

➤ The Baltimore Colts became the Indianapolis Colts

➤ The Oakland Raiders became the Los Angeles Raiders

➤ The St. Louis Cardinals became the Arizona Cardinals

➤ The Los Angeles Raiders became the Oakland Raiders

➤ The Los Angeles Rams became the St. Louis Rams

➤ The Cleveland Browns became the Baltimore Ravens

➤ The Houston Oilers are moving to Nashville in 1998

The most shocking move was when the Browns announced their move to Baltimore. Art Modell, the owner of the team, needed a new stadium (with luxury boxes) to compete for players. The city of Cleveland didn't provide one fast enough and Baltimore came in with a great offer.

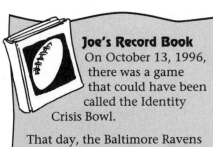

Joe's Record Book
On October 13, 1996, there was a game that could have been called the Identity Crisis Bowl.

That day, the Baltimore Ravens (formerly the Cleveland Browns) played the Indianapolis Colts (formerly the Baltimore Colts). The coach of the Ravens was Ted Marchibroda, who the previous year coached the Indianapolis Colts. Previously, Marchibroda also coached the Baltimore Colts.

The Indianapolis Colts beat the Baltimore Ravens 26-21. And that made fans in Cleveland happy.

Browns fans were very loyal, and very upset. Cleveland had consistently had the highest television ratings of any NFL city. Just 40 miles from the birthplace of professional football (Canton, Ohio), Cleveland looked upon its football team as a sort of religion. Rabid cannot begin to describe what fans there were like on Sundays. And heartbroken cannot begin to describe how they felt when the team moved.

But maybe something good came from the move. It has brought some economic stability to the league, as a number of teams have found stadium deals that can keep them financially sound. The NFL has even cut a deal with the city of Cleveland. The city is building a new stadium (with luxury boxes) and the NFL will put another team in Cleveland by 1999. It may be a team moving, or it may be an expansion team. It will definitely be called the Cleveland Browns. To all the folks in Cleveland who dressed up in dog masks and barked like maniacs at me when I played, I say to them, we can't wait to have you back. From me to you, *woof!*

Money on the Outside—Gambling

Let's see. How can I put this? You can bet some folks are gambling. Look in almost any newspaper every week and you will find the *latest line,* which is a compilation of what Las Vegas oddsmakers have guessed will be the winning margin of each game. One team is favored to win by a certain number of points. The number of points that one team is favored to win by is called the *point spread.* So if Dallas is favored to beat Tampa Bay by 11 points, the point spread is 11. If they win by more than 11—also called covering the spread—they not only win the game, but they win the bet as well. If they win by less than 11, or actually lose the game, they lose the bet. Bets are made on this stuff.

The NFL does not condone gambling. Professional football players are not allowed to gamble. Period.

But folks gamble. The Super Bowl is the biggest gambling day of the year, and on that day you can bet on virtually anything. You can bet the over/under on how many catches a certain person will have. In other words, if the over/under is 5, you are betting the player will either catch more than 5 passes, or less than 5. You can obviously bet who will win the game, how many points will be scored by each team in a quarter, or even who will win the coin toss. Some of the bets that Las Vegas casinos take are funny:

➤ In Super Bowl XXXI, bettors could bet that Brett Favre minus 115 yards would have more passing yards than Tiger Woods has total strokes in the Phoenix Open. In other words, you could take Brett Farve's total passing yardage, subtract 115, and bet it would exceed Woods' total strokes.

➤ Also in Super Bowl XXXI, bettors could wager on whether the Green Bay Packers (plus 3 points) would score more points than the Packers scored in the first Super Bowl, when they beat the Kansas City Chiefs 35-10.

➤ In Super Bowl XXX, bettors could bet whether Michael Jordan would score more points against the Phoenix Suns than the Dallas Cowboys would score against the Pittsburgh Steelers.

Gambling is interesting and it heightens the interest in the game of football. There is no denying it. Fans even follow games that do not involve their favorite team if they have a little wager on the game. It's not a secret. Although the NFL wants nothing to do with gambling, it grudgingly acknowledges it exists.

How expert are these *bookmakers* (gambling statisticians)? You'd be surprised. They study football like astronomers study the sky. They do in-depth statistical analyses of everything possible (things like home wins on cold-weather days versus West Coast teams with left-handed quarterbacks), and then somehow come up with a number for the point spread.

I am amazed at how good they are. A great example of this was Super Bowl XXXI when the Green Bay Packers were favored to beat the New England Patriots by 14 points. The Packers beat the Patriots 35-21.

Bookmakers are usually close to the score, but not always. They are wrong enough to make it interesting. Their most famous wrong guess was Super Bowl III, when the power-house Baltimore Colts were favored by 19 points to beat Joe Namath's New York Jets. Namath was insulted and guaranteed victory. And then he delivered, and the Jets won 16-7, costing a lot of bettors a lot of money, and making a lot for a bunch of others.

Pools

Your place of work may have a *pool* from week to week, in which everyone who wants bets a dollar or two and picks every game against the point spread. Whoever has the most games right wins all the money entered. The tie-breaker is usually picking the score of the Monday night game. These pools can be fun and you don't need to know a lot to make guesses. Football outcomes are not hard science. The ball is shaped weirdly, anything can happen. Folks have been known to win pools based on theories such as *"I'd rather live in this city than that one,"* or *"I like the colors of this team's uniforms more than the color of the other team's uniforms."*

There are also pools at Super Bowl time. These can get complex and innovative. One of the most usual ones is when folks pick the final score. Another has people picking the scores by quarter. These give fans like you an extra reason to watch the game.

900 Lines

On television, you will see shows in which professional gamblers come on telling you of their sure-fire way to win at betting football games. I am a bit skeptical, but these guys are amusing. *"This is the deal of the century and you've gotta call right now."* There is always a charge to make the call.

Look, I have seen cats pick games on television. Horses, too. And dogs. I have seen games picked by fish who "decide" who they think is going to win by swimming through a hole labeled for a team. I figure, if that fish had a 900 line, it would get some people to think it is an expert, too.

If you need to gamble so much that you will call a 900 line for expert advice, you may want to think about whether gambling is really having a good effect on your life. But then, I've never called a 900 line. What do I know?

The Least You Need to Know

➤ The collective bargaining agreement (CBA) is a union contract between the players and the League. The CBA has instituted a salary cap that allows each team to spend $41.45 million per year on players' salaries.

➤ Television provides the biggest piece of the financial pie (NFL revenue). The NFL uses 62 percent of its revenues to pay players.

➤ Teams can be free agents just like players. Both move for the same reason—someone or some city is offering more money to go there.

➤ NFL players can't gamble, but fans can.

➤ A point spread is the amount of points an oddsmaker in Las Vegas has determined one team should beat another by.

Chapter 24

Television and the Media: The Show about the Show

Some folks say the 1950s were the Golden Age of television. I say football is the Golden Event of television. The role of television is to entertain, and there is nothing more entertaining than the colorful clash that is football. But gosh, football is everywhere. Not just on television. Everywhere! Look around. It's on this network, that network, this cable station, that magazine, the local newspaper, and talk radio. Everyone everywhere has something to say about the game. Even I (yes, shy old me) have been known to throw an opinion around from time to time. Television and football? Heck, just like Mom and apple pie.

This is a chapter about the relationship of media to football, and how television especially is a force bigger than any quarterback, coach, game plan, or anything. Television rules. This chapter will explain the various characters on a broadcast and their jobs, the pre-game and post-game shows, the print media, talk radio, and the changing relationship of players to the media. Oh, by the way, this chapter is just another part of the media about football. That's right, the media of football is so big it extends all the way to this chapter. Right now, you are in the middle of the media of football. There is no escape, so you may as well enjoy it.

Made for Television

Imagine what it would be like to be a professional football player. That's television's role. It serves as your imagination. The camera is so intimate that it can take you inside a player's

Joe's Record Book
There are 56 30-second commercials that air during every 60-minute football game.

world, which most people don't get to experience. It gives you the opportunity through pictures and sound to be able to hear the power and see the speed and sense all the things that make up the game of football: the intense hits, the leaping acrobatics, and the moves that defy physiology. Television is up close, immediate. You feel the emotions, the momentum swings, the ebb and flow of the game. And in between, you watch commercials.

And you stick around, because you know that at the snap of the ball, 22 people will be interacting in a perfect moment of television. Football works on the screen because of what it is—a competitive battle of power, speed, and intelligence. The colors help. The motion and athleticism really do work like poetry on the screen. The rectangle of the field works on the box of the screen. The camera focuses on a 20-or-so-yard chunk of yardage around the LOS. The snap of the ball. It all starts. You should see it.

There's No Business Like Show Business

The hype of football is a full-time, year-round event. Even in April, there is the draft, a marathon session that occurs three months after the Super Bowl and four months before the beginning of the new season. And folks watch. There is no game, just players being picked; the power of potential still seems to roar onto the screen. Dreams are made on Draft Day. What will this guy look like in your uniform?

And that's just April. As the season gets closer, the media likes to take you into the world of the football players. Who are these people? What is their personality? What makes them tick? Society in general is becoming more celebrity oriented and the National Football League is no different. We in the media have a job, and that job is to make sure that the players who have been busting butt to make themselves stars actually become stars. They perform on the field. We let you meet them. The machine churns out stars.

When their acts and actions are exemplary, announcers bring light to it. If a guy makes a catch and the announcer says, "I want to tell you something. Let's look at that again because I want to show you how good of a catch that really is," he has just given that player a higher profile. Soon, a fan will turn to his friend, and say "Did you see what a great catch that receiver made?"

We in the media can influence phrases. For instance, in 1997, it is impossible to go very long without hearing the phrase, "Show me the money," from the movie, *Jerry Maguire*.

> **Joe's Tips**
> Players are media savvy. My friend, Chris Berman, who is known for making up nicknames that play on a player's real name, will actually receive letters from players suggesting a good nickname for themselves. For instance (and this is fictitious), a player named Lionel Train may write suggesting he be called "Choo Choo." Everyone wants more notoriety.

The Other Side of "Up"

Today, the media is in great competition and football players have to deal with it because that competition directly affects their lives. The cult of personality that surrounds superstar football players is a two-edged sword. The rewards of fame are great. But the other side of being up is if something goes wrong. The machine that loves to build up players into icons is equally happy to tell the world about them driving five miles over the speed limit. Everything is scrutinized. The essential rule of fame is, *"Don't have a bad day."*

For this reason, many players have become less cooperative with the media. They don't need the media as much as players from the past, and thus, they want their privacy. Just as the media wants more from the players, the players want to give less to the media. It used to be that players would use the media in order to get their names known. Players wanted to become celebrities because they wanted endorsements in order to make more money. But players make so much money now that they are more interested in maintaining their privacy. Many players tire of repetitive questions from the media.

> **Joe's Tips**
> A stupid question isn't always a stupid question. For instance, a reporter may ask an older player, who is an incredible physical specimen, what he had for breakfast. The player may wonder what his breakfast has to do with football. The reporter may just be wondering if his diet has anything to do with his longevity and physical shape. Sometimes stupid questions don't seem as stupid when you stop and think about them.

Further, not all players understand the media or its role. Some players think the media is just there to serve them. And although, in large part, the media is there specifically to make players stars, it serves a larger purpose. The media's job is to inform people about the players, the teams, and the games. Sometimes, the players will like the information that the media shares with the public. Sometimes, players aren't going to like it. And that's the truth.

The Pre-Game Show—Get Ready, Get Set...

The hype hits a peak about an hour before the first games on Sunday. That's when the pre-game shows start. There are, at last count, four pre-game shows on national television, and those don't count all the local ones that are on across the country. The idea of the pre-game show is to get the fans information about their favorite team, their favorite player, and other players and teams from across the country.

Pre-game shows analyze the matchups, too. Things are put in perspective: player versus player; team versus team; a glance at the history; the meaning of the game. The pre-game show is the time for some of the best journalism in football. Reporters are given time to develop stories, and yet it is all put in the perspective of the immediacy of today's game.

The game is broken down, sometimes to the point of matchups, of player against player. A wide receiver against a specific cornerback. The analysts on the show will tell you why they think one player will have a good game. They will back up their opinion with videotape. And then they will let you draw your own conclusions.

The analysts can draw up the favorite play of a team, or give fans a checklist of things to watch for during the game. The pre-game show will probably give weather reports from around the country, and it will focus on any key injuries. The idea of the pre-game show is to get you ready to watch football.

Sure, I admit a bias here. I work on a pre-game show, and I think it's great. But then, I like anytime anyone is talking football. I especially like it when I get to talk about football. So pull up a barstool. Let me tell you about today's game.

The Game Is On

Football works on television because it feels like you are there. You become so emotionally involved in watching these folks, who are themselves emotionally involved, that you forget for moments at a time that you are merely watching television.

Your man takes the kickoff, heads up the middle, and suddenly the wedge springs him loose at just the right moment as he heads up the right sideline in a race with the other team's kicker. C'mon, this is better than television. Right up the sideline, legs churning—daring that little kicker to try and tackle him. How cool is this?

The announcer tells you *"He...could...go...all...the...way!"* (credit that to my good friend, Chris Berman).

The Post-Game Show—What Happened

Highlights and scores. The post-game shows are not about personalities. They are about performances. It is wrap up—a quick analysis. *"Here is what happened, and you've got to see this play."*

Who Are Those Folks on TV?

Journalists, ex-athletes, and ex-coaches get together on all the shows I just described and talk football. Each brings a different perspective, and the perspective changes from year to year. An ex-athlete will get a new perspective as a member of the media.

I believe ex-athletes have a good perspective to add because we have been there. We know the tolerance an athlete has for questions. We know the ecstasy, the pain. Yet we are all different. One ex-player is not necessarily going to have the same opinion as another. We offer our perspectives. And then you watch and can agree or disagree. That's why football is so much fun. At the water cooler on Monday, you can turn to your friend and say, *"Can you believe what Joe Theismann said yesterday?"*

Joe's Record Book
One of the networks tried broadcasting a game with no announcers. It was generally regarded as unwatchable.

Play-by-Play—The Meat and Potatoes

A game broadcast will usually have either two or three broadcasters, and one of them will be the *play-by-play broadcaster*. His job (it's almost always a man) is to describe the action. That's all. He will tell you the situation (down and distance), keep you apprised of the time, and mention other key statistics that arise as the game goes on. He is supposed to do this in a conversational tone because the idea of football commentary is for it to feel like the announcers are in your living room, sharing their thoughts with you.

The Color Analysts—Why That Happened and Not Something Else

There are many factors that go into every play, and it is the color analyst's job to explain those factors. The *color analyst* is usually someone who was associated with the game, as a player or a coach. I am a color analyst, and when I do the job, I think it is my job to help teach the game. The idea is to do it in a conversational, fun manner. Analysts also get to draw on a *telestrator* to demonstrate what just happened.

> **Joe's Gridiron Talk**
>
> A *telestrator* is a tool with which an announcer can draw right over the action on a replay. If a receiver runs a post pattern, for instance, the announcer can draw out the direction of the post pattern on the telestrator.

With or without a telestrator, analysts try to explain what happened and why it happened. For instance, if a pass was just completed, the analyst examines it and quickly explains his take on what happened. Was it a good drop by the quarterback? Was it good blocking by the offensive line or a poor rush by the defensive line? Was there a good move by the wide receiver? Did he have has hands out or did he catch the ball with his body? Every single pass, there is all that to analyze and more. The analyst helps the fan understand the action better.

A good color analyst has knowledge of the game, knowledge of the players, and the ability to communicate in a succinct manner. There are times when an analyst just has to shut up. I know when I've talked too much. Hey, it happens. When it does, I take a play or two off and let the action catch up. Unless there is a big play, I will be quiet for a while. Color analysts say a lot by saying nothing sometimes.

Sideline Reporters—Eyewitness News

Sideline reporters take you behind the scenes, as close to the team as possible. Although many cut-aways to sideline reporters are for trivial information, the sideline reporter serves an essential role in key situations. Every once in a while, something will happen that requires instantaneous information. It is in those times that the sideline reporter is crucial. If there is an injury, the sideline reporter can find out about it right away. If there is an argument between a coach and a player, the sideline reporter may even hear it. The sideline reporter is there for quick information. Usually, a broadcast will have a sideline reporter with each team.

The Camera Takes You There

Hey, I can talk all I want, but if you can't see what I see then you're not going to care. Television is pictures. You have to see the plays, and a network broadcast of an NFL game will give you many different camera angles.

The different camera angles allow the director to display the game like a concert, letting the action dictate what cameras are used. Games have rhythms, and the television broadcasters are acutely aware of these. A cut in with a *slow-motion instant replay* of sure-handed acrobatics in the midst of a giant hit can work like a violin solo. Just sit back and enjoy.

Another trick is to use a *reverse angle* view in which you view a play from the opposite side of the field than you had been viewing the game. Let's say the game camera is behind the home team's bench. A reverse angle view would be from across the field behind the visiting teams bench. So, if you would normally see a running back running a sweep away from you, the television could cut to a reverse angle so that you see the running back coming toward you. The new angle could show how the linebacker pursued on the play in a way that the normal angles couldn't show. A reverse angle is special when it shows something different.

> **Joe's Record Book**
>
> A typical NFL broadcast will feature between 5 and 15 cameras.

> **Joe's Gridiron Talk**
>
> A *slow-motion instant replay* is a video replay of a play that is slowed down so that every instant can be analyzed. A slow-motion instant replay can make football appear to have the grace of ballet, or it can make it appear to have the impact of a demolition derby.

Newspapers and Magazines

What's better than the Monday sports page after your team wins? C'mon, how good is a winning Monday sports page? Big photographs and blaring headlines—it just doesn't get any better than that.

The print media is all part of it. The hype of football is a round-the-clock, across-all-stages show. People are interested. Football sells. Newspapers serve a different role than television. Newspapers try to be analytical, amusing us with twists of phrases about our favorite or least favorite players. Columnists, who are paid to have opinions, are the juice of the sports pages. They love you when you're winning, but I think they might have more fun ripping you when you lose.

Talk Radio

Sports-talk radio has become huge. Just a few years ago, only the major markets had any sports talk, now there are at least one, and sometimes more, all sports-talk stations in almost every city. It is a barstool conversation on the radio.

Fans call in and talk to a host or two. Often fans will vent frustrations about a team. Radio can be the most powerful medium for fans. It is so immediate that your entire concentration, even imagination, is focused on the sound. Even if you are driving, talk radio gets you involved. And the athletes now know the power of talk radio, and many players have become more defensive. Some will not appear on these shows, and many more are afraid to say anything for risk of becoming fodder for someone who has to fill four hours of air time. Callers also see talk radio as their chance in the sun. When they reach the hosts, they have the ear of the city, and they try to become celebrity callers with their wit and wisdom. Some callers at some stations inevitably do become celebrity callers.

Local and National

Your local media will have a tendency to be *homers,* meaning that they root for their home team and show it in their reporting. Either they throw softball questions or else they are too hardball in trying to show they are not homers. At the same time, local media is probably the most fun for a fan to read because these are the folks who think like you do. They *do* want the team to win. They *do* think these guys are bums when they lose. And they zing great.

The national media, big magazines, and television try to deliver football to the entire country. Their role is different. There is no rooting interest.

Players find the local media pays attention to them no matter what they do. Win or lose, the local folks are around. But the national media only notices if they are good. When a team is good, a player can actually get to the point of almost wishing they weren't quite so good so they wouldn't have to deal with so many members of the media.

Joe's Tips
A 9-7 team has probably the easiest time of any dealing with the media. A 9-7 team is successful enough to keep the wolves away but not successful enough to raise anyone's expectations.

When a team is bad, the national media may only mention it, but the local media will be in a feeding frenzy. They have to write, and there is nothing to write about but this crummy team, this crummy quarterback, this crummy coach, this crummy stadium....

At the same time, the national media can seem to brand an entire team to be troublemakers if one or two high-profile players gets in trouble. Never mind that 45 of 47 players have been model citizens. Sometimes, it only takes a couple of players to tarnish the reputation of a team.

The Least You Need to Know

➤ Football is a great television event in which a play-by-play broadcaster describes the action, a color analyst tells you why it happened, and a sideline reporter brings you breaking news from the sideline.

➤ Different camera angles can give you different perspectives on the same play.

➤ Print media have a longer time to analyze things, and columnists are paid to spout opinions.

➤ While the local media will devote as much attention to a bad team as they would a good one, the national media focuses only on the really good teams.

Part 5
The Essentials of Fandom

This final part of the book is about your job as a fan. I know, it's really not a job. Yet cheering for some teams in some years CAN put a strain on your life in ways that only a bad boss can. But most teams and most games are nothing but pure joy.

This part covers the fun of being a fan, starting with a look at different types of game gear—from officially licensed merchandise to homemade paraphernalia. This part also covers the joy of being a fan, including the art of tailgating and the fun of cheering for a team in a distant city. Finally, this part deals with rivalries, which are the essence of football—trying to beat that one team *because…well, just because.*

Chapter 25

Game Gear: What To Wear

In This Chapter

➤ The ritual of getting dressed

➤ Official gear versus homemade stuff

➤ Joe's Top Five fan outfits in no particular order

If you are a fan, you are a fan of *a particular team.* So if you are going to the game or to a party or club where people are going to watch the game, or even if you are just sitting in your own living room, you cannot help but be a fan of your team. You may, I suppose, wear work clothes if you have no choice (like, let's say, you left work to head directly to the game). Otherwise, you really have to wear clothes that somehow or other identify you with your team. You can even wear a tie, as long as the tie has your team's logo on it. But you have to go in uniform. It's not part of the NFL bylaws (and I hired a crack research team to check), but every good fan abides by it anyway because it's fun.

It can be anything, but it's gotta be something. Every fan knows. You've got a special shirt, jersey, hat, socks, earrings, bandana, jacket, something. Something with your team's colors, logo. Something lucky. It's gotta be something lucky because, after all, victory is in your hands. You dress right, your team wins. No question. No question at all.

And so that's why you have to read this chapter, which will teach you how to dress to win even if, heaven forbid, your team happens to lose. You always want to look like a winner. This chapter will help.

Here I cover official game gear, like jerseys and hats and shirts and jackets, and the art of getting ready. I also cover the various logos in the NFL and why some change and why some will never change. And, I finish by discussing the psychology (as if it needs to be analyzed) of taking off your shirt in Buffalo in mid-December, homemade outfits, and my top five original fan outfits in no particular order.

Get Ready to Watch—the Ritual

I know. See, *I know.* You fans think that we players don't know what you go through. You think we're ignorant of your Sunday ritual, that we don't care and don't understand and don't believe, but that's only what you think. *I know.*

Joe's Record Book
Superstitions differ. I used to ride to games with Redskins defensive tackle Dave Butts. On the ride, he *needed* to drive over road kill. Inevitably, we would swerve and I would hear "thump, thump" as the tires rode over a dead animal. "Gonna be a good game," Dave would say. On the other hand, I only needed a banana split on Saturday night for luck.

It is the same for the players, only they are a little closer to the action. Superstitions live. Things must be done in order. There is no explaining it, it's just *the way it has to be.*

This is like religion to some, like some sort of sacrament or trek up the mountain to the annointed land of NFL action. Sure, it may sound silly if you were talking about one of those other teams, but when it comes to *your team* nothing is silly. There is a plan. Victory is in sight.

Alarm goes off. Socks, underwear, pants, shirt, all in a neat pile. You pass the pile and go in the shower. Then you dress. It is ritual, everything in the same order, left sock, then right (if that's the order), and on and on, feeling the momentum of the day riding on your every little move. When your shoes are tied, the hat is on, and you've played the obligatory get-me-ready song of the day, you may appear in public. *And you think we don't know…oh, the things we know.*

Official Game Gear

The NFL licenses *stuff.* All sorts of stuff. Hats and jackets and jersey and shirts and socks and more. But the best is the jersey—the real thing. You want to be part of the team, you have to feel like you are part of it. The NFL wants you to be part of it, but it licenses its stuff (companies pay fees to the NFL for the right to manufacture and sell the stuff) to make sure that it gets its fair share.

One sure way to do that is to wear the jersey of your favorite player. Put on that number and you suddenly are in there with him every time he carries the ball. If you have a 22 Emmitt Smith Dallas Cowboys jersey, you bounce off tacklers when he does. You move between holes, spin around end, and fall into the end zone right along with him. If you are wearing a 13 Dan Marino Miami Dolphins jersey, you walk with a swagger because your man throws the ball better than anybody in history. That's your arm throwing for all those yards and touchdowns. Just look at the number on your chest.

Joe's Tips
If you find someone selling T-shirts from the trunk of a car, the chances are good that that stuff is not officially licensed NFL merchandise.

Players get it. The superstars, especially, understand. The ones whose jerseys you wear understand why you wear their number, and they feel pride carrying the ball for you. You are with them when they throw passes, catch passes, and sack the quarterback. They understand.

You want to be part of it. You want the players to see that you feel part of it, and the players never miss that. Players love to see fans in team jackets. The support, the feel of *team* is immense, and the connection of colors is very direct. It is pride—our colors.

Joe's Record Book
The NFL has licensed four companies to manufacture hats with NFL logos.

Plus, hats are cool. There is no other way to put it, hats are big business because every male and half the females in America seem to have a hat collection. The NFL understands, and licenses companies to put out a number of different kinds of hats per year.

Merchandising—promoting the team through a variety of products—is a big part of the game. You want your team to be good enough so you can be proud to wear the jacket. Even if they aren't good enough, you wear it anyway because they were good enough once, and they will be again. So you wear it when you travel somewhere. Yes you do. You wear your Bears jacket in Wisconson or a Cowboys coat in Washington. You let people know who you are, where you are from, and what football team represents you. Da Bears? That's right, *da Bears*.

Joe's Record Book
The top five clubs in terms of sales of merchandise are:

1. Dallas Cowboys

2. Green Bay Packers

3. San Francisco 49ers

4. Pittsburgh Steelers

5. Miami Dolphins

The NFL is a fashion show because the NFL moves merchandise. Industry newpapers have reported that the NFL moves $3 billion of merchandise a year. Logos and hats and color combinations are all researched. Certain colors (like black) always sell well. If you put black in a team uniform, you increase the chances of their merchandise being successful. Of course, the thing that sells merchandise more than anything is a winning team. Good teams are popular. Folks like to be associated with winning.

Some Logos Never Change, Some Do

How am I supposed to explain love? That's what fans feel when they see a sacred logo—and some of them have that ancient sacred feel, even though they are really not that old. Before 1950 or so, players wore leather helmets without a logo.

Joe's Record Book
Seven teams have changed their uniforms since 1987. Those teams are:

➤ Denver Broncos

➤ New England Patriots

➤ Philadelphia Eagles

➤ Tampa Bay Buccaneers

➤ San Francisco 49ers

➤ Miami Dolphins

➤ Cincinnati Bengals

Joe's Record Book
When a new logo or uniform is introduced, teams have a fashion show to introduce it. A player will usually be the model.

Still, the logos from the older, traditional teams (a few examples are the Chicago Bears and the Green Bay Packers), are things that just seem like they will never change, and hopefully never will. Yet other logos (recently the Patriots and the Broncos) have changed. Success helps sell a logo. But sometimes, a new logo represents a turning point in the history of the organization. The Patriots changed logos the same year that they changed owners and coaches. On the other hand, a change in logo could simply be a way to sell merchandise. After all, who wants to be caught in last year's logo?

Modern logos tend to have a fast back to signify motion. This means the part that faces towards the back has a curving swoopy back that narrows to a point. This is science. It is important to understand that this is not small business. This is big. Very big. How many people do you know who own merchandise from a sports team? Big business. Sports is business, and you, as a fan, are worth money.

Teams change their logos as a marketing tool. If you already have a hat of my team, you are not likely going to buy a new hat every six months. But if I change the logo and you still want to feel associated with my team, well guess what? I sell a lot of hats.

It's just business, and frankly, it's good business. Besides, some of these new logos look pretty good. A new logo gives a team a new identity, a fresh start. The Patriots' timing for changing their logo was good—at the start of a new era. It is a symbolic move that is made by ownership. To the best of my knowledge, owners don't ask players if they should change logos. Nor should they ask. They don't ask fans either. But, maybe they should.

Protect Yourself Against the Elements

Unless your team plays in a dome, you will have to at least think about weather. Hot weather requires sunglasses, sun screen, hats or visors, and cool, loose clothes. Cold weather requires layers of clothes and special attention to your extremeties. Cover your feet and hands.

Do a little scouting. Which side of the field are you sitting on—the sunny side or the shady? How do conditions differ between 1 p.m. games and 4 p.m. games. Try, if you can, to make sure you're in a seat so you can see over the person in front of you. If you are short and somebody nicknamed "Stretch" is sitting in front of you, you may want consider moving (good luck getting someone to trade with you).

Oh, and maybe I don't need to remind all of you, but be sure to drink plenty of (non-alcoholic) liquids, especially in warm weather. You don't want to become dehydrated.

Homemade Gear

True story: In 1983, a Cleveland Browns fan who transplanted to New England had no Browns gear for the upcoming Browns-Patriots game in New England. So he did what any enterprising fan would—he went to the hardware store and bought a can of orange spray paint. He painted an old white t-shirt, wrapped it around his head like a bandana and went to the game. The Browns beat the Patriots 30-0 and this fan ran through the parking lot yelling, "Can you say zero?"

Incredibly, this idiot is still alive. He helped me write this book. He still has an orange forehead.

But what this story proves (besides the fact that everyone gets lucky once in life) is that you can have just as much fun in homemade gear as you can in the expensive stuff. Remember what I taught you throughout this entire book: Football is a head game. If you believe you are having fun…well, you are.

Who Are These People?

Explaining the folks in the stands is as complex as explaining a 9-7-6 H-post swing (see Chapter 12). Perhaps it is more complex. Everybody wears *something* team related. That's established. But sometimes that *something* is something like a blue "O" painted on a bare chest. Yeah, those folks who seem to show up at every cold weather game. There is never just one of them. They travel in packs. Like our friend with the "O" on his chest could simply be the "O" in a pack that spells B-U-F-F-A-L-O B-I-L-L-S.

The guys without shirts. There are packs of them at every game. Wandering, howling, pretending to be warm. They must migrate every Sunday from chest-painting salons. We laugh. They laugh. We laugh more.

On an Arctic-cold day, you have to be insane to take your shirt off. But some folks do, and if they are not insane, they must have some excuse. My guess is they have a lot of antifreeze in their body. I would hope they have some excuse because this is not a smart thing.

Who are these people? Just folks who want to get on TV. When Andy Warhol said that everyone would get 15 minutes of fame in America, I think he had fans of NFL games precisely in mind. But I bet that Andy understood that if you wear an "O" on your chest in December in Buffalo, a camera will probably find you. See, this book includes football, zaniness, *and* the perspective of a dead icon from the world of modern art. What more could you want? Elvis? Heck, Elvis goes to a lot of the games. Elvis imitators (many singing off-key) are just part of the scenary that makes up the festival that is NFL football.

These people are more than nuts without shirts or Elvis imitators. These people are you people—me too. They include us all. We are all fans, and we are all nuts in our own way because the one thing that we all have in common is our love of the game. Whether you wear an official jersey or something homemade, the experience is essentially the same.

But not completely. You see, there are people who are a little more out there. The Elvises, the shirtless wonders. In every stadium, for instance, there are airhorns. It seems there are always only two airhorns (no more, no less), as if there is a law stating that two and only two airhorns are allowed in the stadium.

> **Joe's Record Book**
> Jerry Glanville, when he was coach of the Atlanta Falcons in the 1980s, left tickets at the gate for Elvis Presley, in the hope that the King would use them. It was never determined if Elvis used them, but it is nice to know that Jerry kept the legend alive.

> **Joe's Record Book**
> When John Riggins ran the ball for the Washington Redskins, his nickname was "the Diesel" because he was like a diesel truck running through the hole. Whenever John ran the ball, a fan would blow an airhorn. Every time. It was a moment. I'd take the snap, give John the handoff, and hear the horn. It meshed beautifully.

Joe's Top Five Original Fan Outfits

I've told you my favorite players—those who I thought were the greatest of all time. Well, I've looked in the stands too. And well, here are my favorite fan outfits.

➤ **The Hogettes.** The Hogettes are a group of a half dozen or so large men who cheer for the Washington Redskins and identify with the offensive line, which was known as the Hogs (see Chapter 8). These men, who I believe work at the Pentagon, wear dresses, flowered hats, and pig noses, and they smoke fat cigars. It gives me a sense of calm to know that these men in dresses and pig noses spend their days trying to preserve world peace.

➤ **The Dawg Pound.** The Dawgs of the Dawg Pound were a vivacious, untamed bunch. The Dawg Pound is an on-hold mythical place that is being reconstructed in Cleveland as the city awaits the rebirth of its team. The Dawg Pound originated in the 1980s when defensive backs Hanford Dixon and Frank Minnifield barked at receivers after they broke up a pass. The fans joined in the barking, and soon dog masks began appearing in the end zone section of the old Cleveland Stadium. This became known as the Dawg Pound.

➤ **The guy with the blue afro in Houston.** He is always on TV. He is famous in my mind.

➤ **Raider fans.** They come with shoulder pads with spikes sticking out of them. And then, my favorite, Darth Raider—dressed like *Star Wars* villain Darth Vader except his face is silver and black and his helmet has the Raider logo.

➤ **The 'Aints of New Orleans.** For years, the New Orleans Saints were so bad that some fans would show up with paper bags over their heads. It made a strong statement and you couldn't help (unless you were on the Saints) laughing.

The Least You Need to Know

➤ If you think that your every action on Sunday morning directly affects how your team plays on Sunday afternoon, you should know that it is true. Just kidding. But its still fun to be superstitious.

➤ Football is a fashion show and logos are designed to sell.

➤ You can make your own outfit and have lots of fun.

➤ The guys who take their shirts off at games travel in packs and often end up on TV.

Chapter 26

The Joy of Being a Fan

In This Chapter

➤ Tailgating requires a plan

➤ Fans from other cities may cross your path

➤ A story that tells you what you mean to players

One year when I played, we went on a losing streak, and the fans who once loved the Redskins seemed not to like us as much. One Sunday, after we had lost to the Philadelphia Eagles, I pulled into a full-service gas station on my way home from the stadium. It was raining. I wasn't in a good mood, but I was in public so I had to be friendly. The gas station attendant came up to the window. He immediately recognized me. "Hey, you're Joe Theismann."

"Yes I am."

"Hey, you guys are doing pretty bad these days."

"Yes we are."

"Didn't you guys lose to the Eagles today?"

"Yes."

"Pump your own gas," he said, and he walked away.

That's the passion of the fans that I have come to respect. Should fans diss players? No, of course not. But that guy at the gas station reminded me in a very personal way that my work had an emotional effect on people's lives. You folks, you fans, have a great time watching and cheering. It really is joy. That's what this chapter is about, about the joy of being a fan, from the tailgating to the challenge of rooting for your hometown team from a foreign city. It also covers how to greet fans of visiting teams, and it features a story about how much fans really matter to the players.

Tailgating Is a Profession, a Craft, and an Art

Show me the food. Show me the beverages. Show me the back of your car and a hibachi grill, and then tell me what you think of that other team's quarterback. As any football fan knows, the finest American dining can only be found in the fall in parking lots of football stadiums across the country. Talk about atmosphere.

Joe's Tips
Cheeseburgers are a delicacy served from coast to coast, from border to border, and if you have doubt as to what is the right thing to cook, you can hardly ever go wrong cooking cheeseburgers. But, if you brought along a vegetarian, you should probably plan an alternate to cheeseburgers. See, always be ready to call an audible.

Close your eyes for a moment. I want you to smell the rest of this chapter. Hot Italian sausage sizzling on a grill. In New England, Portuguese sausage, called *chorico* (delicious, spicy, and reddish), is served on Portuguese bread with hot mustard and crisp garden vegetables, alongside some clam chowder. You can smell the ribs cooking within hundreds of miles of Chicago's Soldier Field, and bratwurst in Green Bay was pre-ordained by ancient prophecies (someone once told me this), sort of like steak in Dallas. But this is America, and America is the land of the cheeseburger. In every stadium parking lot, there are cheeseburgers.

It is almost a science, this party in the parking lot. First of all, the choice of food is obviously a function of region. Although there is the common bond of the humble cheeseburger, each parking lot is very different. That's the beauty of America and football.

It is no coincidence that the ritual of football is most associated with Sunday afternoon. Sunday, after all, is a religious day. I don't mean to be disrespectful because I do know that it's not the same. But still. Football is, in many respects, to a lot of people, a sort of religious experience. It is spiritual. It is emotional. It is pure.

And there is ritual. A ritual in the parking lot, where you had better be by a certain time. Everything must happen in order. Your team's performance is a function of so many things—and you cannot at all discount the parking lot performance of any random group of fans. Hey, who's to say that's not what determines which way the ball bounces? It's gotta be something. I say, it's much safer to stick to your favorite beverage, your favorite food, your favorite people, your favorite jersey, and hope that nothing you did will cause a voodoo-like pain in a certain quarterback's arm. I'm not saying this happens, it's just that I remember a few games when…(I'm just kidding!)

Even if there is nothing to this superstition stuff (I didn't say that), your friends will blame you if you commit any sin of not sticking with tradition and the team loses. You don't have to really believe in superstition. You can blame someone for the loss just for the fun of it. If you want to be around football fans, you don't mess with luck. You just don't—cause there's *something* to it.

> **Joe's Tips**
> Tailgating is pure when it is clean. Be sure to put out your barbecue, throw out your trash, and be careful with your glass containers. After all, part of keeping the stadium parking lot clean is keeping America beautiful. And what's a better part of America than a parking lot at a football stadium. It's *your* parking lot. Show some pride and consideration.

Consumption

I love walking through it. I usually get to a game two hours before broadcast. I like to park in a place where I can walk through the crowd. I love watching the fathers and sons, the guys out throwing the ball around. I love watching them become players from the NFL. You hear the conversation. The ball goes through the air, "Oh, Jerry Rice! What a great catch." And then, foomp, they run into a fender. Just like going over the middle, only in the NFL that fender has an attitude.

A tailgate party is Americana, with the same glow as the Ferris wheel at the state fair. It shines. The whole experience is terrific. There are guys smoking cigars, women smoking cigars, and women with earrings that are little football helmets. The person in the parking lot, whom you've never met and will probably never see again after today, becomes your best friend for the next hour and a half.

And then there are the poor lounge chairs. Oh man. We've all seen them. There's this guy, this big guy

> **Joe's Tips**
> Be alert to such things as weather reports so you have a plan as to how to eat if you cannot cook in rain. Also be ready with wet weather gear or whatever you may need. Again, always be ready to call an audible.

squeezed into this poor little lounge chair. And you feel so sorry for the darn thing as it seems to strain (giving, yes, 110 percent) to hold together and keep this guy comfortable. And is this guy comfortable? Oh man. He is leaned back, his shirt is too small so we all see his belly button, upon which rests a can of beer. In his mouth is a fat, smoking cigar, and in one hand is a huge dripping cheeseburger. On his head is a hat of his team, and your team. Your new friend. "Sure," you say, "I'll have a cheeseburger." You look down at the lounge chair. "But don't get up. I'll get it myself."

Music resonates over the aroma of thousands of barbecues. Footballs fly. There is loud laughter, and inevitably some player's name comes up preceded by one of those *adjectives* that your Mom told you never to use. You know, *that* quarterback. Conversations roll, and I love to listen. This game coming up, and that matchup, and I swear half of you people could be on television. Well, maybe not half. But you all know what you are talking about, and I love to listen. Even if you don't know what you are talking about, I still love to listen. It's football. Who doesn't like talking football?

But at its essence, a tailgate party is a festival of consumption. How much can you consume before the game? This may not be healthy, but it is what I have observed. And if this one day of feasting has a health effect, well, who am I to say? I say happiness has a health effect, too. Hey, cheers. Hope your team wins.

Greeting Fans from a Foreign City

Oh, this is fun. Someone wearing a different jacket comes into *your* parking lot. Oh, this is too much fun. C'mon, this almost isn't fair. Actually, it isn't fair. That's the beauty. These folks come wandering into your stadium, your city, your parking lot, your piece of turf in the world, and they have the nerve to wear the jacket of the opposing team. Who are these people? They should go back to…wherever.

Joe's Tips

If an opposing fan becomes obnoxious in your stadium, politely ask him or her to calm down. Point out to the person the circumstance that they really are in. Show the person the wisdom of mathematics. But if the person insists on being obnoxious, don't do the obvious.

These relationships always change. It takes three hours, but by the end of the game someone has the upper hand. So you go into it knowing that even though the numbers are behind you (70,000 to a few hundred), you know that the other numbers could end up saying anything—those numbers being the score and other game numbers.

But still—70,000 to a few hundred is awfully tempting. So you do a bit of ribbing. *You're not really going to wear that jacket here, are you?*

How to Visit Another City

You grew up here, you landed a job there. You like living there, but you cheer for here's team. Here's team is visiting there. Oh boy.

So how do you get tickets to an away game? There are usually a limited amount of tickets available to a visiting team. The best thing to do is to call your local team's ticket office to find out how you can get them.

Try walking into a stadium of fans wearing the colors of the wrong team and you will understand courage. Okay, I exaggerate—but not too much. To go into another stadium and cheer for your team takes a bit of courage. Moxie. It takes guts to declare, in the face adversity, that you like a certain team, and you don't care what these local yokels from *around here* think. If they knew what you knew, if they grew up where you grew up, they'd understand. But they don't. Hey, their loss.

Joe's Tips
Don't wear all your gear at first if you are in a foreign city. Start with just your hat, and move on up from there. No need to be obnoxious. Let the score dictate your behavior.

We're Number One!

It is like being in the sea, the sea of fans. When you and everyone around you is cheering in unison. You all are wearing essentially the same colors, you grew up in towns and cities that surround this stadium, and you live and work here now, you feel a sort of football karma. Look at us. Ha. Loooooook at usssssssssss.

And then the music starts. That thumpin', bumpin', bring-it-on-home kinda stuff that gets you clapping and gets you screaming in the aisles. "C'mon!" (You yell the quarterback's name). "You bum!" (You mean this in the nicest possible way because you really do think this guy is great and you'll be the very first to say so as soon as the guy throws a darn touchdown pass.) "How come they pay you all that money anyway?" (You've gotta say that because fans must now start all complaints with the subject of money.)

When you shout something out, everyone around you laughs because they all were thinking the exact same thing. How come they pay that guy all that money? And then, that very play, that guy does a deep drop and finds your favorite wide receiver has beaten the cornerback by one step on a post route. And the pass is perfect. And you, maybe, for a moment, have experienced heaven. Perfect fan bliss. "Yeah, that's my guy," you yell as you high-five the entire row behind you. "Heckuva throw, man. I knew you could do it. Yeeeeeeeeeeeeaah!" You raise your arms like Rocky Balboa. And the entire sea of fans does the same thing. It is a moment of Zen.

Do Fans Matter? Consider This Story

In the early 1990s, John Riggins and I were inducted into the *Ring of Honor* in RFK stadium in Washington. We were teammates on the Redskins; we won the Super Bowl together.

We had both been retired about five years, so this was a planned event. I went in a suit and tie and I was brought to the 50 yard-line. The game was against the Philadelphia Eagles. I was standing there, full of anticipation, waiting to be honored. But I looked around and John was nowhere—nowhere to be seen.

> **Joe's Gridiron Talk**
>
> The *Ring of Honor* is an area inside most stadiums in which certain players from the past are honored. This recognizes a player for having reached a certain level of accomplishment for that team.

All of a sudden, out by the Redskins tunnel, you could hear a few fans begin to clap and cheer. And then, like a conquering hero through the streets of Paris, John Riggins ran onto the field in full battle regalia. He's in all of his pads and his 44 jersey, with his helmet under his arm.

The place went crazy. I mean bonkers. I hadn't heard that kind of cheering there in, heck, five years. It was nuts. John ran out into this mass hysteria and he smiled. Yes, he smiled.

He stood next to me and I had to ask, "John, why?"

And he said, "Joe, I needed to hear it one more time."

You want to know if you matter? Yes, you do.

The Least You Need to Know

➤ Tailgating is safe with cheeseburgers, but regional fare makes it even better.

➤ If you exercise every day of the week for five years, you can justify one tailgate party. But then, happiness is a healthy thing. You decide on limits. Have fun.

➤ Fans visiting your stadium are fools. On the other hand, if you visit a foreign stadium, you have great courage.

➤ Players appreciate fans. You have no idea how much.

Chapter 27

Rivalries: The Essence of It All

In This Chapter

➤ Rivalries are macho, neighborhood things

➤ Rivalries are about success

➤ Only George Allen could create a rivalry

Rivalries are about hate, of course, but in the friendliest sense of the word. There is one team that you have to beat, and you would *hate it* if you didn't beat them. Rivalries are about good versus evil, and your team is good. Your team wears those great colors, and it has the coolest insignia ever invented. And it's incredible how, of all the teams in all the world, they put your team in your hometown. C'mon. What are the odds?

The word fan is a root of the word *fanatic*. Think about it. You cheer for your team and somehow or other there is this one other team that just about makes you nuts wanting to beat them. Look. I don't know how to say this except to tell the truth. Not all of you will know what a real rivalry is. It's something special, and not every team in the NFL is good enough or has a rich enough history against one other franchise to have developed a rivalry. But when rivalries are good, they are downright bloody—in the nicest sense of the word. What can I say? Think about the word fanatic, and you will understand the essence of rivalry. I sure would *hate it* if we lost to *that team.*

This final chapter is about the essence of the game, where all the clawing and scratching and fighting and pushing 'til you can't breathe comes to a summit—when you play *that team.* I will examine the various types of rivalries—those based on geography, those based on success, and those based on both. I will tell how George Allen invented a rivalry, and I will tell you of my five favorite rivalries in no particular order.

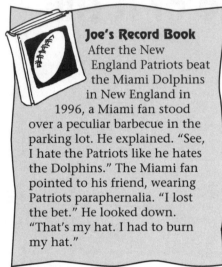

Joe's Record Book
After the New England Patriots beat the Miami Dolphins in New England in 1996, a Miami fan stood over a peculiar barbecue in the parking lot. He explained. "See, I hate the Patriots like he hates the Dolphins." The Miami fan pointed to his friend, wearing Patriots paraphernalia. "I lost the bet." He looked down. "That's my hat. I had to burn my hat."

You and Me, Outside— Right Now!

Look, she's mine! Stay away, just stay the (expletive deleted—hey I learned this phrase living in Washington) away.

See, that's a rivalry. Two guys in the same hometown chasing the same girl. A rivalry is bitter, angry, full of boasts and vengeful thoughts. It is a street fight between two thugs who are usually (but not always) from the same neighborhood. A rivalry is when somebody says, *"You and me outside, now!"*

And the other guy says, *"I can't wait."*

Anytime, Anywhere

If you put tickets on sale right now for a game between the Green Bay Packers and the Chicago Bears to take place say, 25 years from now, it would sell out in a heartbeat. I'm convinced of it. If someone will get me a ticket right now for that game, I will be there, too. C'mon. Bears-Packers. Packers-Bears. You're kidding me. Get outta here. Get me a beer. Listen, that's something to live for, let me tell you. Or how about a Cowboys-Redskins game. Oh, baby! They really don't get any better than that.

Sure, I'm an old Redskin. No, I didn't like the Cowboys. But really, who could? Who would? C'mon. The Cowboys? Yeah, right. Well, maybe a little now.

Rivalries are fun because you can get riled in a half a second, just thinking of the other team. Bring 'em on…anytime, anywhere.

The Toughest Guy in the Neighborhood

It's often a neighborhood thing. Green Bay and Chicago—same neighborhood. Cleveland and Pittsburgh—two Midwest factory towns. When the other team is from the same part of the country as you, you feel something extra when you beat them. It sort of says, *"We rule around here."*

Playing a geographic rival from within your same division can be like facing Armageddon twice a year. It is a matter of municipal *chutzpah*, mutual respect. Which city is better? Why, ours of course. So we rally around the flag of our football team, and we brace for every confrontation with *that other* team, from *that other* city that is (in our quiet, reflective moments we admit) a lot like us. Egads! It's true. They are like us. That's why we want to beat them more than anyone else.

When the terrain looks pretty much the same in your city and my city, but there is just enough cultural difference to make us each a bit condescending (in a playful way, of course) towards the other, that's when you get a good regional rivalry. There must be a long history of competing for the same prize, and there must be epic games and profound moments in that history. If there is all of that, the rivalry will flourish even when most real meaning has been washed from the game. Even if one team is bad, there are still two games that mean a lot to both the good and bad team in a rivalry.

The only problem with all rivalries now is, once again, free agency. Franchise free agency has, in effect, killed a great rivalry between the Pittsburgh Steelers and Cleveland Browns. But free agency as a whole, for players, makes fans identify with teams a little less. It even hurts in identifying the villains. Heck, last year's villain could be this year's wide receiver.

> **Joe's Record Book**
>
> In 1995, when the Cleveland Browns announced the franchise was moving to Baltimore, Browns fans traveled to Pittsburgh for one final Steelers-Browns game. Steelers fans felt sorry for their Cleveland rivals, so they baptized the Browns fans as Steeler fans until Cleveland gets a new team. They were baptized with Iron City Beer. (I couldn't make this stuff up.)

> **Joe's Record Book**
>
> The Green Bay Packers have been playing the Chicago Bears since 1921, when the Bears were known as the Chicago Staleys. The Bears lead the series 81-65-6.

In 1997, defensive tackle Neal Smith, longtime star for the Kansas Chiefs, signed a contract to play with the Chiefs division rival, the Denver Broncos. It even happens with coaches, as New England's coach, Bill Parcells, who brought them to Super Bowl XXXI in

1997, signed a contract to coach the New York Jets, a division rival of the Patriots. In fact, Parcells formerly coached the crosstown team in New York, the Giants, to two Super Bowl championships. The only thing you can root for is *this year*.

A Good Way to Start a Rivalry Is to Meet in the Playoffs

You don't start a rivalry with some team that stinks. A 3-13 team isn't scaring anybody. Beating them doesn't get you a prize. Who cares? If you can almost beat someone or they can almost beat you, that's when it's good. If you stink and they stink and your game is a comedy of errors, there's not much chance for you to get fired up about wanting to beat this team. But if there is a history of playing each other when a season is on the line, and, better yet, the season *is* on the line, there is a good chance you aren't going to like the team you are playing. Because if they beat you, you go home, and you'll remember that.

You will remember that. Thus, the next time you play you will want your team to put a hurt on them even more. See, rivalries occur when you are good and they are good and *winning matters.* It has to have impact in order for the rivalry to flourish. The game doesn't always have to matter in the season for it to matter as a rivalry game. But it has to matter sometimes, or it won't matter at all. Got it?

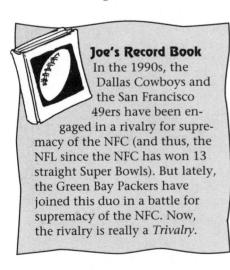

Joe's Record Book
In the 1990s, the Dallas Cowboys and the San Francisco 49ers have been engaged in a rivalry for supremacy of the NFC (and thus, the NFL since the NFC has won 13 straight Super Bowls). But lately, the Green Bay Packers have joined this duo in a battle for supremacy of the NFC. Now, the rivalry is really a *Trivalry*.

In the 1970s, the Pittsburgh Steelers, whose natural rival was the Cleveland Browns, acquired another rival when Bum Phillips built a powerhouse team in Houston. Coach Phillips used the power running of fullback Earl Campbell to try to take on the Steelers. Unfortunately for Phillips, he was right when he declared, "The road to the Super Bowl goes through Pittsburgh." The Oilers never could quite beat the Steelers, who went on to win four Super Bowls. The Oilers never made it past a certain stop on the road. And that's how a rivalry was built. It's not as strong now as it used to be, but it has been replaced by other competitive rivalries.

The Braggin' Bowls

Maybe nobody else in the country cares. There's a bunch of games every week. Who's going to care about your little rivalry when they're not involved? You will, and so will the folks cheering for that other team. Yes, that's right. They care as much as you do. They see it as you see it, which is as a battle of honor. A neighborhood thing, most likely, or a battle for supremacy, or—best case scenario—a neighborhood thing that turns into a battle for supremacy.

When it is Joe Frazier against Muhammed Ali, both claiming with great legitimacy to be the best in the world, the contest itself becomes a tale for the ages. Fans remember stories. Athletes remember stories. Oh heavens, do we remember.

How to Create a Rivalry

My first NFL coach, George Allen, was a master at all things. He was, in fact, a magician who could do things that shouldn't be possible. His career accomplishments are many, and much has been made of how good of a coach he was, but there is another part to George that not many know. He personally created the rivalry between the Dallas Cowboys and Washington Redskins.

George coached the Redskins from 1971 to 1978. His first couple years there, he knew that he had a good football team. He also knew that the Cowboys were a very good football team. So, being a master at public relations, George decided to spice up the NFL.

He asked certain players to incite other certain players. Specifically, he asked my teammates (who will remain nameless) to call Cowboys quarterback Roger Staubach names (I won't tell you those either, in fairness). Well, the idea was to get Roger ticked off. It worked, and some Cowboys began calling names back, and well, people were suddenly *very interested* in the game between the Redskins and Cowboys. And every year this continued, and George built the myth right then and there. It was fun to be a part of.

Joe's Tips
Watch the newspapers for what your rival's players say about your team. Newspaper quotes are often used as motivation.

I never participated. Well, not knowingly, although George told me that one year I caused a bit of a stir. I guess he was right. You see, one year, we were beating the Cowboys 9-3 with only seconds left on the clock. We had the ball on our own 2-yard line. George told me to take the snap from center, run into the end zone and let the clock run out. The idea was to let the clock run out, go out of the end zone, give up a safety, and we win 9-5. Simple. Right? Sure, Einstein.

I backed up into the end zone. I was standing in the end zone watching the clock when it hit :00. Zero. No more time. The game was over. I was ecstatic. I raised my hands. We had won. Except...

Except, the game wasn't over. I didn't run out of the end zone. It was a live ball and I was a live target. The Cowboys thought I was taunting them. Nobody was too pleased by my display, but somebody sure wanted to make me fumble. I mean, when I was hit, I knew for absolutely certain that they wanted me to drop the ball. But I held on, and we still won, 9-5. But wow.

George came up to me afterwards and asked, "Why did you do that?"

"I made a mistake, Coach. I thought the game was over."

"Oh, man. Now how am I gonna explain that."

And the rivalry grew some more.

Joe's Top Five Rivalries

I love rivalries; I love when two teams hate each other. The more they despise each other, the more I like to watch. Here are my five favorite rivalries, in no particular order.

➤ **Washington–Dallas.** Credit for this rivalry goes to George Allen, as I just mentioned, who created it from thin air with a few well-placed comments from a few of his players. It thrived because both teams were good for a long time.

➤ **Kansas City–Oakland.** A non-geographical rivalry that began in the old American Football League, these were the first two AFL teams to go to the Super Bowl, and for many years they battled for AFL or AFC supremacy.

➤ **Green Bay–Chicago.** A rivalry for the ages that began in the era of Curley Lambeau in Green Bay and George Halas in Chicago. This is a cold-weather rivalry built on the frozen tundra and by a wind off the lake. Brrrrrrr.

➤ **Cleveland–Pittsburgh.** This rivalry doesn't even exist right now, but it still makes the list because it is so mythical. Two blue-collar union towns in what is affectionately called *the Rust Belt* doing battle on frozen days. When the Browns return in 1999, so will the rivalry. Count on it.

➤ **Dallas–Philadelphia.** This is a rivalry of recent vintage. It is flourishing because of the excellence of one team, the Cowboys, and the driven nature of the coach of the other team, Ray Rhodes. Ray Rhodes is a driven man, a picture of intensity. But the Cowboys have been the best team in the division. Thus, a rivalry is born.

The Least You Need to Know

➤ There is nothing more fun than beating your rival, just because.

➤ Most rivalries are based on geography because it is often more fun to go after someone just like you.

➤ Some rivalries are based purely on the success of both teams. If two teams are good and meet in a series of meaningful games, a rivalry can soon develop.

➤ The Redskins and the Cowboys rivalry was created single-handedly by George Allen and his legacy lives on.

Gridiron Talk Glossary

beaver   When Pete Carroll was the defensive coordinator of the New York Jets, a stuffed *beaver* was given to the player who made a play that led to a fumble. The beaver, described by many as "the hardest-working animal in the animal kingdom," symbolized a great play. Despite playing for millions of dollars, players took great pride in having possession of the beaver for a week.

blitz adjustment   A *blitz adjustment* is an automatic decision a quarterback must make when he sees a blitz coming from a certain area. The blitz adjustment requires the quarterback to go to the hot receiver.

blitzing   The idea of *blitzing* (bringing more than five defensive players on a rush at the quarterback) is to dictate the tempo of the play. Blitzing is aggressive. It is, quite simply, an attack mode.

blue chip player   One who is considered by scouts to be a player who cannot miss becoming a starter in the league, if not a superstar.

bomb   A *bomb* is one of the most explosive plays in football. A bomb is a long pass and it can be an unparalleled sports work of art.

capologist   The person on an NFL team who is in charge of managing the salary cap. This person is a math whiz who helps the team figure what it can spend on players. Every team knows that one player could make a difference. In the 1990s, the *capologist* is as important as the general manager or coach.

check with me   Is when the quarterback gets in the huddle and calls, "Check with me." What he is saying is, "I'm not going to call a play now. I'll call it at the line." He sets the formation, and then when he gets to the line of scrimmage, he looks at the defense and calls the play.

clearing it out   What a speed guy is often asked to do. This means he is asked to take off down the field in an attempt to get open for a long pass. Even if he doesn't get open, he clears out some defensive players from where a shorter pass or run might go. This is also called *stretching the defense* or *stretching the field.*

collective bargaining agreement (CBA)   The way the NFL splits the pie is with a *collective bargaining agreement,* which is essentially a contract between the league and the players that gives the players a certain amount of the revenue from the game.

color commentator   An announcer on a television broadcast of a game who offers expert analysis of the action that is taking place on the field. Color commentators are often ex-coaches or ex-players.

cornerback   A defensive player whose job is primarily to cover receivers and prevent them from catching passes.

defensive line   The big guys facing the offensive line. Their job is to stop the run and get the quarterback, and occupy offensive linemen so that linebackers can make plays.

double response   When an offensive lineman has a *double response,* he is responsible for a linebacker in front of him and off the ball, and also for an outside linebacker to that side. Normally, only one will rush. The question for the offensive lineman is, which one? He first checks the man in front of him, then checks the outside rusher, and he better do it fast.

draft   How college players are picked for the pros. Every year in the spring, all 30 teams take turns picking players at the annual draft. The worst team from the previous year picks first. The best team picks last.

dummy audibles   Signals that are called by the quarterback at the line of scrimmage that look like an audible but are really meaningless words. The idea is to not let the other team know what you are using as your audible signal, so you call a number of signals that are known by your team to be meaningless. Just more head games.

end zone   The 10-yard area at the end of the field that is the goal of teams. You score touchdowns by getting the ball into the end zone.

fair catch   When a punt returner signals for a *fair catch,* he waves an arm over his head. When he does this it means he plans to catch the ball and promises not to advance it. When he does this, the punting team is not allowed to hit him or interfere with his ability to catch the ball.

field goal   A kick from the field of play that is worth three points. The ball is snapped back seven yards to a player who kneels waiting for it. That player places the ball, pointy end down, on the ground while holding the other pointy end up. The kicker kicks the ball. If it goes through the goal posts, it is worth 3 points. It is usually kicked on fourth down.

first down   Occurs with change of possession of the ball, or when a team moves forward 10 yards from where it began. A team is then given four more plays to move forward another 10 yards. If it does not do so (each play is numbered consecutively) in four downs, the other team is given the ball and it is a first down for them.

flanker   A receiver who usually lines up on the side with the tight end, one yard behind the line of scrimmage.

40 time   How long it takes for a player to run 40 yards. It is the standard measurement of speed in football. It also seems to be the distance most guys run on any given play because everything is run in short bursts. The fastest times are now about 4.1 seconds; 4.5 is average for the NFL, and 5.2 is average for big linemen.

franchise player   A player who the team designates as its most important player. There are actually two types of franchise players. Teams only get one slot for a franchise player. They can choose to use either designation. An "exclusive" franchise player cannot sign with another club. An exclusive franchise player must be offered a minimum of the top five salaries at his position as of April 14, or 120 percent of his previous salary—whichever is greater. If, however, a player is only offered a minimum of the top five salaries *from last season*, he is a franchise player and can negotiate with other clubs. If he receives a higher offer, the old club can match the offer or it can receive two first-round draft choices as compensation if it decides not to match the offer.

front side   The direction the ball carrier runs to start the play. The *back side* is opposite where he is going.

goal posts   The goal posts are the bar-like contraptions at each end of the field. The ball must be kicked over and through the goal posts for extra points and field goals. The goal post consist of a base pole, called *crossbar,* which is the bar perpindicular to the ground that the ball must travel over, and an upright pole on each side of the cross bar. The upright poles are called *uprights*. A successful kick goes *through the goal posts*, or *over the goal posts*, or, in other words (there's lots of ways to say this) *over the crossbar and through the uprights.*

hands team   Includes the guys who normally handle the ball—wide receivers, running backs, and defensive backs. The most important skill for both teams in an onside kick is the ability to grab and hold onto the ball.

hang time   The amount of time a ball is in the air after it is punted. It is the time from when the ball leaves punter's foot until it lands on the ground or in the returner's arms. If you have great hang time (4.0 seconds), the chances of someone returning a punt very far aren't very good.

hard count   When the quarterback yells a signal louder than the other signals he yells in an attempt to fool the defense into thinking the play is beginning. The idea is to get the defense to jump offsides, which is a penalty. The defense cannot cross the line of scrimmage before the play begins.

hashmarks   The lines running along each side of the center of the field signifying one yard on the field. After each play, the ball is always placed between the hashmarks as the starting point for the next play.

head slap   A *head slap* is a move that's not allowed, where one player slaps or bangs around the head of another player. Deacon Jones, who played for the Los Angeles Rams in the 1960s, used it a lot. A lot of old offensive linemen still have headaches from Deacon. Imagine putting a helmet on and having somebody take a baseball bat and banging it upside your head about a dozen times—you just played against Deacon Jones. Ouch.

Heidi Game   The *Heidi Game* took place on November 17, 1968. The New York Jets were leading the Oakland Raiders 32–29 with 50 seconds to go when the time became 7 p.m. NBC put on the scheduled children's movie, *Heidi*, right on time. In the remaining 50 seconds, the Raiders scored two touchdowns. But no one saw it because *Heidi* was on TV.

homefield advantage   What teams have when they play their games in their city. Teams playing before hometown fans win more often.

hot receiver   The receiver who is supposed to get the ball when the defense is blitzing. As soon as the receiver realizes he is hot, he must turn and look for the ball because the quarterback will have limited time to get it to him. There are different hot receivers for different blitzes.

huddle   The meeting on the field that is held by the 11 players before the play begins. On offense, the huddle is run by the quarterback. Huddles can be set up many ways, in a semi-circle or perhaps with the quarterback facing all of his teammates. Most quarterbacks like to have the huddle so they are facing forward to make it easier to visualize the play.

hurry-up offense   An offense teams usually use with two minutes to go in the half. Almost all plays are passing plays designed to get as much yardage as possible and still stop the clock by going out of bounds. Short passes to the sidelines work best. Runs, because the clock continues to tick, are not used often in the hurry-up offense.

I formation   In the *I formation*, because it looks like an I, the quarterback is behind the center and the running backs are in a line behind the quarterback.

immaculate reception   The *immaculate reception* occurred at the end of the first playoff game that the '70s Steelers team ever won. The Steelers were losing to the Oakland Raiders by one point with five seconds to play. Steelers quarterback Terry Bradshaw threw a pass that bounced off of a Raider into the outstretched fingertips of running back Franco Harris. Harris ran the ball in for a touchdown.

inadvertent whistle   When an official blows a whistle by mistake. When this happens, the play stops. Whatever happens after the whistle is insignificant.

interception   An *interception* is a pass that is stolen by the defense.

interference   When a defender hits a receiver as the ball is on its way to him. It is an automatic first down at the point of the penalty.

jumper   A linebacker who starts a few yards back from the LOS and tries to time his leap in the air to coincide with the leap of the running back. Short yardage plays often come down to which player, the running back or the jumper, wins the collision.

linebackers   The best athletes on the team. They line up a few yards behind the defensive line and do everything on defense: get the quarterback, stop the run, and cover receivers.

long arm   The arm of the defensive player that is closest to the quarterback and furthest away from the receiver. In a jump, because of angles, that hand should be able to rise a little higher than the hand nearer the receiver, or *short arm*. The long arm is normally the one used to knock the ball away.

luxury box   An enclosed room with a glass front that is inside many stadiums. These are usually rented to corporations, and are located in some of the prime areas of stadiums. They are rented for tens of thousands of dollars or more per year.

neutral zone   The area between the offensive and defensive lines. It is the length of the ball in width. No player except the center may enter the neutral zone until the ball is snapped.

offensive interference   Occurs when the receiver hits the defender in an effort to not allow him to intercept the pass. It is a 10-yard penalty against the offense.

offensive line   A human wall of five large men between the quarterback and the defense. That block the defense in order to create holes for the running backs to run through or a pocket for the quarterback to pass from.

officials   The guys in the striped shirts who control the chaos. They judge the game and their decision is law. There is no appeal.

open side   The *open side* and *closed side* of a formation are directly related to the placement of the tight end. The open side is the side without the tight end. The closed side has the tight end.

over the crossbar and between the uprights   A ball kicked *over the crossbar and between the uprights* is worth points (the number depends on the situation—see Chapter 3). If it is *wide left*, it flew to the left of the left upright. *Wide right* means it went to the right of the right upright. If it is short, it didn't make it over the crossbar.

pick   Occurs when receivers criss cross and two defensive players run into each other. If an offensive player runs into a defensive player who is covering someone else, it is an illegal pick (if he is caught). If two defensive players run into each other, they're just not very smart.

personal protector   On the kickoff, he is a player who runs right in front of the return man and throws what is hoped to be a key block to bust the return man loose for a long run. The return man follows the personal protector and reads his block as he plans his cuts. When a team is punting, the personal protector lines up between the punter and line, acting as a last line of defense for the punter.

place kicker   The player who kicks kickoffs, field goals, and extra points.

play-by-play announcer   A television announcer whose primary job is to give information about what is happening on a particular play—including who has the ball and the current situation, such as down and distance.

pooch punt   A short, high kick designed to land around the 10-yard line in order to give the punting team a chance to down the ball. As long as the receiving team doesn't touch the ball, the punting team can touch it and down it—making it first down and 10 yards to go for the receiving team at the spot the ball was downed.

prevent defense   At the end of a game or the end of a half, when the defense is worried about a big play, it will often employ what is called a *prevent defense.* The idea is to prevent a big play, but in reality it often prevents the team from winning.

Pro Bowl   The All-Star Game of the National Football League. It is played every year in Honolulu, Hawaii.

punter   A player who holds the ball himself and then drops it in a coordinated manner while, in a continuous motion, kicking it from the air.

quarterback   The player who starts the action. He is the man with the golden arm whose claim to fame is his ability to throw. The quarterback is John Wayne, Babe Ruth, and James Bond, with a few more ingredients thrown in, too.

R back   The *R back* is used by teams that only use one running back. They can call their back a halfback or a fullback, or whatever, but the real name for the one back in a one-back offense is the R back, which stands for "remaining."

red zone   The red zone was named because it represents where a red flashing light should go off. This is where it counts. Don Shula, longtime NFL coach, called it the green zone because that was where the money was made.

redshirt   Means a player doesn't play a certain year when he is in school and he is granted another year of eligibility to play later. This can happen, for instance, if a player gets hurt. He still attends classes and practices, but doesn't play and thus is still eligible to play four years.

ring of honor   An area inside most stadiums in which certain players from the past are honored. This recognizes a player for having reached a certain level of accomplishment for that team.

rivalry   A series of games between two teams that don't like each other.

rubber-band defense   A bend-don't break defense that allows short plays down the field. If the offense has to run a lot of short plays they are sooner or later going to make a mistake, or the rubber-band defense hopes so.

running back   A player who is primarily a ballcarrier. The best ones can control games all by themselves.

sack   A sack occurs when a quarterback is tackled behind the line of scrimmage while he is trying to pass.

safety   When a player is tackled in his own end zone with the football it is a safety, which means it is worth two points for the team without the ball. The team that was tackled in its own End Zone (running out of bounds in your own end zone is also a safety) must then kick the ball to the other team. The kick (it can be a punt or kickoff type kick) is from its own 20-yard line.

safety   A player in the back of the defensive backfield. There are two safeties, a free safety and strong safety. The free safety is usually the furthest player back, and lined up in the middle of the field. The strong safety is also usually far back, but is lined up on the same side as the tight end.

salary cap   The amount of money the NFL designates each team may spend for players. The salary cap for 1997 is $41.45 million per team.

scatback   A small swift running back with elusive moves. They are used a lot in third down situations where they are counted on for their ability to scat here and there, making tacklers miss.

scripting the plays   The San Francisco 49ers, under former Coach Bill Walsh, began every game by knowing which 15 plays the team would run first. This was known as scripting the plays. The idea was to have a good idea how they would begin and then make changes as the game warranted. It was quite successful. Walsh won three Super Bowls, and now many teams script their opening plays.

secondary   The last line of defense. The secondary consists of defensive backs, which includes cornerbacks and safeties. Their primary job is to cover receivers.

set position   Prior to the snap, all offensive linemen must assume a set position without moving their feet, head, or arms, and without swaying their body.

shotgun   A formation in which the quarterback stands five yards behind the center and the center, instead of snapping the ball hand-to-hand, actually snaps the ball through the air to the waiting quarterback. This is primarily in passing downs, and it gives the quarterback an advantage not having to backpedal before throwing.

sleeper   A player who is drafted in the later rounds of the draft who turns out to be something special.

slow-motion instant replay   A video replay of a play that is slowed down so that every instant can be analyzed. A slow-motion instant replay can make football appear to have the grace of ballet, or it can make it appear to have the impact of a demolition derby.

smashmouth football   A simple philosophy—run the ball and then run it again. And then after that, run it again.

snot bubbles   A sensation that is created by a big hit. When you actually have bubbles coming out of your nose after you have been hit, you know you have been hit hard. And, thus, it is a good thing to give another player a case of snot bubbles.

soft spot   An area in a zone defense between defensive players.

spiral   A tight spin on the ball.

split end   A receiver who lines up on the line of scrimmage on the side away from the tight end.

split T formation   A formation where both backs are split behind quarterback. Neither one is directly behind the quarterback.

strength of schedule   Refers to the record from the previous year of the current year's opponents. For instance, a team with six opponents who made the playoffs the previous year probably has a tougher schedule than a team facing only two teams that were in the playoffs the previous year. It is based on the win-loss record of all opponents.

strong side   The strong side of a formation is the side that has the tight end. Usually, the strong side is the right, meaning the tight end lines up next to the right tackle.

subway alumni   Folks who, though they did not attend Notre Dame, for one reason or another have grown to identify with the school. Subway alumni exist for every school.

swoop   A block where a lineman goes by (swoops by) the defensive line to get to the next level of the defense, the linebackers.

tackle box   The area along the line of scrimmage between where the two offensive tackles line up. It includes about three yards on either side of the line of scrimmage and features some interesting battles.

tailgating   A party and cookout in the parking lot of the stadium. It is pure atmosphere and it happens before and after the game.

taking the air out of the football   Running the ball to an extreme. Run after run after run. The idea is to eat the clock in order to get the game to end while your team is in the lead. By avoiding risky passes, teams take the air out of the football.

telestrator   A tool in which an announcer can draw right over the action on a replay. It works like a high-tech Etch-A-Sketch. If a receiver runs a post pattern, for instance, the announcer can draw out the direction of the post pattern on the telestrator.

throwing lanes   The areas between lineman that the quarterback can throw the ball through. There is a misconception about quarterbacks that they must be tall to throw the ball over linemen. In fact, offensive linemen design blocking schemes to create throwing lanes for quarterbacks to throw.

tight end   A big receiver who lines up next to the offensive line. His job is to catch passes and to block like an offensive lineman.

touchdown   When a player has possession of the ball in the opposing team's end zone. It is worth six points.

touchdown dance   A celebration players do in the end zone after scoring a touchdown. There is a fine line between spontaneous joy and arrogant showmanship. A little of both makes for a heck of a dance.

touchdown Jesus   The painting of Jesus that overlooks the Notre Dame Stadium in South Bend, Indiana. In the painting, Jesus has his arms upraised to the heavens (as if, some football fanatics have said, signaling a touchdown).

transition player   A designation given to a player who is one of the best at his position. He must receive an average salary of the top 10 players at his position from the past season. When he becomes a free agent, his old club may match any offer given by another club. Every season, he must receive the average salary of the top 10 players at his position. If the club doesn't offer that money, he loses his transition status and automatically becomes a free agent.

trenches   Think of the term trench warfare and you will get a sense of what the announcer means when he talks of the *trenches* in football. The trenches are where the big guys do battle.

turf toe   The footing on artificial turf is so sure that there is actually an injury called *turf toe*, in which the big toe is jammed into the ground because you have stopped too abruptly. It is like a stubbed toe except you are wearing a shoe.

wedge   A wall of big players who are supposed to form a blocking wall in front of the kick returner. The players get into a formation that resembles a "V," or a wedge. The idea is to throw blocks on the kickoff coverage team in order to spring the kick returner loose for a big return.

wide receiver   A high-glamour job subject to some of the biggest hits in the game. A wide receiver's job is primarily to catch passes.

wild-card team   A team that qualifies for the playoffs without winning its division. The three best non-division winners in each conference qualify as wild-card teams.

National Football League Team Addresses (as of June 1997)

NFL Web site: http://nfl.com

Arizona Cardinals
8701 South Hardy Drive
Tempe, AZ 85284-2800
(602) 379-0101
Fax (602) 379-1819

Atlanta Falcons
2745 Burnette Road
Suwanee, GA 30174
(770) 945-1111
Fax (770) 271-1221

Baltimore Ravens
11001 Owings Mills Road
Owings Mills, MD 21117
(410) 654-6200
Fax (410) 654-6212

Buffalo Bills
One Bills Drive
Orchard Park, NY 14127
(716) 648-1800
Fax (716) 649-6446

Carolina Panthers
800 South Mint Street
Charlotte, NC 28202
(704) 358-7000
Fax (704) 358-0764

Chicago Bears
Halas Hall
250 North Washington
Lake Forest, IL 60045
(847) 295-6600
Fax (847) 295-5238

Cincinnati Bengals
One Bengals Drive
Cincinnati, OH 45024
(513) 621-3550
Fax (513) 621-3570

Dallas Cowboys
One Cowboys Parkway
Irving, TX 75063
(214) 556-9900
Fax (214) 556-9970

Denver Broncos
13655 Broncos Parkway
Englewood, CO 80112
(303) 649-9000
Fax (303) 649-9354

Detroit Lions
1200 Featherstone Road
Pontiac, MI 48342
(313) 335-4131
Fax (313) 335-1403

Green Bay Packers
1265 Lombardi Avenue
Green Bay, WI 54307
(414) 496-5700
Fax (414) 496-5738

Houston Oilers
8030 El Rio
Houston, TX 77054
(713) 881-3500
Fax (713) 881-3527

Indianapolis Colts
7001 W. 56th Street
Indianapolis, IN 46254
(317) 297-2658
Fax (317) 297-8971

Jacksonville Jaguars
One Stadium Place
Jacksonville, FL 32202
(904) 633-6000
Fax (603) 633-6050

Kansas City Chiefs
One Arrowhead Drive
Kansas City, MO 64129
(816) 924-9300
Fax (816) 924-9300

Miami Dolphins
7500 SW 30th Street
Davie, FL 33329
(954) 452-7000
Fax (954) 452-7055

Minnesota Vikings
9520 Viking Drive
Eden Prairie, MN 55344
(612) 828-6500
Fax (612) 828-6541

New England Patriots
60 Washington Street
Foxboro, MA 02035
(508) 543-8200
Fax (508) 543-0285

New Orleans Saints
5800 Airline Highway
Metarie, LA 70003
(504) 731-1799
Fax (504) 731-1888

New York Giants
Giants Stadium
East Rutherford, NJ 07073
(201) 935-8111
Fax (201) 935-8493

New York Jets
1000 Fulton Avenue
Hempstead, NY 11550
(516) 560-8100
Fax (516) 560-8197

Oakland Raiders
1220 Harbor Bay Parkway
Alameda, CA 94501
(510) 567-9000
Fax (510) 864-5134

Philadelphia Eagles
3501 South Broad Street
Philadelphia, PA 19148
(215) 463-2500
Fax (215) 339-5464

Pittsburgh Steelers
300 Stadium Circle
Pittsburgh, PA 15212
(412) 323-1200
Fax (412) 323-1393

St. Louis Rams
1 Rams Way
St. Louis, MO 63044
(314) 982-7267
Fax (314) 770-9261

San Diego Chargers
San Diego Jack Murphy Stadium
San Diego, CA 92160
(619) 280-2111
Fax (619) 280-8107

San Francisco 49ers
4949 Centennial Boulevard
Santa Clara, CA 95054
(408) 562-4949
Fax (408) 727-4937

Seattle Seahawks
11220 NE 53rd Street
Kirkland, WA 98033
(206) 827-9777
Fax (206) 827-9008

Tampa Bay Buccaneers
1 Buccanneer Place
Tampa, FL 33607
(813) 870-2700
Fax (813) 878-0813

Washington Redskins
21300 Redskin Park Drive
Ashburn, VA 20147
(703) 478-8900
Fax (703) 729-7605

Index

Symbols

2-point conversions, 30-32
3-4 defense, 202-203
    alignments, 189
4-3 defense alignments,
    189
5-yard chuck rule, 185
40 time, 305
46 defense, 203-204
900 lines (gambling), 266

A

ACC (Atlantic Coast
    Conference), 231
ace formation (running
    backs), 115
addresses (NFL teams),
    313-316
AFC (American Football
    Conference), 68, 248
Aikman, Troy, 69, 75
'Aints of New Orleans, 287
air-attack offense, 58
alignments (defense), 189
all-star games (NCAA), 233
Allen, George, 299
Ameche, Alan, 65
American Football
    Conference, see AFC
American Football League,
    66
American Professional
    Football Association, 64

analysts, 273-274
    color, 274
    play-by-play
        broadcasters, 273
    pre-game shows, 272
    sideline reporters, 274
arenas (outdoor vs.
    indoor), 24-25
artificial turf (Astroturf),
    22-24
Atlantic Coast Conference,
    see ACC
attacking defenses,
    188-189
audibles, 137
    calling (quarterbacks),
        79-80
    dummy, 304
    offensive strategies,
        137-138

B

back judge, 147
back side, 305
ball carrier, 15
ball design, 14-15
    offical NFL
        specifications, 15
ball-rushing (pass-
    rushing), 167
Baltimore Colts, 65, 67, 69
Baltimore Ravens, 69, 78
Baugh, Sammy, 65
beavers, 303
Berry, Raymond, 106
Big 10 conference, 231
Big East conference, 231
Big West conference, 231

big-play football, 125-126
black audible, 138
Blake, Jeff, 78
Bledsoe, Drew, 166
blitz adjustment, 303
blitzes, 195-196
    offensive strategies,
        140-141
    zone blitz, 210-211
blocking, 86
    pass, 88-89
    run, 88-89
    schemes, 90-92
        cutoff block, 92
        double team, 91
        man-on-man
            blocking, 92
        reach block, 91
        slide block, 91
        trap block, 90
        zone blocks, 92
blue chip players, 244
Blue-Gray Game (all-star
    games), 233
bombs, throwing, 82
Bostic, Jeff, 87
bowl games (NCAA), 232
Bradshaw, Terry, 75, 83
Brown, Gilbert, 162
Brown, Jim, 66, 117
Brown, Paul, 65
broadcasters, 273-274
    color commentators,
        274
    play-by-play, 273
    sideline reporters, 274
Buffalo Bills, 168
bullet passes, 78
Butkus, Dick, 170, 176

C

camera angles, 274-275
Camp, Walter (rugby), 5, 63
capologist, 303
Carolina Panthers, 245
catching passes (running backs), 112
centers (offensive linemen), 44, 87
chains, 21-22
check with me, 303
Chicago Bears, 64, 69, 117, 176-177, 284, 296
chop block (penalties), 89
signal, 155
Cincinnati Bengals, 78
civic connections, 9-11
cleats, 41
Cleveland Browns, 65-66, 69, 117, 263-264, 285, 297
clipping (penalties), 89
signal, 155
clocks (line judge), 147
clothing
homemade gear, 285
Joe's Top Five fan outfits, 287
lack thereof (fans), 285-286
NFL licensed merchandise, 282-284
weather protection, 285
coaching
coordinators, 56-57
designing strategies, 52-53
motivation, 54-56
personalities, 59
scripting plays, 53
studying films, 54

coffin corner kicks, 221
coin-flipping (possession), 36-37
Collective Bargaining Agreement, 258
salary cap, 258-260
college football, 228
all-star games, 233
bowl games, 232
conferences, 231
divisions, 229
draft, 235
Heisman Trophy, 233
NCAA (National Collegiate Athletic Association), 228
Notre Dame, 231
rule differences, 228
vs. professional football, 234
color commentators, 274, 304
combination pass coverages, 207-208
commercials (time-keeping), 34-35
community connections, 9-11
complimentary routes (receivers), 102
Conference USA, 231
conferences (NCAA), 231
confidence (quarterbacks), 76
coordinators, 56-57
offensive strategies, 136
cornerbacks, 46
defensive backs, 181-182
Cosell, Howard, 250
creating rivalries, 299-300
crossbars, 18
crowd noise signal, 150

Csonka, Larry, 68
cutoff block, 92

D

Dallas Cowboys, 69, 117, 167-168, 243, 299
Dawg Pound, 287
dead ball signal, 150
defense
alignments, 189
attacking vs. reacting, 188-189
blitzing, 195-196
linemen, 162-163
Joe's Top Five, 167
stopping the run, 163
tackles, 162
players, 45-46
defensive backs, 180-185
linebackers, 46, 170-176
linemen, 46, 162-163
secondaries, 46
substitutions, 193-194
prevent defense, 128, 197
reading (quarterbacks), 78-79
short-yardage, 196-197
stopping the pass
man-to-man coverage, 192-193
zone coverage, 191-192
stopping the run, 190-191
strategies, 200-205
3-4 defense, 202-203
46 defense, 203-204
double eagle defense, 205

When You're Smart Enough to Know That You Don't Know It All

For all the ups and downs you're sure to encounter in life, The Complete Idiot's Guides give you down-to-earth answers and practical solutions.

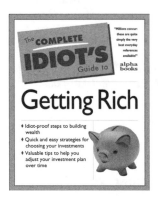

The Complete Idiot's Guide to Learning French on Your Own
ISBN: 0-02-861043-1 ▪ $16.95

The Complete Idiot's Guide to Dating
ISBN: 0-02-861052-0 ▪ $14.95

The Complete Idiot's Guide to Hiking and Camping
ISBN: 0-02-861100-4 ▪ $16.95

The Complete Idiot's Guide to Cooking Basics
ISBN: 1-56761-523-6 ▪ $16.99

The Complete Idiot's Guide to Learning Spanish on Your Own
ISBN: 0-02-861040-7 ▪ $16.95

The Complete Idiot's Guide to Gambling Like a Pro
ISBN: 0-02-861102-0 ▪ $16.95

The Complete Idiot's Guide to Choosing, Training, and Raising a Dog
ISBN: 0-02-861098-9 ▪ $16.95

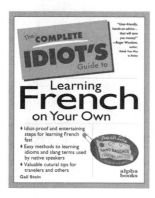

The Complete Idiot's Guide to Trouble-Free Car Care
ISBN: 0-02-861041-5 ▪ $16.95

The Complete Idiot's Guide to the Perfect Wedding
ISBN: 1-56761-532-5 ▪ $16.99

The Complete Idiot's Guide to Getting and Keeping Your Perfect Body
ISBN: 0-286105122 ▪ $16.99

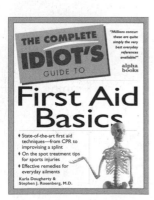

The Complete Idiot's Guide to First Aid Basics
ISBN: 0-02-861099-7 ▪ $16.95

The Complete Idiot's Guide to the Perfect Vacation
ISBN: 1-56761-531-7 ▪ $14.99

The Complete Idiot's Guide to Trouble-Free Home Repair
ISBN: 0-02-861042-3 ▪ $16.95

The Complete Idiot's Guide to Getting into College
ISBN: 1-56761-508-2 ▪ $14.95

You can handle it!